ADAPTATION URBANISM AND RESILIENT COMMUNITIES

Adaptation Urbanism and Resilient Communities outlines and explains adaptation urbanism as a theoretical framework for understanding and evaluating resilience projects in cities and relates it to pressing contemporary policy issues related to urban climate change mitigation and adaptation.

Through a series of detailed case studies, this book uncovers the promise and tensions of a new wave of resilient communities in Europe (Copenhagen, Rotterdam, and London), and the United States (New Orleans and South Florida). In addition, best practice projects in Amsterdam, Barcelona, Delft, Utrecht, and Vancouver are examined. The authors highlight how these communities are reinventing the role of streets and connecting public spaces in adapting to and mitigating climate change through green/blue infrastructure planning, maintaining and enhancing sustainable transportation options, and struggling to ensure equitable development for all residents. The case studies demonstrate that while there are some more universal aspects to encouraging adaptation urbanism, there are also important local characteristics that need to be both acknowledged and celebrated to help local communities thrive in the era of climate change. The book also provides key policy lessons and a roadmap for future research in adaptation urbanism.

Advancing resilience policy discourse through multi-disciplinary framework, this work will be of great interest to students of urban planning, geography, transportation, landscape architecture, and environmental studies, as well as resilience practitioners around the world.

Billy Fields is an Associate Professor of Political Science at Texas State University. His research focuses on understanding the key elements of resilient communities. He is the co-editor of *Transport Beyond Oil* (2013) and leads the International Sustainable Transportation Engagement Program, an annual study-abroad program in the Netherlands exploring best practices in active transportation.

John L. Renne is Professor and Director of the Center for Urban and Environmental Solutions (CUES) in the Department of Urban and Regional Planning at Florida Atlantic University.

ADVANCES IN URBAN SUSTAINABILITY

Urban Sustainability in Theory and Practice
Circles of Sustainability
Paul James

Sustainability Citizenship in Cities
Theory and Practice
Edited by Ralph Horne, John Fien, Beau B. Beza, and Anitra Nelson

Street Fights in Copenhagen
Bicycle and Car Politics in a Green Mobility City
Jason Henderson and Natalie Marie Gulsrud

Adaptation Urbanism and Resilient Communities
Transforming Streets to Address Climate Change
Billy Fields and John L. Renne

For more information about this series, please visit: www.routledge.com/Advances-in-Urban-Sustainability/book-series/AUS

ADAPTATION URBANISM AND RESILIENT COMMUNITIES

Transforming Streets to Address Climate Change

Billy Fields and John L. Renne

earthscan
from Routledge

First published 2021
by Routledge
2 Park Square, Milton Park, Abingdon, Oxon OX14 4RN

and by Routledge
52 Vanderbilt Avenue, New York, NY 10017

Routledge is an imprint of the Taylor & Francis Group, an informa business

British Library Cataloguing-in-Publication Data
A catalogue record for this book is available from the British Library

Library of Congress Cataloging-in-Publication Data
Names: Fields, Billy (Billy M.) author. | Renne, John L., author.
Title: Adaptation urbanism and resilient communities : transforming streets to address climate change / Billy Fields and John L. Renne.
Description: New York : Routledge, 2021. |
Series: Advances in urban sustainability |
Includes bibliographical references and index.
Identifiers: LCCN 2020048257 (print) | LCCN 2020048258 (ebook) |
ISBN 9780367134952 (paperback) | ISBN 9780367134938 (hardback) |
ISBN 9780429026805 (ebook)
Subjects: LCSH: City planning–Environmental aspects. |
Local transit–Planning. | Community development. |
Sustainable urban development.
Classification: LCC HT166 .F474 2021 (print) |
LCC HT166 (ebook) | DDC 307.1/216–dc23
LC record available at https://lccn.loc.gov/2020048257
LC ebook record available at https://lccn.loc.gov/2020048258

ISBN: 978-0-367-13493-8 (hbk)
ISBN: 978-0-367-13495-2 (pbk)
ISBN: 978-0-429-02680-5 (ebk)

Typeset in Bembo
by Newgen Publishing UK

CONTENTS

TABLES AND FIGURES

Tables

Figures

ABOUT THE AUTHORS AND CONTRIBUTORS

Authors

Billy Fields

Billy Fields, Ph.D., is an Associate Professor of Political Science at Texas State University. His research focuses on understanding the key elements of resilient communities. He is the co-editor of *Transport Beyond Oil* (Island Press 2013). He leads the International Sustainable Transportation Engagement Program, an annual study-abroad program in the Netherlands exploring best practices in active transportation. Prior to joining Texas State University, Dr. Fields was Director of the Center for Urban and Public Affairs at the University of New Orleans and Research Director for the Rails-to-Trails Conservancy where he developed and explored the concept of trail-oriented development. Before his academic life, he was also a raft guide in the mountains of North Carolina, an ice cream clerk at Harrods in London, and a food runner at Commander's Palace in New Orleans.

John L. Renne

John L. Renne, Ph.D., AICP, is Professor and Director of the Center for Urban and Environmental Solutions (CUES) in Department of Urban and Regional Planning at Florida Atlantic University, located in Boca Raton, Florida. Dr. Renne is the founder of several companies that focus on transit-oriented development (TOD) real estate development, consulting, investment, and data, including The TOD Group, TOD Group Consulting, Denver TOD Fund, and the TODIndex.com. Renne is the co-editor of *Transport Beyond Oil: Policy Choices for a Multimodal Future* (2013) *and Transit Oriented Development: Making It Happen* (2009).

Contributors

Liliane Geerling

After graduating from the Delft University of Technology (TU Delft) (Industrial Design and Architecture/Built Environment) Liliane worked for the City of Rotterdam in various positions, ranging from urban planner to project manager of urban (re)development projects, among others Kop van Zuid and Loyd district, two former port areas. After that she continued as senior adviser/researcher at BVR advisers for spatial development, where she was involved in many projects on the cutting edge of climate adaptation and participatory planning. She continued her career at the HZ University of Applied Sciences–The Netherlands as senior researcher/lecturer resilience, ecology and spatial planning, climate adaptation planning, disaster risk reduction, and integrated coastal zone management in the study programs of Delta and Water Management. She is managing and developing the Living Lab Water in Surabaya with the Institute for Technology Surabaya and the Living Lab Water Mekong Delta with Can Tho University. Her academic work includes developing circular approaches for plastic pollution in rivers, among others in the Mekong Delta, and a monitoring project for Rijkswaterstaat with Citizen Science in the Southwest Delta (Zeeland). She has ample experience in training young students as well as people from the professional working field.

Tara Tolford

Tara Tolford, AICP, is an urban planner and researcher in New Orleans. She has been a researcher with the University of New Orleans (UNO) Transportation Institute since 2011, specializing in active transportation planning, policy, and data. This has included managing a regional pedestrian and bicycle data initiative, developing and implementing the framework for a statewide pedestrian and bicycle count program, authoring Louisiana's Recreational Trails Program strategic plan, and coordinating the development and application of tools in support of smart growth, growth management, and transit-oriented development. In addition, she is an instructor for UNO's Master of Science in Transportation program, has organized various local and international knowledge-sharing and outreach projects, and serves on numerous local and state committees focused on fostering built environments that support sustainable transportation options, climate mitigation, and equitable use of public space.

ACKNOWLEDGMENTS

This book project has taken us to multiple cities around the world and would not have been possible without the gracious assistance of residents in each of these cities. So many people sat with us and helped to steer us towards a deeper understanding of resilient transportation in their communities. As always in an endeavor like this, any mistakes are ours alone.

With that said, we would like to thank the good people at MobyCon Consulting for working with our students and helping us better understand Dutch streets. We would like to particularly thank Angela van der Kloof for thoughtful, extended conversations that deepened our knowledge and helped us reconsider the potential of streets as places for people. We would also like to thank Cornelia Dinca of Sustainable Amsterdam and Meredith Glaser of the University of Amsterdam for sharing their time and insights about the streets of Amsterdam. We would also like to thank Edwin Koster of Fietsersbond Zwolle for extended bicycle tours of his lovely city. Nico Tillie of the Delft University of Technology (TU Delft) also provided important background information on planning in Rotterdam.

In Copenhagen, we would like to thank Copenhagenize Design Company for providing a window into the city's transportation system. We thank James Thoem and former CEO Morten Kabell for their insights. Thank you to Tine Langsted Krogstrup of SLA and Birgitte Bundesen Svarre and Peter Raaschou-Nielsen of Gehl Architects for helping us dig deeper into resilience planning in Copenhagen. In addition, we thank Rene Sommer Lindsay for meeting in Edinburgh and talking us through the planning process for Tåsinge Plads. James Henderson of San Francisco State University also aided us in better understanding the politics of transportation in Copenhagen.

In London, we thank Lucy Mahoney of C40 Cities, Charles Snead and Andre Neves of Transport for London, and Lucy Saunders of Healthy Streets for providing important background information on transportation and resilience planning. We also would like to thank Lorna King of Oxfordshire Livable Streets and Denver Nixon of the Transport Studies Unit of the School of Geography and Environment at University of Oxford for providing context on transport planning in the UK.

In Vancouver, we thank Arthur Orsini of Vancouver Coastal Health, Anthony Perl of Simon Fraser University, and Paul Lightfoot and Paul Krueger from the City of Vancouver.

In New Orleans, we thank Jennifer Ruley, Dan Jatres, and Mary Kincaid from the City of New Orleans. We also thank David Fields whose photography helped to inspire a rethinking of the role of streets. In South Florida, we thank Amir Koleini, Josh Sawislak, and Colin Polsky of Florida Atlantic University for background on planning efforts. We especially thank Serena Hoermann of the Center for Urban and Environmental Solutions at Florida Atlantic University for exceptional assistance in pulling the final draft of the book together. In addition, we thank planning consultant Tony Hull for hours of background discussions on integrating Dutch street systems into a North American context during planning sessions for the International Sustainable Transportation Engagement (I-STEP) program.

We are also deeply indebted to our collaborators, Liliane Geerling and Tara Tolford. This project would not have been possible without their generous engagement, time, and hard work. Liliane Geerling of HZ University helped us understand the complex water management system of the Netherlands and provided deep insights into resilience planning in Rotterdam. The dialogue that we began several years back was the foundation for this work. Tara Tolford of the University of New Orleans provided important insights into planning in New Orleans and the complexities of knowledge transfer across cities. We are honored that Liliane and Tara worked with us over the years that this book took to come to fruition.

Finally, we thank our families for providing support during our extended and sometimes quixotic travels. Billy Fields would like to thank Tara O'Neill for believing in the project even as it extended into years and Keagan O'Neill Fields for helping to count bikes in the Beestenmarkt in Delft. He would also like to thank his parents, Bill and Linda Fields, for inspiring the sense of inquiry and adventure that is the base for a project like this. John wishes to thank Billy Fields for his vision, drive, and hard work on this book. John contributed to the theory and framing, some of the interviews and editing, and led the chapters on Miami and London. However, Billy led the writing for most of the book and deserves the bulk of the credit for this manuscript.

FOREWORD

Peter Newman AO
Professor of Sustainability, Curtin University, Perth Australia

This is a beautiful book. It's about streets and how they can make more resilient cities. It took me back to a journey I began in 1972 when I went (with my wife) to study in Delft, the Netherlands. We were young, untraveled and had no experience of how different cities could be. It was a cultural shock as the first day after we arrived, we bought a car as we were from Perth and you couldn't live without a car in that city. It was deeply embedded in our psyche. Then we discovered that we hardly ever used the car. We just didn't need it to meet friends or go shopping or do anything really. We ran into our friends in the street, something we had never experienced before.

As we got to know our new city we discovered a big overpass at the entrance to the city that had never been finished. It hung in the sky like a huge, ominous threat. We discovered that Delft, like all cities in the world, had been subject to an American consultant's report that had said unless a major freeway was forced through the city it would never survive economically. The locals however had stopped it.

Instead of adopting the idea of creating more capacity for cars, Dutch cities across the country began to improve the opportunities for walking and biking with *woonerf*, a word that means "living streets." The engineering techniques for these streets included shared space (with priority for walking and biking), some traffic calming with objects like trees, tables, and chairs, and very low speed limits.

It was a powerful cultural education and this book will give you many such examples that are now mainstreaming across the world, especially new case studies in the Netherlands. They show that the approach has worked and continues to be rediscovered in these and other European cities.

But after this experience we had an even deeper one when I went to Stanford to pursue a post doc and we went to live in what is now called the Silicon Valley area. We started off trying to live like we had in Delft and bought two bikes only. They just didn't work to enable us to live properly; most destinations were just too far away. And when we used them, despite bike lanes on and around the campus, we were in constant fear of our lives from the traffic. We had to get a car.

Not long after this, the first oil crisis hit and we witnessed the city go into a traumatic state as gas queues went for miles, people just stayed at home and deeply felt anger, and conspiracies raged about where the oil had been hidden in large caverns in the mountains. There was certainly no resilience strategy and no awareness of the inherent car dependence in the structure of the city with its fabric of bitumen that had been rolled out by the same kind of consultant's reports rejected by the Delft community.

These two experiences shaped my life for the next almost 50 years. We returned to Australia and chose to live in a more Delft-like urban fabric (Fremantle) where we have stayed ever since, and I began life as an academic determined to try and manage the automobile in cities across Australia and the world.

I ran activist campaigns that saved our railway and stopped freeways, and won. This gave me hope that cities could indeed overcome automobile dependence, the term Jeff Kenworthy and I created in 1989, based on data we collected over ten years of travel from 32 global cities.

We soon found that we couldn't just say what was wrong with the dominant traffic-engineering model of creating an endless growth in vehicle-carrying capacity. We had to present alternatives that showed how streets could be reclaimed by traffic calming for people to enjoy rather than being destroyed by traffic, how quality transit could enable cross-city travel even in a car-dependent city, and that we needed to build urban villages in the same way that European cities were doing.

This book shows how such approaches can be done and will improve the economy of cities. They will make people healthier and create solutions to the big problems of automobile dependence, including climate change and vulnerability to resource shocks. But it's not easy. There are always struggles as the culture of car-based planning is deeply set in our perceptions of what is right, even human rights. And these perceptions are embedded in highway-engineering manuals and professional standards.

When Jeff and I started going to cities to speak about our publications we found there were deep-seated objections from the local traffic engineers. For a number of years we never found a single engineer who would countenance the idea of traffic calming. Roads were for cars. We eventually found one in Portland and one in Boulder! A decade later we found one in Sydney. But that didn't mean we didn't help win many battles in the streets of American and Australian cities. The power of communities to see common sense and to achieve political change drove a different vision.

That world continues, though most of the ideas for new city development include traffic calming, more localized urban villages, and electric transit. The third book in our trilogy on automobile dependence suggests that most cities are "moving beyond car-based planning." Indeed COVID and the associated economic collapse seem to be accelerating these changes. So, get on board with the concepts and case studies in this book and start applying them in your own places, as you will find the doors are starting to open.

PROLOGUE

This is a book about streets and how they can be used to help make city life better. Better is, however, complicated. Better for whom? Streets have been defined as spaces for cars, spaces to speed away or towards somewhere else. That vision of streets opened regional development and far-flung neighborhoods where you have your life with a certain set of schools, services, and amenities and I have mine with a different set. As urban developer and scholar Christopher Leinberger (2010, p. xv) argues, "*transportation drives development*. The transportation system our society chooses to invest in will dictate the form of the built environment (italics in original)." Transportation and land use policy also drive segregation (Rothstein 2017) and greenhouse gas (GHG) emissions (Creutzig 2016). While there are multiple intervening variables, the places we build and the opportunities those places offer are defined by the streets we choose to build. We can keep building streets that burn through gas and separate our communities, or we can bounce forward towards something better.

Moments of crisis like the coronavirus pandemic and the emerging climate crisis open moments to rethink the status quo, but the cost of that rethinking is the real pain and suffering of disaster. Disasters are not moments of opportunity, but instead challenging and complex times that call for deep reassessment of the status quo (Walker 2020). This book is about that reassessment, a rethinking of the role of streets and how to create places that better serve community needs.

Resilience: bouncing back is not enough

One of the primary ways to conceptualize crisis response is the emerging paradigm of resilience. During the coronavirus pandemic, for example, individuals and organizations struggled to cope with system failures across multiple sectors. From health care to education to the economy to navigating grocery stores and city streets, systems seemed stretched past the breaking point. Resilience has emerged as a key theme focusing on the capacity of systems to bounce back from shock to create stronger and more robust social, economic, and community networks. During the COVID-19 pandemic, the term was applied to multiple areas from health systems (Legido-Quigley et al. 2020) to supply chain management (Alicke et al. 2020) to food systems (Foley 2020), and the education sector (Brown and Kafka 2020).

The multiple uses and spheres of resilience applications speak to the malleability of the term and its usefulness as a conceptual tool in responding to a world in flux. While resilience is frequently viewed as the capacity of a system to bounce back after a disaster, this approach can, however, limit policy responses to the narrow confines of preexisting pathways. This may be appropriate for places characterized by strong social, environmental, and economic systems, but it is a problematic way to frame crisis response in locations characterized by intense inequality and failing economic and environmental systems. The coronavirus pandemic has, for example, highlighted the unequal landscape of preexisting conditions and health care access that has resulted in significant racial fatality disparities (*New York Times* Editorial Board 2020; Ray 2020). If health care resilience is seen as bouncing back to conditions before the disaster, then the same conditions that created the health storm will be perpetuated. Bouncing back is not enough in the face of failing systems (Shaw 2012).

Community resilience at the street level

In *Adaptation Urbanism and Resilient Communities*, we examine another type of complex system, street systems. Streets have multiple purposes. From acting as the physical location for transportation, water, and electricity infrastructure to creating linkages to your home and neighborhood destinations, street spaces need to accomplish multiple goals simultaneously to help create strong communities. Many streets, however, are not designed to meet these multiple goals equally, but instead privilege the speed of vehicles moving somewhere else over the needs of residents whose front doors open on to these spaces. The result is high crash and pollution rates and social division as highways carve through some neighborhoods to open pathways for others to live in separated enclaves.

As traffic declined during the coronavirus pandemic and the need for safe spaces to walk, bicycle, or use transit at physical distance became more important, many residents looked out their doors and questioned how streets could better serve their community's needs (C40 Cities 2020). In a time when you can't travel very far, making *here* better takes on added significance.

Making here safe for all residents has, however, not historically been a consistent area of emphasis for transportation policymakers. Safe access to quality walking and bicycling infrastructure is often lacking in high-poverty neighborhoods with higher percentages of minority residents (Cradock et al. 2009; Lowe 2016). The result is often high crash fatality rates and vulnerability to pollution in these same neighborhoods. These infrastructure disparities are often compounded by other public space and street concerns that move beyond pollution and the speed and volume of traffic. Cobbs (2020), for example, notes that:

> Livable streets advocates emphasize the need to make streets safer for children and elderly folks. It's time to broaden the definition of livable streets to include public space where all people are free from the threat of violence by the police or racists, as well as interpersonal violence.

Safe streets need to be welcoming places for all residents, and traffic safety is just one component of this larger system.

Instead of focusing on bouncing back after a disaster to streets of speed, pollution, and division, many communities are looking to bounce forward towards streets and public space systems that are better able to handle unexpected shocks like the coronavirus pandemic and, on a daily basis, make local neighborhoods livable places. In *Adaptation Urbanism and Resilient Communities*, we examine this growing movement of cities that are rethinking the role of streets. While most of the book examines the role of streets in addressing another impending shock, climate change, the pandemic has focused growing attention on how to better use street spaces to create safe spaces for movement in a time of physical distancing. Before we begin the deeper evaluation of resilience and how transportation and public space systems can be rethought to address climate change, the emerging transportation response to the pandemic provides an important moment to highlight the growing movement to rethink the large spatial footprint of cars in urban areas and how that space can be repurposed to help meet deeper civic needs to create truly resilient communities.

Car space and the resilient city

In the immediate months of the coronavirus pandemic, the promotion of physical distancing was one of the primary means of containing the outbreak. While limiting movement outside the home was a core component of the physical distancing policy response, transportation for essential workers, trips for critical needs, and, where safe, movement outside the home for exercise and mental health still needed to be safely managed. These needs placed demands on the allocation of city space.

While auto traffic numbers decreased dramatically during the immediate months of crisis, city space was still mostly dedicated to auto traffic. Approximately 30% of urban space is dedicated to streets (UN Habitat 2013) and, when car parking is added to street space, the figure jumps to approximately 50% of all urban space dedicated to car movement (Ellen MacArthur Foundation and McKinsey Center for Business and Environment 2015). Car-dominated cities also produce air pollution that may be a contributing factor in higher fatality risk to COVID-19 (Ogen 2020; Wu et al. 2020). This distribution of space and the negative externalities of transportation system increasingly became contentious issues in many communities as residents sought safe neighborhood spaces for movement for essential needs and access to fresh air outdoors. The question of why street space was being allocated to cars over neighborhood residents was cast in sharp relief.

While most transportation decisions take years to plan and implement, many cities moved quickly to create open streets to allow for greater physical space for neighborhood residents. As of the end of May 2020, the National Association of City Transportation Officials (NACTO 2020a) identified over 100 cities around the world implementing various forms of traffic calming and street closures designed to open streets to create greater space for pedestrians, cyclists, and transit operations. Key guidance to emerge on the creation of these spaces from NACTO (2020b) includes six key principles: support the most vulnerable people first, amplify public health guidance, create safe streets for today and tomorrow, support local economies, bring communities into the process, and act now and adapt over time.

This guidance represents a key shift in planning for streets focusing on safety, local needs, and engagement. Most streets in the past have, however, been planned with radically different goals and processes. Most streets have been planned with limited public engagement and focus on the goals of pushing as many vehicles as possible through neighborhoods at high speeds. Planning to increase the capacity of vehicles and maintaining vehicle speed have been the administrative hallmarks of transportation planning (Hall 2001). While the NACTO principles apply to the pandemic recovery, these same principles can act as springboards for a new type of street planning with broader goals developed with the community based on improving neighborhood quality of life, improving safety, decreasing pollution, and providing access to community goods and services.

The immediate result of the initial interventions and demand from families for safe spaces to walk and bicycle resulted in a boom for active transportation. Headlines from around the world described large growth in bicycling use with pictures of families moving together in the formerly car-filled city streets (Laker 2020). At the same time, air pollution levels dropped significantly as car use plummeted (Ellis-Petersen et al. 2020). The moment for active transportation as a key component of a resilient transportation system seemed to have arrived (Schwedhelm et al. 2020; Vandyke et al. 2020).

As quickly as the moment for active transportation arrived, it was soon followed by larger questions about the future of commuting and transit and even questions about whether cities themselves would survive the crisis. Disasters are shocks to the system and often cause temporary changes and, occasionally, lead to long-term structural change. The 1970s gas crisis, for example, led to a bike boom across the world in the 1970s, but this quickly faded from view as many cities returned to car dominance. In some places, however, the gas crisis led to a radical rethinking of the place of the car in the city. In the Netherlands, for example, the gas crisis was the catalyst for a now decades-long revival of the bicycle as a key component of the transportation system (Wagenbuur 2011; Feddes and de Lange 2019). In Chapter 5 on Rotterdam, we discuss how the Netherlands translated that push into some of the safest and most livable streets in the world. When headlines ask whether the "biking surge" will "last when cities open up again" (Peters 2020), the answer is not predetermined, but instead dependent on what citizens and their political leaders push for. The question today is whether cities will bounce back to the car once the crisis subsides or bounce forward towards a new, healthier transportation system.

While there are many forces at play and early indications from China pointing to a growth in car use to avoid crowded transit systems, there appears to be a growing awareness that bouncing back to the pre-COVID-19 transportation system is not enough. Across Europe, initial polling showed that 68% of surveyed residents in Belgium, France, Germany, Italy, Spain, and the UK wanted "to see air pollution reduction policies—including restrictions on car access to city centers—kept in place" (Posaner et al. 2020). Paris Mayor Anne Hidalgo, for example, argued that polluting cars would not be welcomed back into the city in the same way as before the crisis (Reid 2020b). In a speech before the Paris City Council, Hidalgo said that:

> It will make the health crisis worse. Pollution is already in itself a health crisis and a danger—and pollution joined up with coronavirus is a particularly dangerous cocktail. So it's out of the question to think that arriving in the heart of the city by car is any solution, when it could actually aggravate the situation.
>
> *(quoted in Reid 2020b)*

In the immediate months of the crisis, Hidalgo begun to implement this vision by creating a pop-up network of "corona cycle ways" (Reid 2020a) with the ambition of creating 650 km (403 miles) of new cycle facilities. This expanding network of cycle paths was aimed in the short term to act as a safer temporary substitute for metro trips that would essentially "use streets as public transit" (TransAlt 2020). The plan is the first phase of a long-term effort to improve walking, cycling, and extend transit access in the city (O'Sullivan 2020). These plans call for the creation of connected 15-minute city centers where "all city residents are able to meet most of their needs within a short walk or bicycle ride from their homes" (C40 Cities 2020, p. 30).

Efforts like those in Paris are being replicated in cities around the world. For example, in Italy, Milan has proposed a 15-minute city framework and plans to add 35 km (22 miles) of cycling facilities and enhanced pedestrian connections throughout the city (C40 Cities 2020). Rome, as well, has moved forward with plans to build 150 km (93 miles) of bicycle network improvements (Caballero and Rapin 2020). In North America, Oakland implemented a system of 74 miles (119 km) of slow streets (Lydon 2020). Up the coast, Seattle has created a network of "stay healthy streets" designed to open access for physically distant movement (Davis 2020). Across the continent, New York City, in fits and starts, also implemented a system of 100 miles (160 km) of open streets, but with significant equity issues associated with police enforcement and access in historically disenfranchised communities (Cuba 2020).

In Canada, Montreal planned a pop-up network of over 200 miles (322 km) of extended bicycle and pedestrian facilities (Montreal Gazette 2020) in conjunction with a new network of "family and active streets" (Scott 2020). In the Canadian Northwest, Vancouver opened the iconic Stanley Park roads to bicycles, with bike traffic surging 76%. In the words of a 10-year-old interviewed by the CBC, the results were "fun…I don't have to worry about cars" (Larsen 2020).

Providing access to fun, social movement options is an undervalued component of a resilient transportation system. Streets need to be permitted for freedom for 10-year-olds, 80-year-olds, and everyone in between. That freedom needs to be the same for all residents. Freedom of the street starts with freedom to be who you are and move safely through the community.

Resilient streets are not just movement corridors but can also be places for people, places of community. During the coronavirus crisis, these places should allow ample space for movement away from others. After the crisis, however, these same streets can be made "stickier" to help rebuild community connections. Resilient streets can be adapted to changing conditions quickly and repurposed to meet the needs during a disaster and, when the crisis recedes, help to create communities we are proud to call home.

Operationalizing the moment will take many forms in different places, but core changes that appear to be emerging focus on the promotion of slow, healthy neighborhood streets that provide expanded space for people to walk, bike, and visit local restaurants outdoors (NACTO 2020b). Many streets are being transformed into places for slow movement that encourage safety, health, and commerce. In some ways, this is like a pilot project to show what a healthy, resilient street network could look like. If the pilots are planned with community engagement and well used, they can create constituency for change and an opening to extend these new project types into much broader systems. The crisis response is like a test case of how to create a full network of healthy neighborhood streets, but, if history is any guide, the key will be whether local residents and politicians have the will and power to push through the inertia of the status quo. This process will likely be uneven with some communities springing forward and others snapping back into previous patterns.

In *Adaptation Urbanism and Resilient Communities*, we examine the resilient street transformation process through a series of case studies of resilience leaders in Europe and North America. We examine how Copenhagen, Miami, New Orleans, London, and Rotterdam are rethinking their streets to meet the present challenges of the coronavirus crisis and the emerging climate crisis. The challenges are serious, complicated, and contentious, but the urgency of the present crisis and the impending dimensions of the growing climate crisis are pushing new visions forward (C40 Cities 2020). The disaster experience often upends the possible. Things that seemed to be etched in stone often are not as solid as they once seemed. Possibilities that seemed closed sometimes open.

The transportation question is whether new models of streets can be created to help communities bounce forward to meet these emerging challenges. In *Adaptation Urbanism and Resilient Communities*, we examine the political and institutional forces that are helping to define the answer to these questions and point to potential pathways forward that can help communities build streets that better meet community needs and are truly resilient.

References

Alicke, K., Azcue, X., & Barriball, E. (2020). Supply-Chain Recovery in Coronavirus Times—Plan for Now and the Future. McKinsey. MarchLast accessed 4/15/2020 from www.mckinsey.com/business-functions/operations/our-insights/supply-chain-recovery-in-coronavirus-times-plan-for-now-and-the-future?cid=other-eml-alt-mip-mck&hlkid=53e98fdcbca84440a9da62b8aa318d06&hctky=11800216&hdpid=8044609a-0e2e-4a2a-9818-d7877df47684.

Brown, S., & Kafka, A.C. (2020). Covid-19 Has Worsened the Student Mental-Health Crisis. Can Resilience Training Fix It? *Chronicle of Higher Education*. May 11. Last accessed 7/17/2020 from www.chronicle.com/article/Covid-19-Has-Worsened-the/248753.

C40 Cities. (2020). C40 Mayors' Agenda for a Green and Just Recovery. July 15. Last accessed 7/28/2020 from www.c40.org/other/agenda-for-a-green-and-just-recovery.

Caballero, S., & Rapin, P. (2020). COVID-19 Made Cities More Bike-Friendly—Here's How to Keep Them That Way. *World Economic Forum*. June 19. Last accessed 7/28/2020 from www.weforum.org/agenda/2020/06/covid-19-made-cities-more-bike-friendly-here-s-how-to-keep-them-that-way/.

Cobbs, C. (2020). What's Needed to Address Anti-Black Racism in Urban Planning? *Streetsblog Chicago*. June 14. Last accessed 6/16/2020 from https://chi.streetsblog.org/2020/06/14/whats-needed-to-address-anti-black-racism-in-urban-planning/.

Craddock, A. L., Troped, P. J., Fields, B., Melly, S. J., Simms, S.V. Gimmler, F., & Fowler, M. (2009). Factors Associated with Federal Transportation Funding for Local Pedestrian and Bicycle Programming and Facilities. *Journal of Public Health Policy,* 30, S38–S72.

Creutzig, F. (2016). Evolving Narratives of Low-Carbon Futures in Transportation. *Transport Reviews*, *36*(3), 341–360.

Cuba, J. Mayor's 'Open Streets' Leave Out Neighborhoods That Need It Most. *StreetblogNYC*. Last accessed 6/12/2020 from https://nyc.streetsblog.org/2020/05/21/mayors-open-streets-leave-out-neighborhoods-that-need-it-most/.

Davis, S. Get Ready! 11 More Miles of Stay Healthy Streets Coming Your Way. *City of Seattle SDOT Blog*. Last accessed 6/12/2020 from https://sdotblog.seattle.gov/2020/05/01/get-ready-11-more-miles-of-stay-healthy-streets-coming-your-way/.

Ellen MacArthur Foundation, & McKinsey Center for Business and Environment. (2015). *Growth Within: A Circular Economy Vision for a Competitive Europe*. Cowes, UK: Ellen MacArthur Foundation.

Ellis-Petersen, H., Ratcliffe, R., Cowie, S., Daniels, J. & Kuo, L. (2020). 'It's Positively Alpine!': Disbelief in Big Cities as Air Pollution Falls. *The Guardian*. April 11. Last accessed 5/21/2020 from www.theguardian.com/environment/2020/apr/11/positively-alpine-disbelief-air-pollution-falls-lockdown-coronavirus.

Feddes, F., & de Lange, M. (2019). *Bike City Amsterdam: How Amsterdam Became the Cycling Capital of the World*. Amsterdam: Nieuw Amsterdam.

Foley, M. (2020). COVID-19 and Our Food Supply. *Resilience*. April 3. Last accessed 4/15/2020 from https://school-of-adaptive-agriculture.org/covid-19-and-our-food-supply/.

Hall, F. L. (2001). Traffic Stream Characteristics. In *Traffic Flow Theory: State-of-the Art Report* (N. Gartner, C. J. Messer, & A. K. Rathi, eds.). Amsterdam: Federal Highway Administration/Transportation Research Board/Oak Ridge National Laboratory.

Laker, L. (2020). World Cities Turn Their Streets Over to Walkers and Cyclists. *The Guardian*. April 11. Last accessed 5/21/2020 from www.theguardian.com/world/2020/apr/11/world-cities-turn-their-streets-over-to-walkers-and-cyclists?CMP=Share_AndroidApp_Tweet.

Larsen, K. (2020). Car Ban Sparks Bike Boom in Stanley Park, but What Happens Post-Pandemic? *CBC*. May 16. Last accessed 5/22/2020 from www.cbc.ca/news/canada/british-columbia/car-ban-sparks-bike-boom-in-stanley-park-but-what-happens-post-pandemic-1.5570700.

Legido-Quigley, H., Asgari, N., Teo, Y.Y., Leung, G. M., Oshitani, H., Fukuda, K... & Heymann, D. (2020). Are High-Performing Health Systems Resilient Against the COVID-19 Epidemic? *The Lancet*, *395*(10227), 848–850.

Leinberger, C. B. (2010). *The Option of Urbanism: Investing in a New American Dream*. Washington, DC: Island Press.

Lowe, K. (2016). Environmental Justice and Pedestrianism: Sidewalk Continuity, Race, and Poverty in New Orleans, Louisiana. *Transportation Research Record*, *2598*(1), 119–123.

Lydon, Mike. (2020). COVID19 Livable Streets Response Strategies. Last accessed 6/12/2020 from https://docs.google.com/spreadsheets/d/1tjam1v0NLUWkYedIa4dVOL49pyWIPIyGwRB0DOnm3Ls/edit#gid=0.

Montreal Gazette. (2020). Montreal's Summer Plans: An Extra 327 km of Bike Paths, Pedestrian Lanes. May 16. Last accessed 6/12/2020 from https://montrealgazette.com/news/local-news/montreals-summer-plans-an-extra-327-km-of-bike-paths-pedestrian-lanes/wcm/badcab9b-9a35–461a-8740-a49122748852/.

NACTO. (2020a). COVID-19: Transportation Response Center. Last accessed 4/25/2020 from https://nacto.org/program/covid19/.

NACTO. (2020b). Streets for Pandemic Response & Recovery. Last accessed 7/28/2020 from https://nacto.org/streets-for-pandemic-response-recovery/.

New York Times Editorial Board. (2020). The Cities We Need. May 11. Last accessed 5/21/2020 from www.nytimes.com/2020/05/11/opinion/sunday/coronavirus-us-cities-inequality.html.

Ogen, Y. (2020). Assessing Nitrogen Dioxide (NO_2) Levels as a Contributing Factor to the Coronavirus (COVID-19) Fatality Rate. *Science of the Total Environment*, 726, 15 July, 2020138605.

O'Sullivan, Fergus. (2020). Paris Has a Plan to Keep Cars Out After Lockdown. *Citylab*. April 29. Last accessed 5/18/2020 from www.citylab.com/transportation/2020/04/paris-cars-air-pollution-health-public-transit-bike-lanes/610861/.

Peters, A. (2020). Coronavirus is Causing a Biking Surge—Can it Last When Cities Open Up Again? *FastCompay*. April 2. Last accessed 5/21/2020 from www.fastcompany.com/90484691/coronavirus-is-causing-a-biking-surge-can-it-last-when-cities-open-up-again.

Posaner, J., Cokelaere, H., & Hernandez-Morales, A. (2020). Life After COVID: Europeans Want to Keep Their Cities Car-Free. *Politico Europe Edition*. Last accessed 6/13/2020 from www.politico.eu/article/life-after-covid-europeans-want-to-keep-their-cities-car-free/.

Ray, Rashawn. (2020). Why Are Blacks Dying at Higher Rates From COVID-19? *Brooking*. April 9. Last accessed 4/25/2020 from www.brookings.edu/blog/fixgov/2020/04/09/why-are-blacks-dying-at-higher-rates-from-covid-19/.

Reid, Carlton. (2020a). Paris to Create 650 Kilometers of Post-Lockdown Cycleways. *Forbes*. April 22. Last accessed 5/18/2020 from www.forbes.com/sites/carltonreid/2020/04/22/paris-to-create-650-kilometers-of-pop-up-corona-cycleways-for-post-lockdown-travel/#532aed7754d4.

Reid, Carlton. (2020b). Au Revoir les Automobiles: Paris Closes Rue de Rivoli to Cars. *Forbes*. April 30. Last accessed 5/17/2020 from www.forbes.com/sites/carltonreid/2020/04/30/au-revoir-les-automobiles-paris-to-close-major-boulevard-to-cars/#2b41a77d9b0c.

Rothstein, R. (2017). *The Color of Law: A Forgotten History of How Our Government Segregated America*. New York, NY: Liveright Publishing.

Schwedhelm, Alejandro, Li, Wei, Harms, Lucas, & Adriazola-Steil, Claudia. (2020). Biking Provides a Critical Lifeline During the Coronavirus Crisis. *World Resources Institute*. April 17. Last accessed 5/29/2020 from www.wri.org/blog/2020/04/coronavirus-biking-critical-in-cities.

Scott, M. (2020). Coronavirus: "Family and Active Streets" Open in Plateau. *Montreal Gazette*. May 3. Last accessed 6/12/2020 from https://montrealgazette.com/news/local-news/coronavirus-family-and-active-streets-open-in-plateau.

Shaw, K. (2012). "Reframing" Resilience: Challenges for Planning Theory and Practice. *Planning Theory and Practice*, *13*(2), 308–312.

TransAlt. (2020). Op-Ed: Here Are Some Cities Getting Open Streets Right. *StreetsBlog USA*. May 1. Last accessed 5/22/2020 from https://usa.streetsblog.org/2020/05/01/op-ed-heres-some-cities-getting-open-streets-right/.

UN Habitat. (2013). *Streets as Public Spaces and Drivers of Urban Prosperity*. Nairobi, Kenya: UN Habitat. https://unhabitat.org/streets-as-public-spaces-and-drivers-of-urban-prosperity.

Vandyke, Nancy, Sarriera, Javier, & Sehmi, Gurpreet Singh. (2020). A Roadmap Toward Sustainable Mobility: What we Already Knew, and What We're Learning from the Pandemic. *World Bank Blogs*. Last accessed 6/1/2020 from https://blogs.worldbank.org/transport/roadmap-toward-sustainable-mobility-what-we-already-knew-and-what-were-learning-pandemic.

Wagenbuur, M. (2011). How the Dutch Got Their Cycling Infrastructure. *Bicycle Dutch*. October 20. Last accessed 6/13/2020 from https://bicycledutch.wordpress.com/2011/10/20/how-the-dutch-got-their-cycling-infrastructure/.

Walker, A. (2020). Coronavirus is Not Fuel for Urbanist Fantasies. *Curbed*. May 20. Last accessed 6/10/2020 from www.curbed.com/2020/5/20/21263319/coronavirus-future-city-urban-covid-19.

Wu, X., Nethery, R. C., Sabath, B. M., Braun, D., & Dominici, F. (2020). Exposure to Air Pollution and COVID-19 Mortality in the United States. *medRxiv*. April 9. doi: https://doi.org/10.1101/2020.04.05.20054502.

1

INTRODUCTION

Rising tides and flooded streets

The ocean has begun to wash into the streets of South Florida on sunny days when the breeze barely ripples the palm fronds. On Southlake Drive in Hollywood, FL, the tidal lakes push higher, and residents expect saltwater in the streets and in their yards during the highest tides of the year. These King Tides, combined with a slowing Gulf Stream and rising seas, push water up into the lakes and through the drainage system into city streets, making many areas impassable for hours at a time. Residents move their cars out of the way, watch water rise into their yards, and wait for the ocean tide to recede. It has become increasingly clear, however, that over the next several decades the water is not going to recede. Instead, what once seemed like an anomaly now seems like a harbinger of a future where climate change threatens to push the ocean into the streets, homes, and businesses of low-lying coastal communities around the globe.

Across the Atlantic Ocean in northern Europe, once-rare cloudburst events, when near tropical levels of rain fall in a short time, have become more frequent. On July 2, 2011, almost 6 inches (150 mm) of rain fell in Copenhagen in approximately 2 hours. The sheer physical quantity of the rain outstripped drainage capacity and flooded basements and streets with about $800 million (6 billion DKK) in damages (City of Copenhagen 2012). With climate change altering the temperature and humidity levels, these cloudburst events and, conversely, drought and heatwaves are becoming more common depending on the region (EASAC 2013). Managing water, both too much and too little, has become a key urban issue.

If the challenge of urban planning in addressing climate change were a singular problem for Hollywood, FL, or Copenhagen, a wise course of action might be to focus solely on adapting the lowest-lying and most flood-prone areas to withstand sea level rise and increasing heavy rain events. If the problem were localized, a fair though painful process could be crafted, and the residents of Hollywood or Copenhagen could move forward.

The complicated challenge that confronts coastal residents and planners, however, is that the scale of the impending crisis is global, and the extent of the sea level rise and intensity of storms is dependent on how much more carbon is emitted. Adapting a single community to rising seas and heavier rains is necessary and complicated, but insufficient given the scale of the challenge.

The Intergovernmental Panel on Climate Change (IPCC), the United Nations body for assessing the science related to climate change, calls for measures to contain global warming to a 1.5°C average increase in global temperature by 2030–2052 (IPCC 2018). This corresponds to a rise in sea levels of 1–2 feet (30–60 cm) by the year 2100 (IPCC 2019). However, this goal will not be reached without widespread adoption of low- to zero-carbon lifestyles. A 2.0°C increase in the average global temperature, for example, corresponds to a likely 2–3.6-feet (61–110-cm) sea level rise over the next 80 years (IPCC 2019). Local adaptations in coastal communities will literally be swamped by the widening climate crisis without focused and lasting efforts to decarbonize urban systems.

The policy challenge, then, for coastal urban planning is to equitably adapt cities to withstand already-projected sea level rise and other climate impacts and simultaneously build landscapes designed to decrease greenhouse gas (GHG) emissions to mitigate potentially even more catastrophic impacts.

While planning for community abandonment and migration resulting from increasing sea levels and climate-induced disasters may also become more common during the 21st century, *Adaptation Urbanism* focuses on plans and policies to reduce carbon emissions and adapt streets and communities with the goal of making coastal communities safer, minimizing the need for abandonment. In other words, this book is about implementable solutions that can make cities more livable and resilient while protecting the sunk investments in real estate and infrastructure in coastal communities.

This challenge is large, difficult, fraught with uncertainty (Scott 2013), and simultaneously requires creating political capital necessary to *push* change. Business-as-usual transportation and land use policies, the bureaucratic pillars of how we build our cities, are not only ineffective at addressing the problems, but are often actively making the climate crisis worse. While pushing aside the bureaucratic and conceptual inertia of the present moment can seem daunting, a growing number of cities are innovating and creating highly livable, low-carbon communities that are being adapted to withstand the demands of a changing climate. These cities are increasingly opening new pathways forward to address the climate crisis. While this book addresses serious deep-seated problems, there is hope for a resilient future through overcoming fossil fuel dependence to foster inclusive, healthy, and biophilic cities (Newman, Beatley, and Boyer, 2017).

Adaptation urbanism: redesigning coastal cities for climate change

In *Adaptation Urbanism*, we examine two interlocking dimensions of the urban climate policy: (1) whether and how streets and connected public spaces can be reconceptualized to help cities better adapt and decrease emission levels to mitigate climate change; and (2) how these policies are being politically negotiated at the urban level. We thus examine the technical capacity to use streets and public space to manage climate change and the climate politics of urban transportation policy.

The promising news is that our review of policy efforts from leading coastal cities in Europe and North America finds that streets can be redesigned to help manage carbon emissions and better adapt urban areas to withstand more powerful and potentially frequent storms. Specifically, analysis of the case study cities of Copenhagen, London, Miami, New Orleans, and Rotterdam highlights efforts to rethink urban movement and the space dedicated to mobility in cities. Our analysis of these case study cities and other innovative communities in Europe and North America such as Barcelona, Vancouver, Amsterdam, Delft, and Utrecht finds evidence of a growing movement to reposition streets as central tools in adapting to and mitigating climate change. New designs are being developed that prioritize low-carbon transportation options and incorporate green and blue infrastructure and connected public spaces to minimize flooding and pollution runoff and enhance quality of life.[1] These changes achieve important climate policy goals and, importantly, create new neighborhood amenities that improve the quality of life for residents. In addition, we find that if this process is strategically managed with broad citizen engagement, it can help to create the political capital necessary to create momentum for change. We define this movement as adaptation urbanism, where streets and public spaces are redesigned to manage and minimize climate impacts and enhance urban quality of life.

Analysis of case study cities shows the current opportunities and struggles in changing the role of streets and public spaces in transport policy and highlights key weaknesses of current approaches, particularly in terms of the need to enhance equity outcomes and better negotiate the political barriers to change. In essence, current technology can significantly decrease transportation emission levels, adapt to more intense storms, and improve quality of life, but political barriers are slowing and often halting the transition to more climate-resilient urban outcomes related to transportation and public space. While enhanced technology will help improve outcomes, the current technology of urbanism that exists today can already significantly decrease GHG emissions and make safer, highly livable and sustainable communities that can better withstand a changing climate. What is often lacking, however, is the political will and robust governance structures to implement these proven approaches for the benefit of all residents. In this introductory chapter, we lay out the basic structures of this case and provide a roadmap for the rest of the book.

Streets: a hidden resource that occupies 30% of cities

The need to rethink urban transportation is pressing as the overlapping climate, public health, and spatial impacts of the current transportation system threaten long-term sustainability. To summarize the data presented below, the design of streets is a driving force behind climate change and a leading cause of premature death from crashes and air pollution. The way we design our streets is helping to propel a climate and public health crisis. The data are not hidden, but the issue is nearly invisible from most policy discussions. Rethinking the role of streets can help to address these serious issues and help improve the quality of life of cities and position streets as central places within our communities. William Whyte (1988, p. 7) summarizes this view by arguing that: "And of the primacy of the street. It is the river of life of the city, the place where we come together, the pathway to the center. It is the primary place."

The transportation sector is the single largest source of emissions in the United States, generating about 30% of total GHG emissions (EPA 2019). When indirect sources of GHG emissions from the transportation sector such as fuel drilling and processing are included, the overall contribution of transportation rises to about 40% of all emissions in the United States (Replogle 2019).

The consequences of inaction on climate and the potential impact on coastal residents can be quantified down to the rising tides. Strauss et al. (2015), for example, model baseline and lower emission scenarios for risk in United States coastal populations. Their findings suggest that business-as-usual emission scenarios will result in high-tide flooding of 1,596 US cities with a population of 27.4 million people by 2100. Lower-emission scenarios across multiple sectors can help prevent 900 US cities with a total population of 15.8 million people from being subject to flooding at high tides by the year 2100. Overall, Strauss et al. (2015) conclude that "rapid and deep cuts in carbon emissions could help many hundreds of coastal US municipalities avoid extreme future difficulties." From a coastal planning standpoint, the implications are stark. Business-as-usual emissions scenarios will result in high-tide flooding for millions of residents and, even with deep cuts in GHG emissions, just under 12 million Americans will be subject to high-tide flooding by 2100. Coastal communities need to lead in significantly cutting GHG emissions to limit projected impacts and simultaneously begin to adapt at-risk populations for near-term projected flooding.

While detailed analysis points to the impacts in one country, the impact on the US coastal populations is just one small part of the global impact of sea level rise as North American coastal populations represent less than 5% of the total global at-risk coastal population (Strauss et al. 2015). The impending impact of these calculations will ripple across coastal communities around the globe where action or inaction will be measured in the high-tide lines and determine who is safe and who is at risk.

While the climate impacts from the transportation system are coming into focus, the public health impacts of the current transportation system are becoming more dire. In the United States, there were 37,133 fatalities and an additional

2.7 million injuries resulting from transportation crashes in 2017 (California State Transportation Agency 2020). Analysis of air pollution data by Caiazzo et al. (2013) estimates an additional 53,000 premature deaths per year in the United States are due to transportation-related air pollution. Worldwide, 1.35 million fatalities resulted from crashes in the transportation sector in 2016 (WHO 2018a). Outdoor air pollution from multiple sources including transportation results in 4.2 million premature deaths per year (WHO 2018b). Transportation's impact on air pollution varies by region but is a significant and growing contributor in areas with high auto use like North America, Europe, and increasingly many parts of Asia (Watts et al. 2018). This air pollution, as was previously discussed, also may be a contributing factor to higher fatality risk to COVID-19 (Ogen 2020). Overall, five of the top ten leading causes of preventable death and injury result from transportation pollution and crashes (Global Road Safety Facility The World Bank 2014, p. 22).

While the current health impacts of the transportation system are significant, the impending health impacts resulting from a changed climate are deeply worrying, with increasing susceptibility to infectious diseases, drought, heatwaves, storms, and flooding putting pressure on public health systems (Watts et al. 2018). The result is what the Global Climate and Health Forum (2018) described as a "global health emergency" where "Climate Change threatens to undo decades of health and development gains." While the coronavirus pandemic is, hopefully, a once-in-a-generation disaster, climate change threatens to become a long-term, cascading catastrophe. These serious impacts have caused the World Health Organization (2015) to describe "[c]limate change [as] the greatest threat to public health in the 21st century."

The pressing public health demands are, however, only another important link in a chain of problems with the present transportation system. More intense rainfalls and rising seas due to climate change present a physical challenge for cities to find more space to store and channel water away from homes and businesses. Analysis of the extent of space required for transportation in cities reveals that streets and car parking are currently the dominant land use category in many cities. While the space dedicated to streets varies, analysis of 30 leading global cities puts the overall average at around 30% of urban space dedicated to streets (UN Habitat 2013). When parking spaces are added, the figure jumps to approximately 50% of all urban space allotted to streets and car parking (Ellen MacArthur Foundation and McKinsey Center for Business and Environment 2015).

To put this directly, up to 50% of urban space is predominantly dedicated to automobile use. Donald Shoup from UCLA has shown that cars are parked about 95% of the time and occupy more land area in the United States than housing (Shoup 2017). In a specific analysis of San Jose, CA, Shoup found that "[f]or many land uses, the parking lots are bigger than the buildings they serve…there is more space for parking than for people" (Shoup 2018, p. 9). Scharnhorst (2018, p. 1) discovered similar results and reported that in Seattle population density is less than half that of parking density. In addition to the high spatial cost of parking, Shoup (2018, p. 13) found that "the U.S. probably spends more to subsidize parking than for all the rest of its transportation infrastructure combined" with total costs for transportation infrastructure in 2002 estimated at $190 billion and the costs for parking estimated to be $127–374 billion.

While our streets and car parking dominate the physical geography of cities, the sheer quantity of space dedicated to these land uses remains almost hidden from most policy discussions. Street space is mostly seen as a needed sacrifice zone for movement away from and towards someplace else. Street space and parking areas are rarely seen as physical assets that could be changed to meet broader policy needs of housing affordability, active transportation access, or green and blue spaces to manage water and improve neighborhood quality of life. Our budgets and urban space could be more efficiently used to meet the needs of people rather than the needs of cars.

While the demands of car culture push at city budgets and space, an entirely different view of the role of the street and the underlying components of urban life has begun to emerge to challenge the status quo. As discussed previously, the COVID-19 emergency has highlighted the spatial disparities of our streets and begun to move many city leaders to question whether street space could be better used to create more opportunities for local accessibility. The COVID-19 response and growing climate awareness could combine to create a powerful rationale for reevaluating the role of streets in creating safer, healthier cities.

The increasing focus on rethinking streets can draw from a long lineage of scholars and practitioners who have laid the conceptual and practical groundwork for change. Instead of the street as a space of speed and division, the quote that begins this section by William Whyte speaks to how the street can (and should) be the central place of the city. Whyte's pioneering work laid out the underlying social, environmental, economic, and spatial problems with the dominant approach to transportation planning and pointed to a different way of viewing the street and planning for livable neighborhoods where the street has both a movement and place function. Whyte's work, along with that of Jane Jacobs, Jan Gehl, Kevin Lynch, Donald Appleyard, Allan Jacobs, and many others, has helped to trace the outlines of a new way of seeing city streets.

This new way of understanding the street is more important today as the spatial, public health, and emissions implications of the current transportation system come into greater focus. Policy debates about the size, design, and overall role of streets are increasingly becoming front-line issues in urban political battles to adapt and mitigate against climate change. Instead of accepting the status quo limits on city space, many cities are seeing the extent of street space as emerging spatial resources that can be redesigned to meet the needs of local residents. For example, former New York City Department of Transportation Director, Janette Sadik-Khan has noted that "streets are some of the most valuable resource[s] that a city has and yet it's an asset that is hidden in plain sight" (Sadik-Khan 2013). By rethinking the use of these community spaces, cities could begin to bend transportation emissions trends downward and simultaneously create green places that could become important community resources for adaptation and improved quality of life. Streets can have movement, place, and climate resilience roles. Put another way, imagine that 30–50% of city space has the potential to be transformed from privatized spaces of speed and division into truly public spaces for the community. These repurposed streets could then be used to address our most pressing problems and simultaneously add livability into the heart of the city. Streets are public spaces that can be transformed to meet community needs.

Instead of starting from the status quo framework that focuses on the auto-orientation of city space, many cities are reimagining streets and searching for opportunities to connect zero-carbon transportation options for short journeys and dedicated public transportation and rail for longer trips. Because these forms of travel are more spatially efficient than auto-oriented approaches, this transition opens additional room for parks and greenways that could store water during intense storms and act as community amenities and active transportation corridors during calm days. This vision of improved efficiency, safety, quality of life, and climate security does not require new technology. Instead, this vision demands rethinking how we distribute urban space in the transportation sector and requires generation of the political capital to *push* change to move beyond the status quo transportation system.

Streets of the past/streets of the future

On a recent trip to Amsterdam, we toured the city with Cornelia Dinca of Sustainable Amsterdam. She took us to what she called "the street of the future" (Figure 1.1). Plantage Middenlaan, a street next to the botanical garden not far from Centraal Station in the core of Amsterdam, was redeveloped over the course of several decades from a typical road engineered for cars to one that accommodated bicycles on the fringe, and then finally to a street with transit in the green center median with bicycles and pedestrian options on both sides. Sections of the street outside this zone allow slow-speed access to cars, but the design focus is centered on expanding transit and active transportation and improving quality of life.

The capacity for moving people on the street has increased with light rail (locally known as trams) moving 100 or more people in a single, almost silent train and pedestrians and cyclists steadily moving by on the sides of the green center median. Data from the National Association of City Transportation Officials (NACTO) *Transit Street Design Guide* (2016) show how efficient these types of streets can be compared to car-only designs (Table 1.1). Rather than focusing exclusively on car-only lanes that can carry 600–1,600 vehicles per lane/hour, green transit streets can carry 4,000–8,000 people per 10-foot (3-m) lane area. When a green transit street is linked with potential pedestrian loads of 9,000 people per hour and cycle tracks at 7,500 people per hour, even greater spatial efficiency of movement is achieved. When you couple this with the fact that each of these transit and active transportation users does not require a car-parking space at the beginning and end of the journey, the true spatial efficiency of the green transit street comes into focus. In addition to increasing capacity for moving people, the new design opens up space

FIGURE 1.1 Plantage Middenlaan Amsterdam: "the street of the future."

TABLE 1.1 Hourly person lane capacity

Mode	*Hourly person capacity (10-ft (3-m) lane)*
Cars	600–1,600
Mixed traffic (cars and buses)	1,000–2,800
Two-way protected cycle track	7,500
Dedicated transit lanes	4,000–8,000
Sidewalk	9,000
On-street transitway (bus or rail)	10,000–25,000

to manage water through the insertion of more permeable surfaces, helps to address the urban heat island effect, and significantly decreases emissions by privileging transit and active transportation. The quiet efficiency of the street of the future also becomes a neighborhood amenity, a place, where flows of people pass along a park-like corridor.

In terms of tradeoffs, the street design makes driving vehicles across Amsterdam more complicated and time consuming. The design of the green transit street forces cars to take a short bypass around the area, but allows bicycles, pedestrians, and trams direct access to the multi-block long green corridor. The tradeoff is made more politically palatable through faster connections via transit and cycling and the enhanced quality of place generated by the new design. With new street designs like this, the transportation consumer can choose between faster connections for transit and active transportation and slower, private auto connections. By making the efficient choice for short trips the climate-positive choice, Amsterdam achieves one of the world's highest bike modal shares of 53%, a transit mode share of 21%, and 24% of trips by car (Frame et al. 2017). This helps to decrease the transportation climate footprint of the city.

Green transit streets like this also create beautiful, livable city neighborhoods (an amenity advantage) that help to build political capital for change even in the face of contentious political debates. The Amsterdam of bicycles and green transit streets was, in fact, not the Amsterdam of the 1970s when plans for large highways and a high child transportation fatality rate were the norm. The green Amsterdam of today with its street of the future is the product of strong political coalitions that pushed for change to overcome the same bureaucratic and political barriers that seem to dominate most transportation policy debates around the world (Feddes and de Lange 2019).

The street of the future in Amsterdam is only one of many examples of a new wave of streets that we found in our research. We found many good examples of complete streets that prioritize pedestrians and bicyclists while still allowing slow-speed access for cars and trucks. Such streets also serve water management and urban heat island reduction goals through landscape design.

These streets of the future are the first examples of resilient streets designed to be better adapted to a changing climate and simultaneously minimize GHG emissions (Table 1.2). Some of the examples are fully formed resilient streets with both adaptation and mitigation components woven together. Many other examples represent beginning attempts to tie these resilience concerns together. Subsequent chapters in this book examine key components of these streets in more depth, but it is important at the outset to understand that a new template for what streets can be is emerging in cities around the world.

While the *streets of the future* are taking shape in Amsterdam and a select set of other cities, the *streets of the past*, paradoxically, continue to be built as part of

TABLE 1.2 Emerging examples of streets of the future

Streets of the future	*Location*	*Streets of the future*	*Location*
Plantage Middenlaan	Amsterdam	Hof van Delft (Klimaastraat)	Delft
Frans Halenstraat	Amsterdam	Exmouth Market	London
Bellamyplein	Amsterdam	Orford Road	London
Super Ilas	Barcelona	Cherokee Street	New Orleans
Bülowsvej	Copenhagen	Ackney Street	Portland
Hans Tavsens Gade	Copenhagen	Spoorsingel	Rotterdam
Sankt Kjelds Plads	Copenhagen	Catharijnesingel	Utrecht
Sankt Annae Plads	Copenhagen	Bute Street	Vancouver
Westerstraat Neighborhood	Delft	Union/Adanac Streets	Vancouver

standard practice in most cities around the world today. The bureaucratic inertia and political power of auto-oriented interests continue to perpetuate street designs that could have been drawn up 75 years ago. At the edges of metropolitan areas, particularly in the sprawling Sunbelt of the United States, new, wide residential streets are rolled out in pop-up suburbs. Moreover, overly wide streets and excessive parking standards have been institutionalized in planning, engineering, and fire department regulations in municipalities across the United States, Australia, and other nations. Such regulations inhibit compact infill development projects, transit-oriented developments, and other forms of sustainable development.

In Leander, TX, 27 miles from downtown Austin, Texas, for example, 30-foot-wide (9-m-wide) residential streets are being built to connect into a high-speed network of arterials and highways. At the corner of True Grit Cove and Painted Sky Bend, new homes are being manufactured and plugged into a street network straight out of planning documents from the 1950s. The mode share for walking, biking, and transit together is only 1.7% (Census 2019). There are almost no destinations close enough or safe enough to walk or bike to, and, with extremely limited transit options, almost no transit connectivity. Thus, the private car becomes necessary for virtually all activities. When periodic intense rains come, the hillside streets cascade with water. Continuing to build these streets of the past in fast-growing places locks in high emissions and flooding problems for years to come. Such business-as-usual decisions for transportation infrastructure and land use practices are projected to result in 20–50% more transport GHG emissions compared with more comprehensive and progressive transportation policy approaches (Creutzig 2016, p. 348).

The wide, fast roads are, in fact, achieving the very tasks that they were originally designed to accomplish. The sprawling road template of today is an almost exact model of the vision of the future from the 1930s. Modernist architect Le Corbusier (1964, p. 120) argued that the multi-purpose street where people and vehicles mixed was "an obsolete notion." He instead argued for a new road system of high-speed mobility where he would

> live 30 miles from my office in one direction, under a pine tree; my secretary will live 30 miles away from it too, in the other direction, under another pine tree. We shall both have our own car. We shall use up tires, wear out road surfaces and gears, consume oil and gasoline.

This vision became the template of the *streets of the past* as they were designed to create a fossil fuel economy based intentionally on burning through oil, wilderness, and space, creating class divisions as suburbs were sorted by wealth (Wells 2013). While the planning paradigm of "a city of infinite mobility" (Hall 2014, p. 9) has broadly changed since Le Corbusier's prophetic quotation, the physical design of streets has not changed much in the last 75 years. The world has changed, but our roads remain stuck in the past.

In *Adaptation Urbanism*, we argue that streets of the past cannot be used to usher in a new era of resilience. The design of streets of the past fundamentally privileges

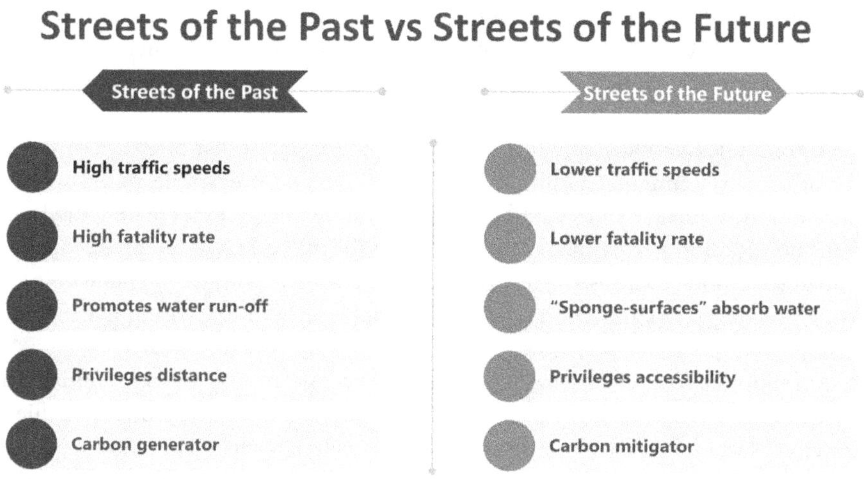

FIGURE 1.2 Streets of the past/streets of the future.

high-speed mobility that empirically has resulted in high fatality rates, high carbon emissions, and high levels of impervious cover that accentuate flooding and contribute to the urban heat island effect (Figure 1.2). The result in the United States, for example, is the third largest per capita transportation emissions in the world (over three times the European Union average) and the second lowest population density among OECD countries (World Energy Council 2016; World Bank 2021). While this matches Le Corbusier's vision of burning through energy and space, the unintended, but foreseeable, consequence has been high fatality rates, the highest per capita number of fatalities among developed countries (World Health Organization 2018a).

The vision of the future from the 1930s is not an appropriate guide for addressing the pressing problems of urbanism in the era of climate change (Calthrope 2010). Our streets have been, as former New York City Department of Transportation Commissioner Janette Sadik-Khan argues, in "suspended animation" for too long (Cohen 2016). It is time to rethink streets from places of speed, division, and even death to places of safety, sustainability, livability, and green urbanism.

Competing visions of the future

While evidence suggests that the 1930s vision of the future has reached its limits, a new futurist vision is developing in the form of the potential for electric and/or autonomous vehicle technologies to remake transportation. Popular media accounts point to a new future of driverless, electric cars that promise pollution-free, frictionless movement. We'll discuss this in more depth in Chapter 3, but it's important at the outset of the book to note the limits of this vision before a contemporary Le Corbusier promises that you can live 30 miles from your job and move easily in a wheeled bubble of free time. Making cars more energy-efficient is an important and surprisingly complicated component of decreasing overall carbon emissions but fails to address the underlying spatial demands of vehicles in urban areas discussed earlier in this chapter.

Automobiles are a spatially intensive form of movement that often act to spread out urban development. Calthrope and Walters (2017), for example, point out that autonomous vehicles could "cause congestion, eat up energy, exacerbate sprawl, and emit more carbon per passenger mile." Litman (2018) describes the preoccupation with autonomous vehicles as a technological solution with limited benefits towards reducing congestion and crashes, improving public health, increasing affordability or improved mobility options for non-drivers.

Autonomous and electric vehicles will have a role to play in future cities, but the question is what role they should have and how they should be used to achieve key city-planning goals in a world constrained by climate change (Schlossberg et al. 2018; Green 2019). The goal, after all, is not to create a new type of movement that intensifies the inefficiencies and weaknesses of the streets of the past, but instead to create streets that are better adapted for the demands of climate change and significantly decrease emissions. Without clear policy guidance for how to integrate electric and autonomous vehicles into the transportation system, we could simply be replacing dirty congestion with the "clean congestion" (Winkleman et al. 2019) of electric vehicles. This is not a template for resilient streets. Instead, we need better access to places that improve the quality of life for all city residents, minimize GHG emissions, and adapt the city for climate change. This is the high bar that transportation planning must meet in the face of the unprecedented demands of the new climate era.

With this in mind, moving from vision to practice is likely not a purely technological challenge of replacing one type of vehicle with another. Instead, we need a better vision of the future to address the complex challenge of urbanism in the climate change era. Beatley (2012), for example, calls this a "failure of imagination" to see what is possible. Instead of seeing change as about "deprivation," Beatley argues that "a green urban agenda" needs to be seen in the context of creating "an opportunity for a more lively, livable, rich, and healthy lifestyle with a smaller ecological footprint" (2012, p. 221).

Adaptation Urbanism traces the beginning movements of this new way of thinking about the role of streets that highlights the opportunities of change. Innovative street archetypes like Plantage Middenlaan in Amsterdam are the seeds of a new type of vision for the future with safe streets and green park corridors that privilege walking and bicycling for short trips and other less carbon-intensive modes for longer, higher-speed trips. Overall, this creates a city with slower speeds on city streets, but greater accessibility for both local and regional trips. These green climate streets better manage water and directly insert new green amenity places into the core of neighborhoods.

Resilient streets like this marry the emerging Vision Zero movement's goal of slower, safer, complete streets with resilience planning goals of climate adaptation and mitigation. At this point, Vision Zero and resilience planning are not consciously organized together into a coherent political movement, but instead occasionally overlap in a set of scattered pilot projects and fractured political actions. Chapter 11 details the potential of these movements to work together to create a powerful political coalition that combines expertise and energy from the transportation, public health, equity, design, and environmental communities to help visualize and implement safer, low-emission green streets (Fleming 2019; Sansone et al. 2019).

Right now, the streets of the future are here if you know where to look for them, but they may not be *here* where you are today. William Gibson has pointed out that "The future is already here. It's just not evenly distributed yet" (Kennedy 2012). Some places have jumped forward and some places remain locked in the past.

Paraphrasing William Gibson, the future is unevenly distributed and only actualizes in certain places because of the convergence of vision, politics, and push. The potential to transfer new ideas from city to city to create more livable places is a powerful vision. In this real-life alternate history, the idea of what streets could be starts with a resonance in the mind and slowly transforms the places around us through the push of change agents and the shift of funding and bureaucratic priorities. Each project moves the ideas forward from the foreign planet of Copenhagen or Amsterdam or Vancouver to the city in your region to the street in your neighborhood. Knowledge transfer and alternate histories, disruptors and the status quo, climate change and the tools to manage risk, equity and the uneven distribution of resources: we stand as ever at the precipice of potential and change. As this future remains mostly unwritten, now is the time to examine the potential and underlying tensions of this nascent movement to change city streets.

Creating a meaningful urban policy platform for resilience: adaptation urbanism

Planning and political issues are mediated through conceptual lenses that define how we see the potential and limits of the present moment. These lenses and accompanying planning movements change over time and emphasize different sets of values that can translate into radically different policy proposals (Hall 2014). The discussion above about the streets of the past/future highlights these differing ideals and underscores how climate change is impacting the perceived goals, roles, and design of streets and public spaces.

As discussed in the prologue, one of the most prominent movements to emerge in urban planning over the last two decades is resilience. Resilience planning developed in the early 2000s from environmental sciences as a promising way to help understand how systems can bounce back from shock. With climate change fundamentally challenging the long-term stability of the present system, applications of the resilience concept to urban planning have begun to question whether bouncing back from shock is enough. Instead, many articulations of resilience have called for a type of evolutionary resilience (Davoudi et al. 2013) or bouncing forward towards cities with green infrastructure and sustainable design for resilient cities (Shaw 2012; Infield et al. 2019). This begins to take resilience from a reactive emergency response articulation and towards a more holistic focus on resilient placemaking (Coaffee 2013).

As the resilience movement has become a near ubiquitous conceptual urban planning lens for the climate change era, figuring out how to negotiate its meaning, boundaries, and potential has increasing importance. Resilience is, as Swanstrom argues, "inherently a normative concept... [and] can only be understood with reference to some desirable outcome. Resilience toward what?" (2008, p. 19). We examine resilience at the place level seeking to define what the role of streets and public space *should* be in the emerging resilient city.

We argue that resilient streets and open space in the climate change era should act to both decrease GHG emissions and to create safer, more livable adapted places to a changing climate. Resilient streets have both a movement function that should be designed to limit GHG emissions (climate mitigation) and a place function that helps to create more livable communities that better manage water, heat, and other changing environmental conditions (climate adaptation). Great streets are designed to both enhance the safe movement of people with limited GHG emissions and create livable places that help to manage water through green and blue infrastructure. Bouncing forward towards the great street of the climate change era needs to be one of the central goals of urban resilience and requires planning for both the movement and place functions of streets.

Our analysis of current projects, however, shows that resilience planning for streets and open spaces has, to this point, focused on addressing only half of the central climate change equation. Existing transportation resilience projects have focused almost exclusively on the climate adaptation element of resilience and have failed to address the need for climate mitigation to fundamentally reshape the carbon generation components embedded in current roadway design. Transportation climate mitigation has often been seen as national level concern focused on improving fuel economy rather than a local planning issue that could be addressed through changing street design policy. As the examples at the beginning of the chapter explain, adapting to climate change is a necessary but insufficient policy response to the scale of the climate crisis. Cities need to adapt to climate change and simultaneously decrease emissions.

Our analysis of resilience projects has, however, also uncovered an emerging wave of projects currently in development that begin to connect climate mitigation and adaptation concerns in a more integrated fashion. These types of projects increasingly combine both green/blue infrastructure systems in ways designed to adapt cities to a changing climate and simultaneously accentuate urban mitigation potential by facilitating highly livable, compact development. At the city level, we call this emerging wave of resilience projects *adaptation urbanism*, where streets and public spaces are intentionally designed to encourage walking, bicycling, and transit to mitigate GHG emissions and adapt the city to climate change through the use of green and blue infrastructure. Adaptation urbanism is the developing physical form of resilient streets and public spaces that links climate adaptation, mitigation, and placemaking together as the foundation for the safe/climate/spatially efficient and equitable city. As the example of Amsterdam discussed earlier shows, resilient streets make the low-carbon transportation options the safest, easiest, and least expensive choices while adapting the landscape to better places that handle the stresses of a changing climate.

Chapter overview

To accomplish these aims, *Adaptation Urbanism* identifies key strengths/weaknesses of the current policy approaches to urban resilience (Chapter 2) and situates these developments within the planning structures for streets and water management (Chapter 3). We then create an exploratory normative evaluation model to determine how well or how far cities are from integrating adaptation/mitigation components into the urban street and public space projects (Chapter 4). We use this adaptation urbanism framework as an applied method that links the broader resilience literature directly to urban transportation policy to help steer cities towards addressing the short-term impacts of climate change through adaptation of streets and contribute to longer-term solutions through climate mitigation by decreasing transportation emissions.

Studying a nascent movement like adaptation urbanism presents challenges and opportunities. Most of the project examples we analyze in the chapters are not fully formed, but instead represent different component parts of the adaptation urbanism framework. For example, some projects may emphasize the transportation features designed to increase active transportation accessibility, while other projects emphasize the climate adaptation components of improved water management. Different city departments and funding streams often emphasize divergent resilience project characteristics. Some may directly focus on climate mitigation, while others may focus on climate adaptation. Climate adaptation and mitigation components, at this juncture, are only rarely actively woven together in specific city projects. The result is that there are few fully formed resilient streets emerging from standard practice at this point in time.

While we point to the central need to weave climate adaptation and mitigation together, our own training and background are more in the transportation sector. *Adaptation Urbanism* builds from a transportation analysis of the policymaking and bureaucratic structures and then looks towards linkages with the public space and water management sectors. For water management and park and open space professionals, this may seem to overemphasize transportation policy issues. Building multi-disciplinary knowledge is vital to bridging disciplinary divides that can act to silo projects and limit the potential power of projects to achieve both climate mitigation and adaptation goals simultaneously. We encourage water and park and open space professionals and their transportation counterparts to begin to build interdisciplinary bridges to push multi-sector projects forward.

We argue that the adaptation urbanism analysis framework can help to build those bridges by focusing on the need to tie climate adaptation and mitigation together at the project level. Adaptation urbanism links safe streets focused on decreasing GHG emissions with improved public places that act to better manage water. Linking street and public space design to water management expands the design focus of streets from a pure movement focus to a broader purpose of addressing rainwater and, vitally, improving neighborhood quality of life. This creates a new mission for streets and public spaces in the age of climate change and helps provide a compelling new set of goals for street, water, and public space designers as they come to terms with the pressing new demands of the climate crisis. Our analysis of case study cities in Chapters 5 through 9 of Rotterdam, Copenhagen, London, New Orleans, and Miami shows a diversity of responses currently in development in Europe and North America. While no individual city currently represents all of the potentialities of adaptation urbanism, the case cities taken as a whole present a strong set of examples that can point the way forward for an urbanized resilience.

We recognize that our case study cities provide only a small sample of the universe of new and innovative efforts to improve the resilience of streets and open space systems. In Chapter 10, we take a wider view of developments in adaptation urbanism by examining projects from Barcelona, Vancouver, and around the Netherlands (Amsterdam, Utrecht, and Delft). These European and North American examples show the development of adaptation urbanism within a Global North planning framework. More detailed work on resilient streets and green infrastructure from a Global South context is needed (Moyer and Becerra 2018; Vasquez et. al. 2019). With this background examined, we propose a targeted policy approach geared towards Global North cities to plan for and implement adaptation urbanism projects (Chapter 11). We close (Chapter 12) with a final synthesis of the challenges and possibilities that face urban planning in the climate change era.

Note

1 We examine the broader conceptual foundations of green and blue infrastructure in Chapter 3. The basic framework is that green space and water areas can be used specifically as a form of community infrastructure to achieve multiple benefits, including water management, environmental conservation, and enhanced livability. Green and blue infrastructure is often contrasted with gray infrastructure like drainage pipes that are buried and designed to hide water and move it away. Green and blue infrastructure can be seen as a "a new living with water framework that focuses on" creating systems that act "in concert with structural engineering systems" (Fields et al. 2017). Lawson et al. (2014) provide a useful list of key blue and green infrastructure components, including the blue infrastructure components of "ponds, flowing waterways, wet detention basins and wetlands that exist within the drainage network" and the green infrastructure components of "natural land and plant based ecological treatment systems and processes. This comprises open spaces, parks, recreation grounds, woodlands, gardens, green corridors, vegetated ephemeral waterways and planted drainage assets that undergo a wet/dry cycle due to runoff flow, e.g. green roofs and street trees."

References

Beatley, T. (2012). Conclusion: Green Cities of Europe as Compelling Models. In *Green Cities of Europe* (Beatley, T. ed). Washington, DC: Island Press.

Caiazzo, F., Ashok, A., Waitz, I. A., Yim, S. H., & Barrett, S. R. (2013). Air Pollution and Early Deaths in the United States. Part I: Quantifying the Impact of Major Sectors in 2005. *Atmospheric Environment, 79*, 198–208.

California State Transportation Agency. (2020). CalSTA Report of Findings AB 2363 Zero Traffic Fatalities Task Force. January. Last accessed 3/27/2020 from https://calsta.ca.gov/-/media/calsta-media/documents/calsta-report-of-findings-ab-2363-zero-traffic-fatalities-task-force-a11y.pdf.

Calthorpe, P. (2010). *Urbanism in the Age of Climate Change*. Washington, D.C.: Island Press.

Calthrope, P. & Walters, J. (2017). Autonomous Vehicles: Hype and Potential. *Urban Land*. Last accessed 12/30/2019 from: https://urbanland.uli.org/industry-sectors/infrastructure-transit/autonomous-vehicles-hype-potential/.

Census. (2019). *2013–2017 American Community Survey 5-Year Estimates*. City of Leander, Texas. Last accessed 12/30/19 from: https://factfinder.census.gov/.

City of Copenhagen. (2012). *Cloudburst Management Plan 2012*. Copenhagen: The City of Copenhagen, Technical and Environmental Administration.

Coaffee, Jon. (2013). Towards Next-Generation Urban Resilience in Planning Practice: From Securitization to Integrated Place Making. *Planning Practice & Research*, 28(3), 323–339.

Cohen, Josh. (2016). The Case for Changing the World by Changing Street Design. *NextCity*. March 8. Last accessed 3/27/2020 from https://nextcity.org/daily/entry/janette-sadik-khan-interview-complete-streets.

Creutzig, F. (2016). Evolving Narratives of Low-Carbon Futures in Transportation. *Transport Reviews, 36*(3), 341–360.

Davoudi, Simin, Brooks, Elizabeth, and Mehmood, Abid. (2013). Evolutionary Resilience and Strategies for Climate Adaptation. *Planning Practice & Research*, 28(3), 307–322.

EASAC (European Academies Science Advisory Council). (2013). Trends in Extreme Weather Events in Europe: Implications for National and European Union Adaptation Strategies. EASAC Policy Report. November 22. Halle, Germany: EASAC. ISBN: 978-3-8047-3239-1.

Ellen MacArthur Foundation, & McKinsey Center for Business and Environment. (2015). *Growth Within: A Circular Economy Vision for a Competitive Europe*. Cowes, UK: Ellen MacArthur Foundation.

Environmental Protection Agency (EPA). (2019). Sources of Greenhouse Gas Emissions. Last accessed 12/27/2019 from www.epa.gov/ghgemissions/sources-greenhouse-gas-emissions.

Feddes, F., & de Lange, M. (2019). *Bike City Amsterdam: How Amsterdam Became the Cycling Capital of the World*. Amsterdam: Nieuw Amsterdam.

Fields, B., Thomas, J., & Wagner, J. A. (2017). Living with Water in the Era of Climate Change: Lessons from the Lafitte Greenway in Post-Katrina New Orleans. *Journal of Planning Educationj and Research, 37*(3), 309–321.

Fleming, B. (2019). Design and the Green New Deal. *Places Journal*. April 2019. Last accessed 3/27/2020 from https://placesjournal.org/article/design-and-the-green-new-deal/?cn-reloaded=1.

Frame, Gladys, Ardila, Arturo, & Chen, Yang. (2017). The Kingdom of the Bicycle: What Wuhan Can Learn From Amsterdam. Transportation Research Procedia. 25. 5044-5062. 10.1016/j.trpro.2017.05.203.

Global Climate and Health Forum. (2018). A Call to Action on Climate and Health. Last accessed 4/2/2020 from www.globalclimateandhealthforum.org/call-to-action.

Global Road Safety Facility, The World Bank; Institute for Health Metrics and Evaluation. (2014). *Transport for Health: The Global Burden of Disease from Motorized Road Transport.* Seattle, WA: IHME; Washington, DC: The World Bank.

Green, B. (2019). *The Smart Enough City: Putting Technology in its Place to Reclaim our Urban Future.* Cambridge, MA: MIT Press.

Hall, P. (2014). *Cities of Tomorrow: An Intellectual History of Urban Planning and Design Since 1880.* Hoboken, NJ: John Wiley.

Infield, E. M. H., Abunnasr, Y., & Ryan, R. (2019). *Planning for Climate Change: A Reader in Green Infrastructure and Sustainable Design for Resilient Cities.* New York: Routledge.

IPCC (2018). Summary for Policymakers. In: Global Warming of 1.5°C. An IPCC Special Report on the Impacts of Global Warming of 1.5°C Above Pre-Industrial Levels and Related Global Greenhouse Gas Emission Pathways, in the Context of Strengthening the Global Response to the Threat of Climate Change, Sustainable Development, and Efforts to Eradicate Poverty (V. Masson-Delmotte, P. Zhai, H.-O. Pörtner, D. Roberts, J. Skea, P. R. Shukla, A. Pirani, W. Moufouma-Okia, C. Péan, R. Pidcock, S. Connors, J. B. R. Matthews, Y. Chen, X. Zhou, M. I. Gomis, E. Lonnoy, T. Maycock, M. Tignor, & T. Waterfield, eds.). Geneva: IPCC.

IPCC. (2019). Summary for Policymakers. In: *IPCC Special Report on the Ocean and Cryosphere in a Changing Climate* (H.-O. Pörtner, D. C. Roberts, V. Masson-Delmotte, P. Zhai, M. Tignor, E. Poloczanska, K. Mintenbeck, A. Alegría, M. Nicolai, A. Okem, J. Petzold, B. Rama, & N. M. Weyer (eds.)). Geneva: IPCC.

Kennedy, Pagan. (2012). *William Gibson's Future is Now. New York Times.* January 13.

Lawson, E., Thorne, C., Ahilan, S., Allen, D., Arthur, S., Everett, G., & Wright, N. (2014). Delivering and Evaluating the Multiple Flood Risk Benefits in Blue–Green Cities: An Interdisciplinary Approach. *Flood Recovery, Innovation and Response IV,* 184, 113–124.

Le Corbusier. (1964). *The Radiant City.* New York: The Orion Press.

Litman, T. (2018). Win-Win Solutions for Climate Protection and Health. *Planetizen.* Last accessed 4/2/2020 from www.planetizen.com/blogs/100874-win-win-solutions-climate-protection-and-health.

Moyer, E. & Becerra, A. (2018). Building Resilience Through Transportation and Infrastructure. *NRDC.* October 30. Last accessed 6/11/2020 from www.nrdc.org/experts/erika-moyer/building-resilience-through-transportation-infrastructure.

National Association of City Transportation Officials. (2016). *Transit Street Design Guide.* New York, NY: Island Press.

Newman, Peter, Beatley, Timothy, & Boyer, Heather. (2017). *Resilient Cities: Overcoming Fossil Fuel Dependence.* Washington, D.C.: Island Press.

Ogen, Y. (2020). Assessing Nitrogen Dioxide (NO_2) Levels as a Contributing Factor to the Coronavirus (COVID-19) Fatality Rate. *Science of the Total Environment,* 726, 15 July, 2020138605.

Replogle, M. (2019). *Testimony before the Senate Committee on Environment and Public Works on Infrastrcture Investment.* United States Senate March 6. Last accessed 1/11/21 from www.epw.senate.gov/public/_cache/files/c/b/cb50379a-5710-412e-a939-5af70161065e/89E04E200A7DD6ADF92751A045565F90.03.06.2019-replogle-testimony.pdf.

Sadik-Khan, Janette. (2013). New York Streets? Not So Mean Anymore. *TED City 2.0.* September. Last accessed 02/05/2020 from www.ted.com/talks/janette_sadik_khan_new_york_s_streets_not_so_mean_any_more.

Sansone, C., Sadowski, J., & Chriqui, J. F. (2019). *Public Health Engagement in Complete Streets Initiatives: Examples and Lessons Learned.* Chicago, IL: Institute for Health Research and

Policy, University of Illinois at Chicago. Last accessed 1/11/2021 from https://go.uic.edu/CompleteStreetsPH.

Scharnhorst, E. (2018). Quantified Parking: Comprehensive Parking Inventories for Five U.S. Cities. Research Institute for Housing America Special Report, Mortgages Bankers Association. Last accessed 4/01/2021 from: www.mba.org/news-research-and-resources/research-and-economics/research-institute-for-housing-america.

Schlossberg, M., Millard-Ball, A., Shay, E., & Riggs, W. B. (2018). Rethinking the Street in an Era of Driverless Cars. UrbanismNext. University of Oregon. Last accessed 3/18/20 from https://scholarsbank.uoregon.edu/xmlui/bitstream/handle/1794/23331/UrbanismNext_ResearchBrief_003.pdf?sequence=1.

Scott, M. (2013). Living with Flood Risk. *Planning Theory & Practice*, 14(1), 103–106.

Shaw, K. (2012). "Reframing" Resilience: Challenges for Planning Theory and Practice. *Planning Theory and Practice*, *13*(2), 308–312.

Shoup, Donald. (2017). *The High Cost of Free Parking: Updated Edition*. New York: Routledge.

Shoup, Donald. (2018). *Parking and the City*. New York: Routledge.

Strauss, B. H., Kulp, S., & Levermann, A. (2015). Carbon Choices Determine US Cities Committed to Futures Below Sea Level. *Proceedings of the National Academy of Sciences*, *112*(44), 13508–13513.

Swanstrom, T. (2008). *Regional Resilience: A Critical Examination of the Ecological Framework*. IURD Working Paper Series. Berkeley, CA: Institute of Urban and Regional Development, UC Berkeley.

UN Habitat. (2013). *Streets as Public Spaces and Drivers of Urban Prosperity*. Nairobi, Kenya: UN Habitat. https://unhabitat.org/streets-as-public-spaces-and-drivers-of-urban-prosperity.

Vásquez, A., Giannotti, E., Galdámez, E., Velásquez, P., & Devoto, C. (2019). Green Infrastructure Planning to Tackle Climate Change in Latin American Cities. In *Urban Climates in Latin America* (pp. 329–354). Cham: Springer.

Watts, Nick, Amann, Markus, Arnell, Nigel, Ayeb-Karlsson, Sonja, Belesova, Kristine, Berry, Helen, Bouley, Timothy, et al. (2018). The 2018 Report of the Lancet Countdown on Health and Climate Change: Shaping the Health of Nations for Centuries to Come. *The Lancet* 392(10163), 2479–2514.

Wells, Christopher W. (2013). *Car Country: An Environmental History*. Seattle, WA: University of Washington Press.

Whyte, W. H. (1988). *City: Rediscovering the Center*. Ann Arbor, MI: The University of Michigan.

Winkleman, S., Deweese, J., and El-Geneidy, A. (2019). Car-Oriented Sprawl Increases Driving and GHGs in Greater Montreal. Green Resilience Strategies. Last accessed 4/1/2020 from www.greenresilience.com/montreal-sprawl.

World Energy Council. (2016). Energy Efficiency Indicators. May. Last accessed 3/27/2020 from wec-indicators.enerdata.net/transport-co2-emissions-per-capita.html.

World Health Organization. (2015). WHO Calls for Urgent Action to Protect Health From Climate Change—Sign the Call. Last accessed 4/2/2020 from www.who.int/globalchange/global-campaign/cop21/en/.

World Health Organization. (2018a). Global Status Report on Road Safety 2018. Last accessed 1/31/2020 from www.who.int/violence_injury_prevention/road_safety_status/2018/en/.

World Health Organization. (2018b). Ambient (Outdoor) Air Pollution. May 2. Last accessed 1/31/2020 from www.who.int/en/news-room/fact-sheets/detail/ambient-(outdoor)-air-quality-and-health.

2

COASTAL URBAN RESILIENCE

Coastal urban resilience: a paradigm for managing change

Coastal, delta cities, where rivers meet the ocean's tides, are places of change. Throughout history, delta cities have been known as gateways for trade and the exchange of ideas and culture. Built on the unstable interface between land, sea, and river, these cities both thrive and are simultaneously threatened because of easy access to water. These areas and their immediate coastal neighbors are estimated to contain 480 million people worldwide and, if viewed as part of a system including upstream river networks, combine for almost half of the world's population (Tessler et al. 2015).

While coastal cities historically have been challenged with flooding, the edges of the sea have become literally more fluid as sea level rise redraws the boundaries of continents. The people who live here, the economies that depend on that access, and the historical meaning of places built on this interface are threatened.

Coastal cities, these centers of continual transformation, will need to change at a faster rate than ever before to maintain the trade, commerce, and culture that justify their precarious position. The questions of how these places should change and who benefits from these changes are core issues to understand urbanism in an era of climate change. Vale (2014, p. 195) succinctly identifies the underlying equity challenges when he argues that "climate change yields lots of losers, but not everyone loses equally."

Resilience, a flexible and contested heuristic (Meerow et al. 2016), has emerged as a key framework for understanding and managing the tensions of climate-induced change. Bloomberg Philanthropy's C40 Cities, ICLEI's Resilient Cities Congress, National Association of City Transportation Officials' (NACTO's) Global Designing Cities Initiative, and the recently concluded 100 Resilient Cities (Bliss 2019), among others, are helping local communities begin to envision and enact innovative approaches to address urban resilience. Powered by these new partnerships and the speed of the internet, resilience planning ideas have been embedded in the popular discourse of city building around the world.

As this movement has grown and spread, however, concerns about how to manage change and who benefits from the more resilient city have also grown (Derickson 2016; Bohland et al. 2018). At a fundamental level, how we define resilience, whether it is bouncing back to the status quo or bouncing forward to a new future (Shaw 2012; Renne et al. 2020), helps to articulate the scope and direction of planning processes and policy choices. In addition, *who* is allowed at the table to help define resilience policy is vital to determining equity outcomes (Meerow et al. 2016; Harris et al. 2018).

This chapter explores the resilience planning literature to help better understand the key concepts and implications of this growing movement. The chapter is broken down into two main sections. First, we provide a broad overview of the resilience conceptual framework to define the term within a set of urban-oriented tensions outlined by Meerow et al. (2016). This broad articulation provides a theoretical base for understanding resilience. In the second section, we work to convert this theoretical base into an actionable policy framework suitable for urban planning practitioners. Issues associated with density and the built environment, transportation planning, and overarching issues of equity are examined through an urbanist lens to highlight key unresolved tensions that underpin resilience planning at the current moment. We conclude that urban resilience needs to be seen not as a mechanism for maintaining the status quo, but instead as a key policy tool to manage the dynamic non-equilibrium condition of climate flux that defines this era (Meerow et al. 2016).

Resilience: a conceptual lens for understanding planning in the age of climate change

In the late 1980s and 1990s, resilience planning was a nascent movement that had not made a significant impression on urban planning. By the late 2010s, however, resilience literature citations had grown dramatically. Meerow and Newell (2015) review the literature on resilience across multiple fields and point to a dramatic rise in its use since about the year 2000.

In terms of the growth of resilience in urban planning and transportation journals, we conducted a similar broad term search to examine the use of the resilience concept. We reviewed the Reuters Web of Science citation database for resilience and variations on the term resilience in urban studies, regional planning, transportation, and transportation science technology-focused journals (Figure 2.1). We also found a dramatic increase in the use of the term from one total citation during the decade of the 1980s to 3,949 citations during the 2010s (2010–2019). From the decade of the 2000s to 2010s, there was an 877% increase in the use of resilience in urban studies/planning/ transportation articles. We also found a similar increase in the use of resilience concepts in the water resource area with use of the term increasing from 308 citations in the 2000s to 3,334 in the 2010s.[1]

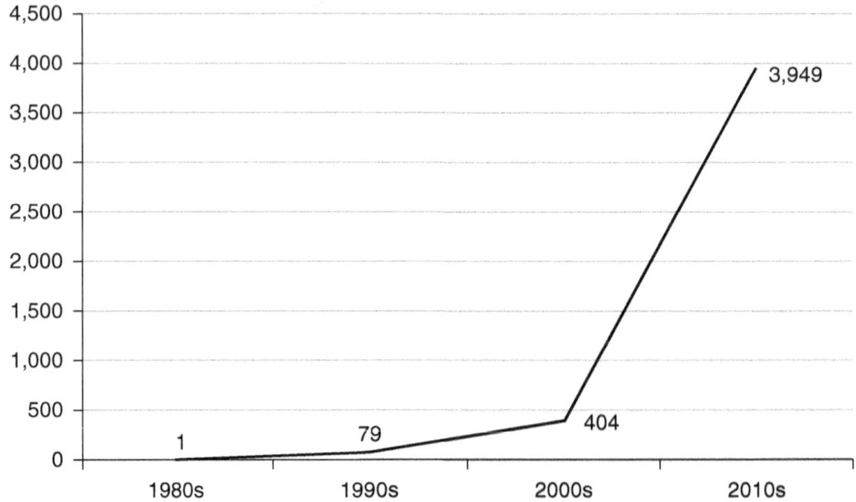

FIGURE 2.1 Growth in resilience use in urban studies/planning/transportation-oriented journals: 1980s to 2010s.

While this basic descriptive analysis shows the growth of the use of resilience in urban planning, transportation, and water resources sectors, conceptual consensus on its exact meaning and implications for urban planning has not directly followed. It remains a concept with multiple meanings and uncertain boundaries. In many ways, resilience has grown in importance not in spite of the lack of conceptual clarity, but often because of its malleable meaning (Bohland et al. 2018). Resilience has proven to be a term that reaches across disciplines and provides a broad aim for the planning profession, especially as a tool for planning for climate change (Hamin Infield et al. 2018).

While this broad banner provides room for multiple meanings, the lack of clarity threatens to make resilience a weak device for planning. Like sustainability, however, resilience can be made a useful lens by serving as a tool to highlight the underlying tensions of the planning process and highlighting clear pathways towards resolving these tensions. Scott Campbell, the author of one of the most influential pieces on sustainability tensions, provides a conceptual path showing how planning movements like sustainability and resilience can be used to successfully confront climate change. Campbell (2016) argues that:

> *If we once focused on the shift from 1970s environmentalism to 1990s environmental sustainability, we must now shift from 1990s sustainability to today's adaptation, mitigation, and resilience in an era of vulnerability to sea level rise, drought, rising temperatures, and increasingly violent storms. Global climate change will remap the social and spatial distribution of risk and reward of urban development, and our planning maps need to keep apace.*
>
> *(Campbell 2016, p. 395)*

Defining resilience: articulating tensions, identifying opportunities

For resilience to be a valuable conceptual lens, it must help us negotiate the tensions of urban planning in the age of climate change, particularly in terms of addressing equity issues (Fainstein 2018). To address these issues, we map out the underlying tensions of urban resilience in order to provide a strong working definition for the concept.

One of the most rigorous examinations of the underlying tensions of resilience is undertaken by Meerow et al. (2016). The authors conduct a comprehensive bibliometric analysis of resilience literature and identified both multiple conceptual meanings of resilience and a set of potential tensions that flow from these differing interpretations.

Meerow et al. (2016) identify 25 major conceptual definitions of resilience. These definitions range from the succinct to more specific iterations of systems components. A representative definition from the listing is Campanella's (2006) definition of resilience discussed in relation to the disaster recovery of Hurricane Katrina. Campanella (2006, p. 141) defines resilience as "the capacity of a city to rebound from destruction." While this definition is fairly simplistic, the discussion in the article explores the complexities of cities and what makes them resilient. Campanella argues that cities are much more than their physical infrastructure of building stocks and roadways, but instead are "thick concatenations of social and cultural matter" that "endow[s] a place with its defining essence and identity" (Campanella 2006, p. 142). Resilience in this sense is about much more than infrastructure and its physical systems, but instead the meaning of resilience should be widened to include the social and cultural connections of cities that often resist being measured and neatly placed in engineering formulas.

Campanella's (2006) article begins to outline the complexities of urban resilience theory and the difficulties of articulating a clear definition of what makes a city resilient. While these complexities make Campanella's and many of the other scholarly definitions conceptually thought provoking, the lack of a fully articulated definition can be limiting from an urban planning and management perspective. As the old saying goes, what gets measured, gets managed. Resilience planning needs to be distilled into a functional framework if it is to be utilized to steer administrative resources and guide policy decisions.

Meerow et al.'s (2016) analysis helps to provide a foundation for those type of delineations. From the broad literature and definitional analysis, Meerow et al. (2016) identify a series of six major unresolved tensions that run through the literature (Table 2.1).

These six broad categories define a universe of potential tensions for urban resilience scholarship and practice. Meerow et al. (2016) use this analysis of tensions to help articulate a refined definition of resilience. From this analysis, they argue that resilience should be defined as:

TABLE 2.1 Unresolved urban resilience tensions

Urban resilience tensions
1. Meaning and scope of what is urban
2. Clarifying notions of equilibrium
3. Defining the normative dimensions of resilience
4. Articulating the pathways to urban resilience
5. Describing types of adaptation
6. Defining the timescale of intervention

> *the ability of an urban system—and all its constituent socio-ecological and socio-technical networks across temporal and spatial scales—to maintain or rapidly return to desired functions in the face of a disturbance, to adapt to change, and to quickly transform systems that limit current or future adaptive capacity.*
>
> (*Meerow et al. 2016, p. 45*)

While the definition is a bit wordy, the underlying logic is strong. They argue that "[u]rban resilience operates in non-equilibrium, is viewed as a desirable state, recognizes multiple change pathways (persistence, transition, and transformation) and emphasizes the importance of adaptive capacity and timescales" (Meerow et al. 2016, p. 45).[2] This distillation is a type of roadmap to key issues that cities will face as they work towards planning for and implementing urban resilience. Each tension is related and forms a complex set of tightly linked issue areas that will challenge resilience planners.

To better explain the urban policy implications of these tensions, we focus in more depth on the issues related to notions of equilibrium and the normative dimensions of resilience. These tensions help provide grounding for understanding the complex and shifting role of culture and equity outlined by Campanella (2006) and situate these issues within an analytic frame that can be used to enhance urban resilience policy dialogues. The other tensions outlined by Meerow et al. (2016) (defining urban, pathways to resilience, and types and timescale of adaptation) are discussed as they emerge in the discussion particularly in relation to the adaptation/mitigation divide discussed below.

Bouncing back or bouncing forward?

One of the most contested components of the definitions of resilience revolves around the notion of equilibrium. From the review, Meerow et al. (2016) identify three basic types of equilibrium orientations: single-state, multiple-state, and dynamic non-equilibrium frameworks. Each articulation is premised on identifying the appropriate balance point for a resilient system.

The most common and widely used articulation, particularly in disaster management, has been the single-state equilibrium model. In this framing, resilience connotes "the capacity of a system to revert to a previous equilibrium" (Meerow et al. 2016, p. 43) after a disaster or other punctuated moment of disruption. The example definition used earlier in the chapter by Campanella (2006, p. 141) falls into this category as it posits a "capacity" to "rebound from destruction."

While definitions of resilience that focus attention on the broad need to rebound or bounce back from a disaster add important meaning to disaster recovery theory, they are often unclear about what condition cities should bounce back to. This lack of clarity presents two overarching problems. First, the assumption is that there is an equilibrium state to return to. In a world challenged by a changing climate, returning a community's urban systems to the standards of previous environmental condition is highly problematic. In relation to the discussion of streets in Chapter 1, for example, returning to the street designs of the past locks in increasing emissions, safety problems, and broader water management issues for another generation. Vale (2014, p. 195) sums up the weaknesses with this type of resilience articulation by arguing that, "Most societies are not in anything like an ecological equilibrium at the moment just before the latest disaster strikes."

A second interlocking problem with this conception of resilience is that many communities are characterized by highly unequal resource distributions. Reverting back to the status quo means returning to a potentially inequitable system. Derickson (2016, p. 162) argues that this formulation of resilience threatens to become "a celebration of the status quo" where deep underlying problems are ignored. He argues, instead, for a conception of resilience that focuses on creating "the will for different futures" through fostering "civic infrastructure...the social and institutional processes and relationships we have in place that help us make futures" (Derickson 2016, p. 165).

As researchers have begun to examine resilience theory more deeply identifying these problems, they have begun to move away from this single-state equilibrium frame. A more nuanced iteration is the multiple-state equilibrium or ecological resilience frame. In this iteration, systems are seen as having "different stable states" that can transform from one stable iteration to another (Meerow et al. 2016, p. 43). While this iteration introduces the element of changing systems into the core of the conceptual frame, it still focuses on an equilibrium state that ignores underlying social, economic, and environmental weaknesses that are almost inherent to urban planning in the present moment.

Given the state of instability of the present moment, the most promising definitional framework to emerge over the last decade from an urban climate change perspective is the dynamic non-equilibrium systems approach. This approach argues that "systems undergo constant change and have no stable state" (Meerow et al. 2016, p. 43). Defining resilience in the state of flux focuses attention not only on *what was* before a disaster or punctuated event, but also focuses attention on *what should be* in the future. This moves resilience from bouncing back to bouncing forward (Shaw 2012, p. 309). It, therefore, inserts the normative component directly into the heart of the resilience definition and forces observers to redefine the type of future conditions that are desired and for whom these structures benefit.

For example, our current urban system is premised on cheap access to fossil fuels to power transportation and economic transactions. Meerow et al. (2016, p. 44) point out that "fossil fuel dependence" is "highly undesirable yet quite resilient." It is a condition that can persist for quite a long time, but still have powerfully negative impacts (discussed in more detail in Chapter 1).

In transportation planning, articulations of resilience have most often focused on adapting infrastructure to changing conditions and improving hazard mitigation of infrastructure without focusing on the need to decrease greenhouse gas (GHG) emissions through a process of climate mitigation (Weilant et al. 2019). After a disaster, for instance, bridges might be adapted to be made higher or roadways raised so as to avoid damage in the next storm. This type of "bouncing back" logic following a disaster is a type of urban adaptation that deals with immediate climate change issues while ignoring the status quo fossil fuel dependence. The climate adaptation component is, in itself, a complicated and difficult process to find the resources to build higher and stronger, but the inclination to build back what was in place prior to a disaster as quickly as possible (Olshansky et al. 2012) acts to entrench the very systems that are perpetuating the climate problem.

The *bounce back* approach to transportation resilience fails to identify the important need to plan for and implement a transportation system designed to mitigate climate impacts by decreasing carbon emissions that are spurring the stronger and more frequent storms to begin with. To truly *bounce forward* (Shaw 2012, p. 309), communities need to adapt infrastructure for climate change and simultaneously focus on climate mitigation measures to decrease carbon emissions. Focusing on these dual goals of climate adaptation and mitigation opens up new potential pathways to reenvision a transportation infrastructure that is both more adapted to climate change and focused on lower to zero carbon emissions. It, thus, opens up pathways to plan for and implement the *streets of the future* that will be needed for cities to thrive in the decades to come. Rebuilding streets adapted to a changing climate must be coupled with the imperative to build streets that mitigate GHG emissions. We have begun to factor in rising sea levels into road-building calculations but have not begun to factor in carbon emissions into street-building calculations. Both climate adaptation and mitigation must be included in resilience infrastructure planning.

This process will be deeply contentious as parts of the status quo that are reliant on fossil fuels must be challenged to change while other components of the system must be radically re-envisioned. In the bridge example above, rail and active transportation linkages may be added to the climate-adapted bridge to help mitigate GHG emissions. These new climate-mitigating features will only be included if new resources and truly resilient planning approaches are developed and institutionalized. At present, budgeting, disaster management regulations, and overall resource allocation and planning processes all act to limit truly resilient pathways of action (Fields et al. 2017).

To more effectively manage this process, communities need, as Derickson (2016, p. 165) points out, a strong "civic infrastructure" premised on broad and deep citizen engagement. One way to help focus attention on the need to build this new civic infrastructure is to conceptualize resilience less as a specific state and more as a process. Harris et al. (2018), for example, make a strong case that "resilience thinking must be reframed as a process of negotiation, rather than as a definitive goal or outcome." They argue that this process "will necessarily be uneven, political and contested, and will point to complex trade-offs rather than win–win–win scenarios" (Harris et al. 2018, p. 2). They call this process "negotiated resilience," where resilience applications focus on the process of "iterative engagement with diverse actors, interests and across time and governance scales" (Harris et al. 2018, p. 2). From this perspective, resilience theory and practice offer, in the words of Meerow et al. (2016, p. 47), "no right or easy answers," but instead focus on "grappling with" these difficult questions "collectively through an inclusive and open discourse."

Outlining the urban resilience climate policy problem: an urbanist view of resilience

Meerow et al.'s (2016) overarching examination of resilience tensions helps to identify the broad challenges of urban resilience. In the previous section, we began to situate these challenges within the urban policy sphere, but, for many practitioners, simply identifying these tensions and challenges may not provide an actionable urban policy framework to improve decision making. Urban planners and policymakers are attuned to working in a specific set of issue areas such as land use and zoning, transportation, economic development, citizen participation, and equity. To operationalize urban resilience tensions and highlight key potential urban policy dimensions of the problem, we drill down to these types of nuts-and-bolts urban issues where these broad resilience tensions manifest.

"Urbanizing" climate resilience

While most discussions of urban climate resilience acknowledge the need for both adaptation and mitigation measures, there is often a failure to recognize the importance of urban form and "good" urbanism itself as mechanisms to achieve policy goals. Cities that have pedestrian-oriented streets, moderate to higher density of housing and business opportunities, and strong transit systems are the backbone of lower urban GHG emissions, but technological innovations are often touted as singular pathways forward towards resilience (Green 2019). The urban policy result is that technological optimism for emission-free energy sources is often substituted for time-tested urban approaches to managing transportation GHG emissions. As discussed in Chapter 1, transportation energy use can be effectively managed with the existing urban policy tools that help to shape the built environment, transit opportunities, and overall roadway design (Schlossberg et al. 2018).

After reviewing the literature on resilience literature focused on climate mitigation/adaptation, we identify a set of key issue areas that expose the complexity of urban resilience planning. These issue areas are not intended to replace the overarching conceptual tensions outlined by Meerow et al. (2016), but instead are designed to show how those tensions play out in urban policy issue areas that planners are accustomed to addressing. These three key urban issue areas are:

1. Planning for the built environment
2. Citizen participation and politics of development
3. Equity.

Current applications of resilience planning for the three issue areas help to limit the capacity for reshaping urban landscapes to minimize carbon emissions and create a technical, project-oriented culture that often focuses on technological solutions. Planning for these technological solutions often results in tightly limited scope that ignores key equity impacts and other potential pathways that could help a community bounce forward. The following section addresses these issue areas and then shifts towards constructing targeted responses to weaknesses in urban resilience dialogue and points to specific urban policy tools to manage these areas.

Urban resilience issue 1: planning for the built environment

While resilience policy planning has broadly acknowledged the role of climate mitigation and, increasingly, adaptation at the urban level (Meerow and Woodruff 2020), minimizing GHG emissions through modal shift away from automobiles has often been discounted in favor of improved fuel efficiency and electric vehicle uptake. With these technological and efficiency shifts being driven by higher levels of government, the perceived role of urban resilience in the transportation sector then often shifts towards hardening critical infrastructure from climate risk (City of Austin Sustainability Office 2018, p. 27). The result is that, particularly in urban areas in the United States, resilience policymakers have focused on adapting transportation infrastructure to a changing climate but have broadly failed to acknowledge the role of that same infrastructure in perpetuating high GHG emissions. This is an important blind spot in current urban resilience planning (Baca 2019; Weissman and Casale 2019). In addition to the technological optimism noted above, reasons for this appear to be related to a limited understanding of the potential impact of urban form on GHG emissions and policy differences over the proper sphere for action.

Research has begun to point to the connection between built environment characteristics and travel behavior and GHG levels (Ewing et al. 2008, 2014; Newman, Beatley, and Boyer 2009; Handy 2017). Broadly speaking, this research finds that there is a strong link between built environment characteristics like development dispersion and auto-centric transportation policy and higher emission levels. Conversely, the research finds that a focus on connecting a compact city with transit and active transportation decreases emissions. The conclusion that sprawling places consume more transportation energy and more compact places limit energy use is almost intuitive but is backed up by strong research (Ewing and Cervero 2010, 2017).

The implications for long-term resilience are stark. Policies designed to encourage more compact urban form need to be integrated into the overall resilience agenda. Recent research from the McKinsey Center for Business and the Environment and C40 Cities, for example, points to the potential of improved transportation and land use accessibility as a central strategy for urban areas to meet GHG emissions targets. The study found that as much as 20–45% of overall emission reduction goals could be achieved through what they called "focused acceleration" of strategies addressing this sector (McKinsey Center/C40Cities 2017).

While this research has emerged over the last decade, it has not widely been integrated into policy planning for transportation and land use in the United States as these areas are often highly complex, rule-bound, and prone to institutional inertia in decision making. The current mobility paradigm often favors speed of vehicles over safety and livability and focuses on expanding roadway capacity as central policy solution to roadway congestion (Bellis 2020). Addressing climate change, livability, and equity are not central features of the dominant transportation policy discourse.

In addition to the transportation and land use policy resistance to change, another key reason why the built environment is not a central component of resilience mitigation project implementation in cities to date is that most applications of resilience do not address transportation climate mitigation directly at the urban level. Governments have broadly focused on climate mitigation as a national level concern that is negotiated through multinational treaties and, in the transportation sector, addressed through improved auto efficiency or shifts to electric vehicles. Implementation is often unclear at local or regional levels. There has been a broad acknowledgment of the need for climate mitigation to be included at the national level, but efforts to tie mitigation and adaptation together have proven more contentious as the scale descends to the urban level. The goals of mitigation and adaptation are often perceived as of such a different scale that they are seen as incompatible and potentially competing when proposed together for urban projects (Walsh et al. 2011; Stead 2014). While significant work has been done in tracking emissions and creating mitigation strategies for other sectors (Meerow and Woodruff 2020), strategies focusing on the connection between the transportation sector and the built environment have been undervalued in urban resilience planning.

In addition, climate adaptation is often an easier political "sell" than targeted transportation climate mitigation policies. As the Hollywood, FL, flooding example that starts the book highlights, local politicians who are concerned about limiting immediate threats like flooding, particularly in the United States, often turn to a resilience framework with a narrow focus on adapting infrastructure. Long-term changes to the transportation and land use systems that address GHG emissions are complex and politically fraught and often remain underdeveloped in urban resilience planning policy dialogues.

For these reasons, climate adaptation policy in the transportation sector is often more advanced at the urban level than that of climate mitigation strategies focused on integrated land use/transportation design changes. Climate adaptation and mitigation goals can, however, be synergistic. One of the most promising emerging areas that can help to tie these two components together is the application of green infrastructure. Hamin Infield et al. (2018) note that green infrastructure is a tangible form of resilience planning that can be examined at the site, city, and regional scales to address climate change. They note:

> *In just the last few years, these two big ideas have come together: using green infrastructure to address climate change. Green infrastructure, along with other regulatory and social actions and grey infrastructure where needed, provide a set of solutions that can reduce greenhouse gas emission and improve adaptation to future climate change in urban areas.*
>
> *(Hamin Infield et al. 2018, p. 2)*

Urban resilience issue 2: citizen participation and politics of development

A second tension involves the land use politics of changing the built environment. Balancing multiple interests and overlapping policy areas in this era of climate change is immensely challenging because of the lack of clarity about how resilience should be operationalized and at what governmental level. The resilience framing debate has implications about what types of projects are selected to be implemented at the urban level. As Vale (2014) notes, resilience is "intimately tied up with deeply political choices" that help to determine "which parts of the built environment should receive investment and, therefore, which people should benefit" (p. 194).

For example, there is intense debate about what types and how much development/redevelopment to encourage in cities in connection to resilience policy (Fainstein 2018). As resilience policy seeks to enhance the safety of some areas, it could lead to increasing costs that push others towards more dangerous environmental zones. Whitehead (2013) provides a broader theoretical extension of this by arguing that resilience policies currently deployed represent a form of "neoliberal urban environmentalism" (p. 1349) designed around narrow economic development and capital accumulation goals to the exclusion of more social equity goals. The result, Whitehead argues, is that certain areas will increasingly be adapted to climate change with increased development and increasing cost of living for those lucky or wealthy enough to live in these safe zones. This process of "climatological gentrification" (Whitehead 2013, p. 1362) poses a significant challenge as societal benefits can accrue to the wealthy, forcing affordable housing to the less adapted (and less safe) fringes.

Building upon Molotch's (1976) concept of the "urban growth machine," Bohland et al.'s (2018) *The Resilience Machine* examines "different ways in which neoliberal mentalities are fed through the rhetoric of resilience practices, policies and development projects and explore the often invisible effects of resilience strategies" (p. 1). Rogers (2018) argues in Chapter 8 of *The Resilience Machine* that the long-term project of resilience, affecting all of civil society, is the need to "balance privitasation of responsibility inherent in neoliberal governance with the empowerment at the heart of collaborative and participatory forms of community building" (p. 141).

While broader critiques of neoliberalism make serious and useful arguments about the equity implications of development, the climate mitigation potential of compact urban form is often lost in the rhetorical blur of the neoliberal critique. Whitehead (2013), for example, discounts the mitigation potential of compact, urban areas themselves in the broader resilience policy arena. The operationalization of the neoliberal critique often takes the form of growth minimization proposals that are focused on limiting new development. In urban areas, this can translate into policies that limit the supply of core area affordable housing and redevelopment. Such policies also often result in higher housing costs in core areas, which limit affordable housing, exacerbate equity outcomes, and push affordable housing to the periphery. Kelbaugh (2014) notes the "ecological paradox of urbanism" where limiting core area development can actually result in increased GHG emissions and habitat destruction as development is dispersed. Countering this are proponents of urbanism (old and new) who argue for using the climate mitigation potential of more compact urban settings. Duany and Talen (2013), for example, argue that "walkability [is] the essential element that made urbanism intrinsically sustainable" (p. 5).

The study of the urban politics of densification as a climate mitigation strategy is just emerging but is providing an important window into the complexity of landscape-based resilience strategies. Filion (2018), for example, explores policy efforts in suburban Toronto to promote denser land use along designated transit-oriented development corridors. He finds that there are "durable automobility-related features at the heart of the North American suburban phenomenon" (Filion 2018, p. 5) that promote a politicized culture of automobility. Reliance on the automobile often promotes a zero-sum development dynamic where increases in density are seen to come at the expense of existing residents in form of congestion and perceived declines in property values. The politics of density in suburban areas often coalesces around NIMBY (not in my backyard) efforts to defend "the low-density character of the suburb in the face of densification initiatives" (Filion 2018, p. 7). While Filion's case focuses on Toronto, growing networks of NIMBY political activists have challenged densification efforts in Austin, TX, and around the United States (Hankinson 2018; Kimble 2019).

While political battles rage over density and gentrification, efforts to rethink street space are making slow, but significant, progress in many cities. As we will see in Chapter 6 on Copenhagen, small changes to street space carried out over time may be a politically acceptable way forward. Copenhagen, for example, decreased parking by 2–3% every year starting in the 1960s (Newman et al. 1997). This opened up space for increases in the bicycle network and has dramatically shifted the overall mode share of the city over time. A North American example of this same type of slow process of changing street space is developing in Portland. The City of Portland is proposing increasing the percent of street space allotted to pedestrians, bicyclists, and transit an additional 2% and decreasing parking by a small percent each year. Changing the city's use of the right way is designed to increase the "people moving capacity" of street by 60% (City of Portland Bureau of Transportation 2019, p. 5). Vancouver, BC, has also begun linking transportation funding with active transportation and transit mode share goals. More detail on these efforts is explored in Chapter 10.

Urban resilience issue 3: equity as an afterthought

A third and related weakness of current urban resilience practice is the failure to integrate equity concerns directly into the core of planning and practice. As the neoliberal critique makes clear, resilience planning is often portrayed as an apolitical, technical exercise when it is in fact a potentially dramatic social and economic restructuring that provides safety, livability, and enhanced amenity value to a select set of residents. On the other side of the equation, some hazardous areas will increasingly become less valued as climate impacts become clearer. These issues are particularly acute in coastal areas. With approximately 30% of the US population living within coastal counties (Wilson and Fischetti 2010), these issues help to define who is in harm's way and who is, literally, sheltered. In this way, resilience projects can be seen as a new type of amenity that simultaneously makes some citizens safer with increasingly valuable housing stock and potentially pushes some citizens into less attractive and unsafe areas.

For example, Fainstein (2018) shows how urban green space and park planning that adapts cities for climate change can also add to the amenity value of neighborhoods, increasing housing cost. She links urban growth machine politics to resilience by pointedly arguing that "the move to create resilience converges with these [growth] interests in developing parks that will absorb flooding from nearby waterways" (Fainstein 2018, p. 4). The result, she argues, is that "resilience planning, even while it has enhanced the city's ability to survive flooding, has contributed to the interests of the growth machine" (p. 6).

To counter these potential inequities in development politics will require targeted direction of citizen engagement in selecting priorities for resilience. The process of resilience planning and decision making need not be a purely technical exercise, but instead must be paired with citizen-led "assessments of investment priorities" (Fainstein 2018, p. 4).

To put this directly, resilient streets need to be just and equitable places where all community members feel safe not just from cars, climate change, and pollution, but from crime and state-sanctioned violence as well. Policies for the design and management of these places need to be constructed through open dialogue with the community. This is the base. Everything else rests on this. If streets aren't just and safe, they aren't resilient.

From market-oriented to adaptation urbanism resilience

With this background in mind, it is important to clearly address equity implications of resilience planning. Without a clear process of citizen engagement and affordable housing assistance, urban resilience projects could exacerbate current inequities and result in increased safety for some and increased risk for others (Meerow and Woodruff 2019). The trend lines of a resilience planning process premised on current development practices are direct and challenging.

We envision this type of market-oriented process for climate adaptation projects in Figure 2.2. The siloed focus of climate adaptation developments begins with a narrow set of laudable goals targeted on, in coastal settings, decreasing susceptibility to flooding through the use of multi-purpose open space planning. While these goals are vital, they broadly ignore affordability concerns that could result from the projects and focus on only one-half of the climate resilience question (climate adaptation). While flooding risk diminishes, housing costs can increase because of the added amenity value and improved safety of the green and blue infrastructure projects. Because of a narrow, siloed focus on only climate adaptation, streets remain unsafe and continue to generate high GHG emissions and other pollution. These impacts are hidden in the background as they were not seen as part of the scope of the project. This process shows how market-oriented resilience's singular focus on adaptation can increase safety and livability for some but leave others behind.

For urban resilience to be more than an extrapolation of the current urban political trendlines of inequity and high GHG emissions, it must be crafted as a socio-political process that, as Derickson (2016, p. 165) argues, directly "mitigate[s] this uneven capacity, in order to seed the conditions for envisioning and engendering socially just futures." Mitigation, in this sense, is not just to climate change, but to the broader patterns of uneven development.

In coming chapters, we discuss how affordable housing priorities and climate mitigation can be integrated with green and blue infrastructure development to help ensure more equitable outcomes and broader community resilience (Rigolon and Nemeth 2018). This is operationalized as the adaptation urbanism resilience

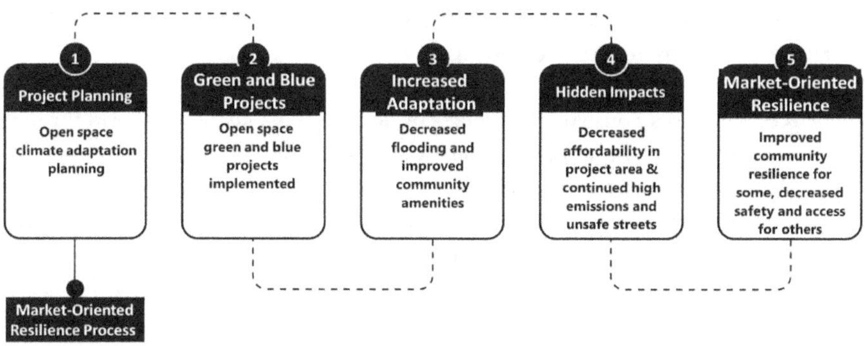

FIGURE 2.2 Market-oriented resilience process.

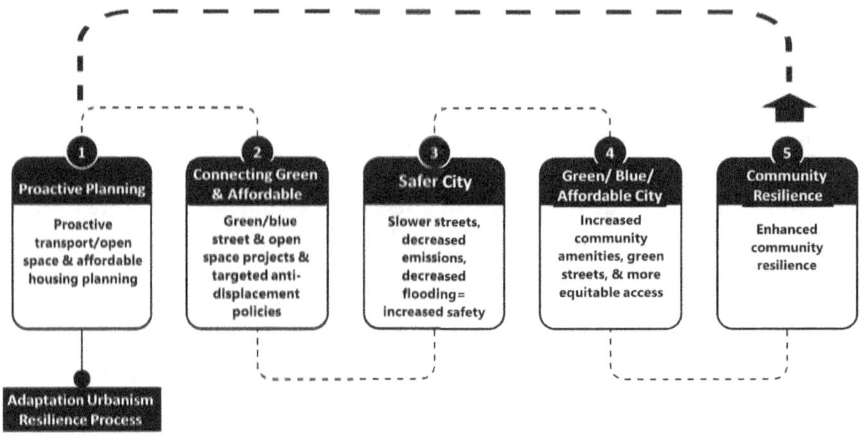

FIGURE 2.3 Adaptation urbanism resilience process.

process (Figure 2.3), where citizens engage in setting the vision from the start. This is seen as an iterative, long-term process of building towards community resilience with climate adaptation, mitigation, and equity brought together as key goals for transportation and open space planning. Instead of urban resilience planning operating in a narrow silo, the goal is to work across sectors (open space, water management, transportation, public health, and housing) to help create a much more holistic practice of community resilience planning. While this iterative process is complicated and contested, the process is crafted to move communities towards a resilience system that helps to build the safer/green/blue/affordable city. This is the promise and challenge of adaptation urbanism.

Urban resilience summary

This chapter surveys the meaning and tensions associated with urban resilience practice. While there are numerous definitional frameworks for resilience developed in the literature, we find Meerow et al's (2016) articulation helpful as it situates urban resilience practice within a set of tensions drawn from the wider resilience literature. To slightly restate Meerow et al's (2016, p. 45) definition:

> Resilience is a constructive process of negotiating a changing world through, depending on the situation, "persistence, transition, and transformation" by focusing on a process of adaptation across multiple timescales. It is not a technical end state condition, but rather a way of visioning the city and engaging constituencies in sustaining and reshaping the future city.
>
> *(modified definition from Meerow et al. 2016)*

In the second section of the chapter, we situate this broad resilience articulation within a set of issues familiar to urban planners. Climate change is pressing planners to transform the built environment to decrease GHG emissions and withstand (and thrive) in a changing climate while also negotiating planning politics and working to address serious equity issues. While the climate change component is a relatively new urban policy issue, the underlying issues of managing change are core issues of urban planning. Resilience policymakers can draw on the deep research and theoretical foundation of the urban planning profession to manage change and create more livable, equitable cities.

At its core, urban resilience is about articulating the "good city," a city built to last, but designed to change through negotiated processes and practices of engagement. We recognize that the aims are lofty, and that the practice is messy and often fails to meet these high standards. Urban planners, particularly in the United States, operate within a neoliberal structure that limits governmental actions and often relies on private capital to lead development. These structural conditions are worthy of critique, discussion, and contested action, but they are the proverbial river that planners swim in. Planners are, thus, aiming for just and negotiated outcomes, but often lack clear mechanisms to achieve these ends.

Planners need tools to bend the boundaries of these structures, to negotiate these structural tensions to improve outcomes for all residents. Urban resilience practice offers an opportunity to engage in this process of critical professional evaluation and situate urban planning at the center of urban policy responses to climate change. "Good" urbanism itself should be one of the core strategies to address climate change, but only if planners and a broad urban coalition steadfastly articulate the goals and build the political capital necessary to structure this new urban future. Such goals and outcomes need to benefit all members in society, not just the wealthy who can afford such protection. We outline these tensions in Figures 2.2 and 2.3 to conceptually center the tensions between market-oriented resilience and a more holistic adaptation urbanism process.

We engage the difficult challenge in Chapter 3 by outlining a new, resilient vision for urban streets. This urban-centered approach to resilience focuses squarely on how streets can be planned to reduce GHG emissions and, simultaneously, be used to adapt the city to a changing climate. As discussed later in this book, such benefits aim to promote more sustainable and just outcomes by encouraging investments in local infrastructure that reduce GHGs, increase safety, and promote greater livability and improved public health that is accessible to all members of society. This is the adaptation urbanism process.

Notes

1 It should be noted that we conducted a basic, descriptive analysis of the use of the terms resilience, resilient, or resiliency in selected-area focused publications. We did not include geography, environmental sciences, or other related fields. Meerow and Newell (2015) conduct a much more detailed analysis of the use of the terms and their relationship to cross-disciplinary research. Our effort here is simply to show the growth of the use of the terms in the urban planning, transportation, and water resources fields.

2 In an applied context, this means that resilience planners cannot assume that the prior state was in balance (non-equilibrium) and that they will need to work to create a positive vision with local residents to, depending on the circumstances, persist, transition, or transform key policy areas over time.

References

Baca, Alex. (2019). The Green New Deal's Huge Flaw. *Slate*. February 7. Last accessed 12/10/2019 from https://slate.com/business/2019/02/green-new-deal-alexandria-ocasio-cortez-flaw-land-use.html.

Bellis, Rayla. (2020). The Congestion Con: How More Lanes and More Money Equals More Congestion. Washington, DC: T4America. Last accessed 3/6/2020 from http://t4america.org/maps-tools/congestion-con/.

Bliss, Laura. (2019). The Rise, Fall, and Possible Rebirth of 100 Resilient Cities. Last accessed 4/1/2020 from www.citylab.com/environment/2019/06/climate-change-resilience-cities-rockefeller-foundation/589861/.

Bohland, J., Davoudi, S., & Lawrence, J. L. (Eds.). (2018). *The Resilience Machine*. New York, NY: Routledge.

Campanella, T. J. (2006). Urban Resilience and the Recovery of New Orleans. *Journal of the American Planning Association, 72*(2), 141–146.

Campbell, S. D. (2016). The Planner's Triangle Revisited: Sustainability and the Evolution of a Planning Ideal That Can't Stand Still. *Journal of the American Planning Association, 82*(4), 388–397.

City of Austin Sustainability Office. (2018). Climate Resilience Action Plan. https://austintexas.gov/sites/default/files/files/Sustainability/Climate_Resilience_Action_Plan.compressed.pdf.

City of Portland Bureau of Transportation. (2019). Transportation for Everyone: Central City in Motion Implementation Plan. Last accessed 12/11/2019 from www.portlandoregon.gov/transportation/71158.

Derickson, K. D. (2016). Resilience is Not Enough. *City, 20*(1), 161–166.

Duany, A., & Talen, E. (Eds.). (2013). *Landscape Urbanism and its Discontents: Dissimulating the Sustainable City*. Gabriola Island, BC, Canada: New Society Publishers.

Ewing, R., & Cervero, R. (2010). Travel and the Built Environment: A Meta-Analysis. *Journal of the American Planning Association, 76*(3), 265–294.

Ewing, R., & Cervero, R. (2017). "Does Compact Development Make People Drive Less?" The Answer is Yes. *Journal of the American Planning Association, 83*(1), 19–25.

Ewing, R., Bartholomew, K., Winkelman, S., Walters, J., Chen, D., Mccann, B., & Goldberg, D. (2008). *Growing Cooler: The Evidence on Urban Development and Climate Change*. Washington, DC: Urban Land Institute.

Ewing, R., Tian, G., Goates, J. P., Zhang, M., Greenwald, M. J., & Greene, W. (2014). Varying Influences of the Built Environment on Household Travel in 15 Diverse Regions of the United States. *Urban Studies*, 52(13), 2330–2348.

Fainstein, S. S. (2018). Resilience and Justice: Planning for New York City. *Urban Geography, 39*(8), 1268–1275.

Fields, B., Thomas, J., & Wagner, J. A. (2017). Living with Water in the Era of Climate Change: Lessons from the Lafitte Greenway in Post-Katrina New Orleans. *Journal of Planning Education and Research, 37*(3), 309–321.

Filion, P. (2018). Enduring Features of the North American Suburb: Built Form, Automobile Orientation, Suburban Culture and Political Mobilization. *Urban Planning, 3*(4), 4–14.

Green, B. (2019). *The Smart Enough City: Putting Technology in its Place to Reclaim Our Urban Future*. Cambridge, MA: MIT Press.

Handy, S. (2017). Thoughts on the Meaning of Mark Stevens's Meta-Analysis. *Journal of the American Planning Association, 83*(1), 26–28.

Hankinson, M. (2018). When do Renters Behave Like Homeowners? High Rent, Price Anxiety, and NIMBYism. *American Political Science Review, 112*(3), 473–493.

Harris, L. M., Chu, E. K., & Ziervogel, G. (2018). Negotiated Resilience. *Resilience, 6*(3), 196–214.

Infield, E. M. H., Abunnasr, Y., & Ryan, R. L. (eds.). (2018). *Planning for Climate Change: A Reader in Green Infrastructure and Sustainable Design for Resilient Cities*. New York, NY: Routledge.

Kelbaugh, Douglas. (2014). The Environmental Paradox of the City, Landscape Urbanism, and New Urbanism. *Consilience: The Journal of Sustainable Development*. 13(1), 1–15.

Kimble, Megan. (2019). The Fight to Make Austin Affordable. *Texas Observer.* December 6. Last accessed 3/17/20 from www.texasobserver.org/the-fight-to-make-austin-affordable-housing/.

McKinsey Center/C40Cities. (2017). Focused Acceleration: A Strategic Approach for Climate Action in Cities to 2030. McKinsey Center for Business and Environment and C40 Cities. Last accessed 3/18/20 from www.c40.org/researches/mckinsey-center-for-business-and-environment.

Meerow, S., & Newell, J. P. (2015). Resilience and Complexity: A Bibliometric Review and Prospects for Industrial Ecology. *Journal of Industrial Ecology, 19*(2), 236–251.

Meerow, S., & Woodruff, S. C. (2020). Seven Principles of Strong Climate Change Planning. *Journal of the American Planning Association, 86*(1), 39–46.

Meerow, S., Newell, J. P., & Stults, M. (2016). Defining Urban Resilience: A Review. *Landscape and Urban Planning, 147*, 38–49.

Molotch, H. (1976). The City as a Growth Machine: Toward a Political Economy of Place. *American Journal of Sociology, 82*(2), 309–332.

Newman, P., Beatley, T., & Boyer, H. (2009). *Resilient Cities: Responding to Peak Oil and Climate Change.* Washington, DC: Island Press.

Newman, P., Kenworthy, J., Scheurer, J., Beirad, L., Hartelius-Jensen, M., Broberg, S., Larsen, A. K., Pölkow, B., Hansen, B., Søndergaard, B., Møller, C., Sun, M., Holm, D., Holm, D., Witt, G., Winslaw, L., & Jensen, M. (1997). 'Car-free' Copenhagen: Perspective and Ideas for Reducing Car Dependence in Cophenhagen. Department of Design, Royal Danish Academy of Fine Arts, Copenhagen and Institute for Science and Technology Policy; Perth, Australia: Murdoch University.

Olshansky, R. B., Hopkins, L. D., & Johnson, L. A. (2012). Disaster and Recovery: Processes Compressed in Time. *Natual Hazards Review*, 13(3), 173–178.

Renne, J., Wolshon, B., Murray-Tuite, P., & Pande, A. (2020). Emergence of Resilience as a Framework for State Departments of Transportation (DOTs) in the United States. *Transportation Research Part D: Transport and Environment, 82*, 102178.

Rigolon, A., & Németh, J. (2018). "We're Not in the Business of Housing": Environmental Gentrification and the Nonprofitization of Green Infrastructure Projects. *Cities, 81*, 71–80.

Rogers, P. (2018). The Resilient City: Where do we go from Here? In *The Resilience Machine* (pp. 125–144). (J. Bohland, S. Davoudi, & J. L. Lawrence, eds.). New York: Routledge.

Schlossberg, M., Millard-Ball, A., Shay, E., & Riggs, W. B. (2018). Rethinking the Street in an Era of Driverless Cars. *UrbanismNext*. University of Oregon. Last accessed 3/18/2020 from https://scholarsbank.uoregon.edu/xmlui/bitstream/handle/1794/23331/UrbanismNext_ResearchBrief_003.pdf?sequence=1.

Shaw, K. (2012). "Reframing" Resilience: Challenges for Planning Theory and Practice. *Planning Theory and Practice*, *13*(2), 308–312.

Stead, Dominik. (2014). Urban Planning, Water Management and Climate Change Strategies: Adaptation, Mitigation and Resilience Narratives in the Netherlands. *International Journal of Sustainable Development & World Ecology*, 21(1), 15–27.

Tessler, Z. D., Vörösmarty, C. J., Grossberg, M., Gladkova, I., Aizenman, H., Syvitski, J. P. M., & Foufoula-Georgiou, E. (2015). Profiling Risk and Sustainability in Coastal Deltas of the World. *Science*, *349*(6248), 638–643.

Vale, Lawrence J. (2014). The Politics of Resilient Cities: Whose Resilience and Whose City? *Building Research & Information*, 42(2), 191–201.

Walsh, C. L., Dawson, R. J., Hall, J. W., Barr, S. L., Batty, M., Bristow, A. L., & Tight, M. R. (2011). Assessment of Climate Change Mitigation and Adaptation in Cities. *Proceedings of the Institution of Civil Engineers-Urban Design and Planning*, *164*(2), 75–84.

Weilant, Sarah, Strong, Aaron, & Miller, Benjamin M. (2019). *Incorporating Resilience into Transportation Planning and Assessment*. Santa Monica, CA: RAND Corporation. Last accessed 3/26/2020 from www.rand.org/pubs/research_reports/RR3038.html.

Weissman, G., & Casale, M. (2019). Highway Boondoggles 5: Big Projects, Bigger Price Tags, Limited Benefits. U.S. PIRG Education Fund and Frontier Group. Last accessed 3/18/2020 from https://uspirg.org/sites/pirg/files/reports/USP%20Highway%20Report%20Jun19%20web%20rev1.pdf.

Whitehead, M. (2013). Neoliberal Urban Environmentalism and the Adaptive City: Towards a Critical Urban Theory and Climate Change. *Urban Studies*, *50*(7), 1348–1367.

Wilson, S. G., & Fischetti, T. R. (2010). *Coastline Population Trends in the United States 1960 to 2008*. Washington, DC: US Department of Commerce, Economics and Statistics Administration, US Census Bureau.

3

FROM URBAN RESILIENCE TO STREET RESILIENCE

Rethinking the role of streets in the climate-adapted city

Addressing urban resilience tensions: towards adaptation urbanism

The tensions on display in current iterations of urban resilience provide a complex and difficult foundation on which to build a new urban agenda. Our contention is that urban resilience is not a value-free end state condition, but instead a process of change that can be guided to help enhance safety, decrease carbon emissions, and encourage more equitable outcomes (Meerow et al. 2016; Harris et al. 2018). While the process will involve tensions, urban resilience need not be a zero-sum game where some residents benefit from safer and more attractive places and others are suborned to edges of safety. We argue that this makes urban resilience both a technical challenge to effectively and efficiently modify cities to better withstand and mitigate climate change and a process challenge where multiple voices need to be integrated into discussions about how best to achieve these goals. This, as Healey (2009, p. 840) argues, is the place governance challenge where "place discourses jostle" over how best to develop the evolving city form. There is no one perfect, technical solution to these problems, but instead a process of engagement where communities build policy solutions to fit local conditions and create places with long-term value and meaning. This is the foundation of a "negotiated resilience" (Harris et al. 2018, p. 2).

In this chapter, we unpack the meaning of resilience in the context of street and open space planning. We find that current transportation and water management practices are constrained by bureaucratic structures that limit innovation and result in privileging status quo practices over more resilient alternatives. The administrative and technical features of the current system are brought forward to help highlight key barriers to more resilient theory and practice. This provides the foundation for establishing a new policy framework we call *adaptation urbanism*, detailed further in Chapter 4.

Because discussions of transportation and water systems can be terminologically dense, we begin by centering the dialog in a set of real-world places to help show how rethinking resilience can work to make safer, healthier, and more equitable cities. In this way, we seek to define what a new resilient city might look like and who gets to benefit from these new resilient places.

From personal choices to climate resilience

The design of our cities impacts climate emissions levels. Cities both are the source of the largest concentrations of greenhouse gas (GHG) emissions, with 70% of CO_2 emissions being generated for urban energy production and transportation (UN Habitat 2016), and, paradoxically, have the potential to act as a vital management tool in decreasing emissions. As was discussed in Chapter 2, climate policy solutions have traditionally been scaled from the national level down to the local. There is, however, increasing evidence that planning from the local level up through the underlying design of cities can also be an effective way to manage GHG emissions.

As an example, try to think about how you traveled to work or school today. Most people think about the length and/or the cost of the trip and how stressful or even how pleasant the trip was. These individual factors help to influence how far you decide to live from work or school and, because commuting can be a large budgetary expense, significantly impact your personal finances. A good way to think about these factors is as a series of potential variables that impact your transportation choices. Ewing and Cervero (2010) analyze the impact of series of variables (the so-called "D" variables after the first initial of each term) and find that the design, diversity, density, destination accessibility, distance to transit, and demand management of the land use and transportation systems impact travel behavior and modal choice. These "D" variables help to define the structures that either limit or open individual transportation choices.

These individual decisions, when added up, do something else as well. When scaled up, they help to determine how much your city and region contributes to the problem of climate change. Cities with more compact development and good connections to transit, walking, and bicycling use less energy in the transportation sector. As we pointed out in Chapter 1, this can be 20–50% lower transport GHG emissions than in cities that are more spread out and car-reliant (Creutzig 2016, p. 348).

Let's think about a typical trip and how the way we build our cities and transportation systems impacts travel choices and GHG emissions. Imagine you are sitting in a coffee shop in a large Sunbelt city in the United States on a warm October day. To get there, you drove several miles through moderate traffic on a four-lane road with cars moving at 40 miles per hour (64 km/hour) to reach the shopping area. While you may have wanted to limit your transportation fossil fuel use, walking and biking were not safe and it would have taken too long to take a bus because of infrequent service. Because of the structures of the transportation system that made it both unsafe and inefficient to walk/bike or use transit and simultaneously made it easy to drive with free parking and low fuel costs, you may have made the rational choice given the system characteristics and driven for your trip. Conversely, if you did not have enough money to own a car or took a principled stand to limit GHG emissions, you were subjected to a safety tax of navigating high-speed roads with limited active transportation infrastructure.

Now imagine a similar scenario in a city such as Copenhagen. Although the hints of summer have already given way to the darker and colder season ahead, the chilly street is still lively with people walking and biking past the windows. The people around you could have driven to the coffee shop but, truthfully, it did not occur to most of them as 66% of all trips within inner-Copenhagen are by bike, walking, or transit (Danish Cyclist Federation 2017). It was so much easier and faster to jump into the flow of bikes, walk, or take the metro or bus to get to the destination. As car parking was both limited and fairly expensive in the center city, driving would have cost more money and taken more time than walking, biking, or transit. The rational choice was, as was the case in Amsterdam example from Chapter 1, the low-carbon choice. Because the city is set up to encourage these types of low-GHG choices, there is no need to take a principled stand for the climate and fight through high-speed car traffic to reach your destination. In addition, owning a car is not a cost for access to the city. The safety tax has been repealed and instead you have been given a low-carbon transportation bonus that makes walking, biking, and transit the more efficient choice.

You probably have experienced some elements of this little thought experiment in practice. Your transportation habits are different depending on whether you are in a car-dependent city with a safety and efficiency tax on transit and active transportation or living or visiting a city with a more integrated, multi-modal system. This is not some type of policy revelation, but a reasonable place to start thinking about how the built environment opens or often closes potential choices. Moreover, in the car-dependent neighborhoods and cities of countries like Australia and the United States, many residents have never experienced life without a car and often have a negative view of public transport. However, when they visit cities in Europe or even places like New York, San Francisco, Sydney, or Melbourne, they happily travel by foot and transit, not realizing the overarching land use and transportation conditions encouraging them to do so.

As policymakers begin to address how to make cities more resilient to a changing climate, opportunities to utilize the street design and the built environment as integrated tools in transitioning towards a low-carbon transportation system should become increasingly important policy responses (Boarnet and Handy 2017). One of the important factors that influences the potential to use these low-carbon transportation modes is that most trips are fairly short. In the United States, for example, half of all trips are under 3 miles (5 km) in length. Flusche (2010) describes this as the 30–40–50 distance concept, where 30% of trips are under 1 mile, 40% of trips are under 2 miles, and 50% of trips under 3 miles. This places half of all journeys within easy range for walking, biking, e-biking, or even an e-scooter trip. The low-carbon choice could be easy, fast, and affordable with the provision of safe facilities. When combined with public transport and trains for longer trips, the outlines of a truly low-carbon transportation begin to come into view.

Deconstructing the transportation bureaucratic state: implications of induced demand

While the future of a new, low-carbon transportation system is beginning to emerge, streets of the past continue to dominate the landscapes of many cities around the world. Over the last 75 or so years, land use and transportation policy in many cities and nations have focused on privileging a lower-density, more car-dependent built environment. Through the use of an integrated set of rules and codes, building lower-density land uses (Levine 2006) and constructing road systems based on car-oriented principles (Lee and Handy 2018) have become the standardized norm. The codes, rules, and underlying bureaucratic funding and rule-making systems act to create an intricate web of public management structures that need to be dislodged to open significant opportunities for addressing the urban climate crisis.

At the core of modern transportation system management is the use of a series of metrics that measure flow and speed of traffic. Measures such as level of service, average daily traffic, and overall speed of traffic flowing through the system speak to a narrow focus of transportation as an engineering problem to solve (Green 2019). In this engineering problem, increasing space in the system opens more room for traffic to flow and helps to increase the number and speed of vehicles in an effort to limit congestion, usually at peak hours. In this bureaucratic system, competing priorities for use of public space are negated by the administrative power sphere of traffic engineers. This places traffic engineers as the key arbiter of spatial use in the city (Aldred et al. 2019).[1] This intuitive, reductionist approach to understanding movement in cities has significant policy implications as the traffic engineers seek to maximize speed and auto throughput by building wider intersections, adding flyovers to decrease system friction, and adding additional lanes to increase system capacity, and "having drivers crowdsource speed limits via the 85th percentile rule" (Taylor and Hwang 2020, p. 10). Every few years, government-mandated transportation models are reworked and, not at all surprisingly, show that increases in population and traffic in the system require additional road expansion. We have built larger and larger roads for 75 years and the system remains clogged.

One of the primary reasons why traffic-engineering solutions have failed is because transportation is not simply an engineering problem of limited space, but an economic problem of an unpriced service. The concept of induced demand explains the economic consequences of adding unpriced roadway capacity and expecting it to "solve" congestion. The new, "free" transportation lanes are essentially an invitation for transportation consumers to use more of the product. As the product is free once you own a car, consumers can alter where they live and how they travel and consume more distance in the equivalent time. This encourages development of new residential opportunities on the periphery and expands the footprint of the city. As more trips are taken to an ever-expanding city footprint, the roadway again becomes clogged and the cycle of transportation modeling, planning, and expansion continues again. Lee and Handy (2018) describe this process as the "congestion–capacity–congestion cycle" (p. 24).

The economic logic and empirical impact of this induced demand process have been solidly analyzed over the last 50 years. In a review of induced demand scholarship, Noland and Hanson (2013) conclude that studies show that "one cannot reduce congestion through new road projects, and building new roads that access undeveloped land will result in increased vehicle travel. Our review of empirical studies finds conclusive evidence of this theoretical relationship" (p. 81). The policy implication, Noland and Hanson (2013) conclude, is that decreasing congestion cannot legitimately be used as rationale for road building. This, they argue, should "shift the debate to whether development should be dispersed or, on the other hand, made more concentrated and amenable to non-motorized modes of travel" (p. 81). Lee and Handy (2018) argue similarly that breaking the induced demand cycle "requires addressing the demand for travel, which is inextricably linked with the accessibility provided by land development patterns" (p. 24).

Understanding the policy implications of induced demand provides a pivot point for opening a new understanding of the goals of transportation planning and the potential to create streets as places of value. If we take induced demand seriously, the question is not whether and how to decrease congestion through the present system, but instead how to build a city that increases accessibility to quality homes and employment and decreases GHG emissions that are fueling the climate crisis. Taking induced demand seriously requires reevaluating the underlying structures of transportation planning and funding and opening new pathways for conceptualizing resilient cities. Instead of building streets to use up resources and expand the spatial footprint of the city, as Le Corbusier suggested (Le Corbusier 1964), the city building "problem" is flipped to determining the best way to build accessibility to places of value. This requires a new view of efficiency focused not only on the limited metrics of speed and auto throughput, but of better managing land use, energy, and safety. Green (2019, p. 21) summarizes this view by pointing out that,

> Because most traffic engineers strive for efficiency—defined solely in terms of automobile travel—they do not measure whether roads meet the needs of pedestrians and transit riders. And what is left out of equations tends to be not just ignored but devalued.

What gets measured, gets managed and we are measuring the wrong metrics.

Safe/climate/spatially efficient: rethinking urban transportation metrics

As discussed in Chapter 1, the streets of the past continue to be built on the edges of cities all around the United States and, increasingly, around the world. Instead of focusing on access to places and the safety of vulnerable road users, measurement

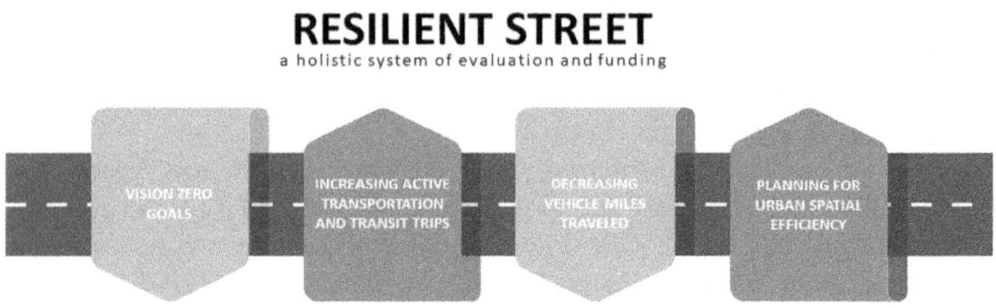

FIGURE 3.1 Resilient street metrics.

metrics and funding continue to emphasize the outputs of automobile flows. Makarewicz et al. (2018, p. 144) summarize this by pointing out that "performance and evaluation metrics used in funding decisions are biased toward regional mobility rather than accessibility." The economic principle of derived demand aligns with an accessibility framework for travel by individuals whereas mobility-based planning focuses on the supply side of travel. While both are important, state Departments of Transportation and many local public works departments have ignored the demand side of transportation and only focus on road building and widening. A focus on accessibility allows for more individual choice, variety, flexibility, competition, and spillover benefits to individuals and communities (Levine et al. 2019).

A body of recent works has begun to deconstruct the interrelationship between measurement metrics and funding mechanisms that perpetuate the modernist transportation system and begun to build countervailing metrics that should be used to evaluate street performance. We focus below on four emerging metrics (transportation safety, decreasing vehicle miles traveled (VMT), active transportation mode share goals, and modal spatial efficiency) that, when combined together, offer the potential to begin measuring (and funding) the *right* things (Piatkowski and Marshall 2018). These new metrics provide the foundation for a truly resilient street (Figure 3.1).

Metrics of success 1: advance Vision Zero goals

One of the most important emerging metrics to evaluate transportation success (or failure) has been the increasing use of Vision Zero policies to evaluate transportation safety. Developed in Sweden in the mid-1990s, Vision Zero policies center on the goal of creating safe systems to reduce and eventually eliminate serious injuries or fatalities from the transportation system. Instead of focusing primarily on the behavior of transportation users, Vision Zero policies begin with a focus on how roads can be built to help prevent a mistake from turning into a fatality or serious injury.

The approach focuses on the limits of the human body to withstand forces in a crash. Kristianssen et al. (2018) succinctly describe Vision Zero as a "policy innovation with a focus on the tolerance of the human body to kinetic energy and that the responsibility for road safety falls on the system designers" (p. 260). Humans, in other words, can only withstand a certain amount of force to the body and survive a crash. Road designers need to design streets in ways that limit the potential of humans to come into contact with deadly forces by focusing, particularly in urban areas, on limiting speed through design interventions. The results from Sweden have been impressive. Since the inception of the program, road fatalities have declined by half (Kristianssen et al. 2018).

A similar approach was also developed in the Netherlands in the mid-1990s, called Sustainable Safety. This approach mirrors the Swedish method in many ways and provides clear guidance on how to design urban roads for safety with a special focus on managing design speeds of roadways and separating vulnerable road users at speeds above about 20 mph (30 km/hour: the upper end speed at which a crash is most likely survivable by a pedestrian or cyclist).

Taken together, Vision Zero and Sustainable Safety policies represent what can be called a Safe Systems approach that is based on four overarching principles. First, the human body has a known and limited ability to tolerate crash forces. Second, people make mistakes that lead to crashes. Third, system designers share responsibility with road users for crash prevention, and fourth, all elements of the system should be strengthened to multiply their effects (Dumbaugh et al. 2019). These types of policies are making in-roads in the United States. A recent survey by Dumbaugh et al. (2018) of the 150 most populous cities in the United States found that 45% of communities have a formal policy or explicit target related to traffic safety, including Vision Zero or Towards Zero Deaths.[2] The Vision Zero/Safe Systems approach is a template for planning streets of the future and will be discussed in more depth in Chapter 5 on Rotterdam and Chapter 6 on Copenhagen.

Metrics of success 2: from level of service to decreasing vehicle miles traveled

While Vision Zero seeks to recenter the transportation system around improved safety outcomes, much of the underlying bureaucratic architecture of the transportation system is based on increasing speed and volume of vehicles, often at the expense of safety. New metrics that challenge these underlying bureaucratic systems are beginning to emerge as well. Lee and Handy (2018), for example, analyze California's efforts to replace level of service with VMT as the central metric for defining project impacts in the effort to decrease GHG emissions. As a result of California's Senate Bill 375 (SB 375), state transportation planners have been forced to reevaluate how project level mitigation measures are determined. The arcane process in the past used to rely on level of service of automobiles and often resulted in increasing capacity of roadways to maintain existing roadway capacity levels. As the induced demand dilemma shows, this process actually led to increasing levels of VMT and increasing GHG emissions.

Pushed by the need to make progress on climate goals by SB 375, California's Global Warming Solutions Act of 2006, many communities in California are now utilizing VMT as a new metric to determine environmental consequences of transportation and development. The act gives the California Air Resources Board authority over GHG emissions from cars and light trucks and encourages cities and counties to develop effective land use plans to achieve long-term emissions targets. Lee and Handy (2018) analyze the technical modeling implications of the shift and point to important changes that begin to take this type of system into wider usage. The underlying policy implications of this shift are, as Lee and Handy (2018) note, that policies to decrease "VMT impacts will require increasing accessibility and decreasing automobile demand, whereas mitigation of automobile delay has largely focused on optimizing traffic operations and increasing automobile capacity at specific intersections or roadway links" (p. 22).

Metrics of success 3: target/fund active transportation and transit mode share goals

Metrics matter in moving away from level of service. Piatkowski and Marshall (2018) extend this logic of counting "what we care about" (p. 60) in a shift from measuring level of service and the number of cars on roadways to a more nuanced proposal for measuring holistic community benefits of active transport investments. The authors argue that moving from mobility to accessibility will require measuring not just movement of pedestrians and cyclists (a type of mobility indicator), but also to broader accessibility-centered indicators focused on community health, environment, and economic variables. This approach, they argue, should focus on beginning with active transportation "mode share goals, which in turn must be accommodated by building appropriate infrastructure" (p. 68) to meet those goals. When transit is added to the equation, the beginnings of a low-cost, low-carbon transportation system that provides more equitable access to the community start to come into focus.

This more holistic approach focuses on planning for community goals and then investing to achieve those goals. This statement is so simple and straightforward that it is difficult to comprehend why we are not doing this already. As we laid out, this basic statement of policy and funding intent runs counter to established transportation-planning practices where the focus is always on minimizing auto congestion through proxies of speed and level of service and then, secondarily, achieving other policy goals. Flipping the equation and actually planning and funding active transportation and transit to meet community goals leads to what Piatkowski and Marshall (2018, p. 68) describe as a virtuous cycle of "induced demand for active modes and holistic benefits" where investments lead to increasing use which leads to increasing investments to meet community goals. Moreover, these scholars argue that this more holistic approach of broader community goals helps to address the underlying "institutional inertia" (Piatkowski and Marshall 2018, p. 64) of the mobility-centered paradigm and push innovation forward. This type of approach also opens the door to valuing the public life benefits of streets that can help transform a space into a place of value (Gehl and Svarre 2013).

The targeted approach to goal setting and funding allocation based on those goals is succinctly captured by the former planning director of Vancouver, Brent Toderian. He succinctly argues that: "If your city's transportation plan doesn't have specific and ambitious mode shift targets, and an action plan to achieve those targets, you don't have a transportation plan" (Toderian 2019). Recently, Cambridge, MA, passed the Cycling Safety Ordinance which mandates inclusion of protected bicycle facilities on major roads whenever a street is resurfaced (Schmitt 2019). These types of approaches start to link planning goals directly with actions and show how cities can begin to push forward faster. Chapter 10 examines these concepts in more depth.

Metrics of success 4: promote spatial efficiency for accessibility/livability/climate adaptation

The rise of electric and autonomous vehicles opens another potential avenue for rethinking the metrics used to evaluate transportation funding and overall mission. Schlossberg et al. (2018), for example, argue that autonomous vehicles will be "likely to disrupt long-established patterns of urban development, transportation choices and the use of streets" and "offer an entry point into society-wide conversations about transportation, the functions of cities, the use of streets, and how all this impacts equity, environment, social cohesion, happiness, economic health, resiliency, and more" (pp. 2 and 3). While the timeline for autonomous vehicle uptake is unclear, the process for planning for their inclusion in the transportation system presents an important opportunity to rethink how communities allocate street space and its underlying societal purpose.

As discussed earlier, streets represent about 30% of city space (UN Habitat 2013) and, when combined with auto parking, could account for up to 50% of all space in cities (Ellen MacArthur Foundation and McKinsey Center for Business and Environment 2015).[3] One way to think about how to prioritize street space is by focusing on the spatial efficiency of differing modes. Spatial efficiency metrics seek to compare the space needed to move people through an area using a suite of different modes. For example, a bus or tram can move 100 or more people in a much more compact area than 100 or more cars. As we discussed in Chapter 1, the space needed to move people in differing modes has been quantified and shows that transit, walking, and bicycling are much more spatially efficient than automobiles (NACTO 2016).

The present moment represents a time to re-envision how that space is allocated. The COVID-19 emergency has opened many new avenues for reprioritizing city space for people over cars with pop-up bike lanes and open-streets plans emerging in cities around the world. While we hope that the need to physically distance from each other will diminish, the public's desire to have safe neighborhood spaces for walking and bicycling appears, at least for the moment, to have grown during the crisis. As cities transition from the COVID-19 crisis to the emerging climate crisis, the new recaptured city space can help provide a launching pad for bouncing forward towards safer and healthier streets.

This transition to more spatially efficient options like walking, bicycling, and transit can allow cities to recapture the local benefits of the public street and use the "saved" space to add green infrastructure (GI) that soaks up water and enhances community livability. This vision of the resilient street preferences the neighborhood benefits of the street to local communities over the regional mobility purpose of speeding vehicles that has dominated our cities for so long.

In terms of the potential rise of electric vehicles, the spatial limits of the number of cars moving in a city is essentially the same whether they are powered by electricity or gasoline. Simply continuing present transportation-planning practices will, as we have argued, replace dirty congestion with the "clean congestion" of electric vehicles (Winkleman et al. 2019). The local benefits of improved livability and climate adaptation will not be realized as we continue the same spatial hierarchy that prioritizes car space above all else.

In terms of autonomous vehicles, it largely depends on what policies are put in place to help determine the spatial efficiency of these new vehicles. Green (2019) presents a sweeping discussion of the normative and political underpinnings of technology and of the use of efficiency as a measurement tool. Efficiency could be seen as moving large numbers of vehicles in a seamless, technologically connected system of autonomous vehicles. This type of system, currently being pushed by technology and car companies, seeks to maintain the dominance of cars in the urban landscape by prioritizing efficient movement of autonomous vehicles at the expense of the "unconnected" pedestrians and bicyclists. Green (2019, p. 8) notes that "efficiency carries the veneer of being objective and socially optimal but can actually generate unexpected and unjust impacts."

Green (2019, p. 10) characterizes the policy challenge of determining appropriate efficiencies as the Smart Enough City where the complex and potentially competing visions of efficiency are negotiated. He argues that the "Smart Enough City place[s] their policy goals at the forefront and, recognize[s] the complexity of people and institutions, think[s] holistically about how to better meet their needs." In other words, technology doesn't solve the underlying resilience political questions and, at worst, can mask those decisions in a veneer of technological objectivity that blinds us to competing potential visions.

Safe/climate/spatially efficient and equitable: adaptation urbanism

The underlying policy question is: what type of efficient city should we plan for? It is a policy choice that we make each day. The current metrics and funding mechanisms support the status quo orientation and are masked in the aura of scientific legitimacy. These structures and the underlying bureaucratic inertia of the transportation policy system prevent the basic policy choices from surfacing and reinforce a normative vision of the city based on, as we have observed, city-building principles from the 1930s and 1940s.[4]

We propose that the foundation of transportation efficiency in the climate change era should center on prioritizing the most spatially, climate, and safety-efficient and equitable transport options. While the auto-efficiency question is about how to move the largest number of vehicles at the highest speeds, the adaptation urbanism efficiency question is about how to maintain and expand safe, climate, spatially efficient transportation options to manage a changing climate and reduce GHG emissions. This new type of system focuses on expanding low- to zero-emission accessibility to the city and maintaining and expanding public space for livability and climate adaptation. Modes of lesser spatial, climate, and safety efficiency should be integrated as a secondary priority. This type of planning system focuses on building lower-speed accessibility to locations over the status quo normative vision of encouraging higher-speed mobility to regional destinations.

A system focused on urban spatial efficiency may sound radical and complicated, but it is not even particularly new or technically difficult to implement. It is currently in use in the Netherlands and has resulted in some of the most livable and safest urban areas in the world. Bruntlett and Bruntlett (2018) note that Utrecht, for one example, has created a "mobility policy that centers on spatial efficiency" (p. 134). This approach is used widely across the Netherlands and focuses on planning for "pedestrians first, then bikes, then public transit, and, finally, at the very bottom, the private automobile" (Bruntlett and Bruntlett 2018, p. 134). Spatially, the street is planned from the edges, where pedestrians and cyclists have dedicated space, to the center, where higher-speed automobiles move. If there are spatial constraints, they should impact the auto space as the active transportation zones are planned first. This flips the traditional transportation spatial hierarchy where car space is dedicated first and the left-over space may be programmed for bicycles, pedestrians, or transit later. While this approach is not always followed strictly in the Netherlands, the basic contours of this spatial efficiency approach can be experienced on Dutch streets.

This approach is in keeping with the Vision Zero/Safe Systems approach and focuses on creating safe places for vulnerable road users through either constrained auto speeds if there is mixing of modes (below about 20 mph or 30 km/hour) or dedicated infrastructure for vulnerable road users on higher-speed roadways. This places safety, efficiency, and climate mitigation first in the policy hierarchy and then allows cars (whether they be electric, autonomous, or gasoline-powered) into the system with limitations. Integrating transit as a key feature of this system helps to link communities to jobs and significantly decreases transportation costs, a key equity dimension.

Amsterdam and a growing number of other European cities are moving even further and planning to limit gasoline-powered vehicles from the city center by 2030 (discussed in more detail in Chapter 10). The result of the hierarchy of planning is a safe and spatially efficient transportation system that prioritizes safety, spatial efficiency, and, increasingly, climate-efficient transportation over less efficient modes. This process also generates highly livable places for people.

Metrics of success: summary

To summarize, recent efforts to create new measurement metrics for transportation open new and important avenues for reenvisioning the role of streets. These recent approaches outlined above link streets to safety outcomes (Vision Zero), to climate policy (VMT and GHG emissions), to targeted active transportation and transit mode share goals, and to the spatial efficiency of different modes of transportation.

While each of the emerging trends is an important individual mechanism for altering the status quo policy system, taken together, these four new metrics and funding trends create a powerful new way to reimagine resilient city streets (Figure 3.1). Imagine that the four streams of emerging metrics (Vision Zero goals, decreasing VMT, increasing active transportation/transit trips, and planning for urban spatial efficiency) were combined together into a holistic system of evaluation and funding to define the resilient street. We will return to the political implications of this type of scenario in Chapter 11, but, for now, imagine that the status quo metrics and funding systems could be altered. Imagine that the 50% of all trips under 3 miles (Flusche 2010) could be moved from cars to a high share of walking, bicycling, and transit trips. Imagine that this policy goal is linked to funding structures designed specifically around accessibility, spatial efficiency, safety, and decreasing VMT. The movement towards measuring the safety, climate, active transportation and transit, and spatial efficiency of differing modes creates a platform for rethinking the role of streets in creating resilient, low-carbon communities. The stakes for reevaluating metrics and funding mechanisms are high.

In some places around the globe, efforts to integrate these new types of metrics have already produced important results in terms of improved safety, reduced GHG emissions, and enhanced community livability. In other places, the political question is how to push these movements forward and begin to really measure what matters.

Adapting streets for changing climate and mitigating GHG emissions through urban form

Pushing towards reenvisioning streets as safe, spatially efficient components of a low-carbon equitable transportation system is, however, only one part of the urban resilience challenge. A second part of the challenge is that the environment is changing and will continue to change from already emitted GHGs. Cities must adapt to address these changing environmental conditions. While there are many environmental challenges, managing water, both too little and too much, is one of the core areas of concern. As discussed in Chapter 1, climate projections suggest that, depending on the region, intense rainfall events and, conversely, droughts will become more common. For example, in tropical areas, Aumann et al. (2018) project that under current climate forecasts intense rainfall events could increase by 60% by the end of this century. For coastal communities, these stresses will be compounded with sea level rise.

This threat combined with long-standing problems of modernist city planning is pushing cities to reexamine how water and public space are managed. During the modernist city expansions of the 20th century, cities turned their figurative backs on water with systems designed to push water out and away from populations as quickly as possible. Flood walls, buried culverts, and pumps were the backbone of the so-called gray infrastructure system. Instead of seeing water as an amenity to be managed, canals and other waterways were buried and often replaced on the surface with roadways that would act, in the biological metaphor, as the new arteries of the city.

In addition to increasing GHG emissions, these new transportation arteries resulted in two important impacts at the landscape level. They generated valuable land away from the city center for new development and resulted in decreasing the value of land in the city center as neighborhoods were demolished and the former multi-purpose canals were paved into high-volume streets that crisscrossed the city. In New Orleans, for example, the canal in the center of Broad Street was buried and replaced with additional travel lanes in the 1930s. The Works Progress Administration's description of the project perfectly encapsulates this philosophy and shows the "construction by [the Works Progress Administration] of a concrete box culvert in Broad Street [that] eliminated an open canal and provided for the widening of the thoroughfare" (New Orleans Public Library 1939). This is the "drained city" with buried stormwater below and space created for the automobile on the surface (Brown et al. 2009).

The result was that the city spread outwards with the higher-speed roads generating higher pollution and GHG emissions. Development potential on the periphery increased with easier access and land values in the center of the city were devalued as the new highway corridors acted as disamenities. Chapter 8 on New Orleans provides a more detailed examination of how these processes worked.

As the 21st century dawned, citizens and urban planners began to reexamine these lost spaces (Trancik 1986) and see potential for city living. As planners and residents worked to decrease the disamenities, land values for city center properties began to increase, creating both increasing demand and, in many communities, potential displacement of existing residents. While this is a complex meta-narrative of cities with many intervening factors, the overall trends mark a significant shift in city planning and a base for reexamining how city space is used and conceived.

At the same time that city centers began to be revalued, environmental conditions began to become more unstable. The modernist infrastructure systems were designed under environmental conditions that do not reflect the new climate realities of the 21st century. In many cities, more intense rainfall events are already stressing the limited capacity of gray infrastructure systems. In Chapter 1, we discussed the flooding that occurred in Copenhagen from a cloudburst storm in 2011. As the rain fell, the below-ground infrastructure filled to beyond capacity, with the result that water physically did not have any place to move but back into the streets and basements of the city. The result was approximately $800 billion in damages and a wakeup call about the limits of the current system (City of Copenhagen 2012).

Using the modernist planning approach to water and city planning, the choice for cities in this type of scenario is to find large budgetary resources to expand the capacity of the pipes and culverts buried beneath the ground to retrofit them for higher volumes of storm runoff or hope that the science is wrong and accept the periodic flooding of the city as the cost of access to the coast. This type of approach is not far off from what many US cities are actually doing right now as limited federal and state resources, climate denial, and a hope that the more stable past is precedent help to set the policy decision framework.

Measurement metrics and the adapted city

While current political structures in many places lend themselves to this type of policy thinking, this form of political narrative pushes a false choice. The problem and the solution for flooding and water storage are how we understand water and use city space. As the limits of the gray infrastructure systems have become more apparent, a growing chorus of planners has begun to focus on green and blue infrastructure systems as a lower-cost, effective, and amenity-based way to address urban water management (O'Donnell et al. 2017). Brown et al. (2009) encapsulate this view by articulating the vision of a water-sensitive city where "the normative values of environmental repair and protection, supply security, flood control, public health, amenity, livability and economic sustainability, amongst others" are used to envision a new relationship to water. In this type of new approach, "[c]ommunities would be driven by the normative values of protecting intergenerational equity with regards to natural resources and ecological integrity, as well as by concern that communities and environments are resilient to climate change" (p. 854).

In many ways, transportation and water management planning are struggling with similar and converging problems that often not only share similar solutions, but actually could share the same physical spaces for transformation. In much the same way that transportation planners have struggled to overcome the institutional inertia of a prior era, water planners have also begun to address how to change existing practices to achieve this more resilient vision. In the same way that transportation planning needs to move away from siloed, technical metrics, so too does water management need to move "from the traditional, linear, 'technocratic' approach to an adaptive, participatory, and integrated approach" (Brown 2008, p. 221).

Measurement metrics and funding practices, just like in the transportation sector, act to privilege the status quo and limit innovation. O'Donnell et al. (2017), in an analysis of barriers and potential pathways to promote more green and blue infrastructure in the UK, note that the top three barriers to change include the "reluctance to novel/new approaches/change practices," "lack of knowledge, education, awareness," and "funding and costs" (p. 3). Underlying these barriers is a rigid system of benefits calculation that limits the inclusion of the cross-sector community benefits of green and blue systems. O'Donnell et al. (2017) note that communities are "not statutorily required to provide the multiple benefits and so find it a challenge to include these in their own business case" (p. 6). Despite these challenges, the area that planners felt was most likely to help push innovation forward was "the promotion of multifunctional space and identification and assessment of the multiple benefits" (p. 4).

Sustainable water management and transportation could be converging on the same physical spaces for innovation and need to find ways to work together to evaluate benefits to potentially partner on multi-sector projects. Using a broader notion of cost/benefits that extends beyond the siloed boundaries of the current bureaucratic structures to include the placemaking potentials of water and transportation could be a promising pathway forward if cities can build more flexible measurement metrics and link these to funding availability.

Green, blue, compact, and urban: the rise of the urban environmentalist

While this convergence between transportation and water management is beginning to develop, conceptual barriers about the role of urbanism and density act as another important potential barrier. Planning and implementation for urban iterations of green and blue infrastructure require overcoming significant "thought" barriers that center around the perceived role of development and density in the environmental movement. Important tensions have developed between traditional environmentalists who favor open space protection focused on climate adaptation and urban environmentalists who tend to focus on the climate mitigation features of more urban environments (Newman and Kenworthy 1999; Waldheim 2006; Duany and Talen 2013).

This debate has been intense in strong market cities like San Francisco and Austin where growth demand, housing affordability, and transportation congestion have seemingly become intractable policy problems (Hankinson 2018). An emerging sprawl-agnostic environmentalist lobby seems to be developing that, in the words of one Austin, TX, advocate, favors land development codes that care "deeply about automobile storage" (Kimble 2019), but seem unconcerned about housing affordability and transportation GHG emissions. The anti-infill environmentalists have often been at odds with a newer, pro-urban development network of activists. As we discussed in Chapter 2, the NIMBY (not in my backyard) vs. YIMBY (yes in my backyard) debates are increasingly prevalent in these cities and offer an important window in the coming political debates over climate adaptation and mitigation (Bliss 2019). The *New York Times* Editorial Board (2019), for example, recently noted that,

> Allowing more people to live in cities could mitigate inequality and reduce carbon emissions. Yet in most places, housing construction remains wildly unpopular. People who think of themselves as progressives, environmentalists

> and egalitarians fight fiercely against urban development, complaining about traffic and shadows and the sanctity of lawns.

In many ways, these tensions flow from conceptual differences about the meaning and role of the environment in cities and, as we argue, a failure to recognize the potential role of urban design in planning for more livable urban places. Conceptually, GI (green infrastructure) grew out of the land conservation movement and efforts to quantify benefits of natural systems. In an influential early work, Benedict and McMahon (2006, p. 1), for example, define GI as "an interconnected network of natural areas and other open spaces that conserves natural ecosystem values and functions, sustains clean air and water, and provides a wide array of benefits to people and wildlife." By conserving strategic natural areas, GI could provide multiple ecosystem benefits, help manage water and flooding, and "guide future growth and future land development and land conservation decisions" (Benedict and McMahon 2006, p. 3). They labeled this type of approach "strategic conservation through green infrastructure" (Benedict and McMahon 2006, p. 11). This approach, they argue, can focus development away from the most hazardous areas into more compact settlements and work in concert with smart growth approaches to land development to create the compact, hazard-resilient city. The focus, they argued, is to articulate the value of ecological resources as needed infrastructural components and not as "an amenity" (Benedict and McMahon 2006, p. 2).

This framing of GI in terms of ecological and conservation values is the dominant view, especially in terms of conceptualizing how climate adaptation projects should be planned and implemented. Matthews et al. (2015), for example, argue that GI should explicitly focus on ecological values. They argue that Benedict and McMahon's conceptualization of GI needs to go further and challenge the very growth structures that are generating the climate crisis. Instead of working within the established economic growth orientation of current urban-planning regimes to show monetary benefits of GI, Matthews et al. (2015) argue that GI should be conceived as seeking to advance primarily ecological values of climate adaptation as a way to address the climate crisis. They argue that, "The role of green infrastructure then is to cope with the adverse side-effects of unchecked economic growth, rather than to promote it" (Matthews et al. 2015, p. 158).

While providing important contributions on how to envision ecological systems and, in the case of Benedict and McMahon, guide development away from hazard zones, both articulations of GI undervalue the role of urban density in managing GHG emissions. Benedict and McMahon (2006) do focus on the use of GI as a tool to limit impacts of sprawl and as a type of conservation hazard zoning, but do not explicitly address climate mitigation potential of urban form in terms of GHG emissions. Matthews et al. (2015) perceive development-centered approaches to urban planning as the central problem of urban climate change and build a conceptualization of GI centered on climate adaptation and growth minimization. At least in terms of open space/transportation sector, this could create a potential false dichotomy between climate adaptation and mitigation. As we noted above, well-designed urban areas with denser clusters of housing and businesses all linked with transit and walking/bicycling infrastructure are key policy tools in managing climate change. Centering the value of GI on land conservation and climate adaptation can lead to tensions as core area redevelopment proposals that would help to limit GHG emissions are potentially seen as at odds with land conservation environmentalism.

The climate change era is forcing more complicated environmental calculations about local vs. global benefits and driving tough choices about urban development. As we discussed in Chapter 2, this is the "ecological paradox of urbanism" where urbanization can result in types of "ecological sacrifice zones" (Kelbaugh 2014, p. 3) that can be justified by the greater good of limiting sprawl and decreasing overall GHG emissions.

While this stark scenario of sacrifice zones of urbanity is a possibility, more nuanced conceptualizations of GI can help address the ecological urbanism paradox and the climate adaptation/mitigation divide. Kelbaugh (2014), for example, goes on to note that "local adaptation and global mitigation strategies are typically complementary" and can help enhance human and ecological habitats while limiting overall GHG emissions. The conceptual foundations of GI planning can be used to protect conservation lands for ecological value on the periphery and guide growth away from hazard zones *and* simultaneously be used as more micro, urban-scale interventions to provide important place, water management, active transportation, and ecological benefits within built-up areas. Our focus throughout the book is more on urban-scale interventions, but it is important to integrate the broader conservation and hazard zoning approaches on the periphery and in key areas of environmental risk to create a holistic GI approach to regional development.

To further illustrate the potential for promoting dense, walkable, and transit-oriented places which help to reduce GHG with enhanced ecological habitats, the Biophilic Cities Network (2018) is working "to conserve and celebrate nature in all its forms and the many important ways in which cities and their inhabitants benefit from the biodiversity and wild urban spaces present in cities." The network includes many leaders working to promote sustainable transportation systems and denser land use patterns.

Copenhagen: green infrastructure as climate adaptation and mitigation

Identifying synergies between climate adaptation and mitigation in GI planning is a promising area and can help to bridge this divide on environmental policy at the urban level. In many ways this is a design challenge of weaving development into green and blue landscapes to promote ecological values, limit GHG emissions, and create safe, healthy, equitable human places. This design challenge is not without historical precedent. GI grows out of a long tradition of urbanization centered around urban parks. From the amenity-driven development of the urban parks of Frederick Law Olmsted to the more recent growth of trail-oriented development

(Fields 2009), urban green spaces have a long design legacy of combining multiple objectives within larger projects. The challenge is to take these historical precedents and apply them explicitly to climate resilience.

In a few places around the world, transportation and water management planners have come together to explore the potential of reimaging both movement and water to enhance resilience. The National Association of City Transportation Officials (NACTO) *Urban Street Stormwater Guide*, for example, identifies "Streets as Ecosystems." The guide states,

> The opportunity is ripe to reimagine how streets function in cities, not just as mobility corridors and public spaces, but as part of the natural ecosystem. With re-urbanization, aging infrastructure, and a changing climate, sustainable stormwater management is a core challenge for resilient cities.
>
> *(NACTO 2017)*

GI components such as bioswales, parks and greenways, and green streets are increasingly being combined with blue infrastructure of canals, small urban ponds, or mini-wetlands to redevelop city spaces into these types of lower-emission, more climate-adapted places that help to foster urban ecosystems (Fields et al. 2017).

A good example to help see these connections in practice is the Tåsinge Plads project in Copenhagen (Cathcart-Keays 2016) that developed in response to the cloudburst flooding in the area. The Tåsinge Plads project focuses on transforming an underutilized parking area in a fairly non-descript Copenhagen neighborhood into a multi-dimensional community amenity with improved water management, increased open space, added amenity value to the community, and reconfigured auto parking to accentuate sustainable travel (Figure 3.2). Through a community engagement process, key elements of the project developed to include a new neighborhood park that would double as water storage with surface water retention and tanks below the park for extra storage. The green filtration decreased pollution and provided new green space for the neighborhood. Local children can also pump the filtered water from below to create a water play space right in their own neighborhood.

This project fits within a broader climate-planning framework of retrofitting streets to address the increased frequency of high-intensity rain events and simultaneously addressing livability issues. As the example in Copenhagen shows, the physical location for this GI transformation can be the street itself.

Projects like Tåsinge Plads that combine street, water, and public space systems show how integrating adaptation and climate mitigation requires pioneering infrastructure systems that are multi-dimensional, focused on accomplishing multiple policy goals simultaneously. They draw from the GI paradigm designed to balance conservation and land development (Benedict and McMahon 2002, p. 5), but focus on streets, parking areas, and other urban open space as the physical location for these infrastructure systems to provide a way to frame water management within a strong, amenity-centered urban park setting. This is exactly what the Tåsinge Plads

FIGURE 3.2 Tåsinge Plads Copenhagen.

project aims to accomplish. While a single project would have a limited impact on regional safety and GHG emission levels, a network of projects like this could help regions adapt to a changing climate and help meet GHG reduction targets through focused redevelopment. We examine this project in connection with the larger resilience-planning efforts in Copenhagen in more detail in Chapter 6.

Conclusion

As the example from Copenhagen shows, project level articulations of synergistic planning for climate mitigation and adaptation are beginning to emerge. As we noted, key conceptual barriers often limit the *thinking* necessary to produce such projects. There are also numerous political and bureaucratic structures that prevent synergistic action. Networks like the Biophilic Cities and technical guidance from professional organizations like NACTO can help local governments begin to break down these institutional barriers.

In this chapter, we have begun to trace a new set of metrics based on evaluating multi-sector benefits that focus on safety, spatial efficiency, equitability, community livability, and limiting GHG emissions. These metrics are still developing but offer opportunities to begin to rethink the underlying purpose of urban infrastructure like streets and public space. Rather than the modernist monoculture of streets as traffic sewers and buried culverts as literal sewers, advances in transportation and water management offer the opportunity to create networks of green streets rimming uncovered canals that manage water and act as community amenities. Rethinking street space offers an opportunity to tie these two emerging trends together to accomplish multiple community goals and simultaneously address pressing climate mitigation and adaptation needs. This type of new thinking is at the core of adaptation urbanism. In the next chapter, we examine this emerging movement and build a set of tools to evaluate the developing practice.

Notes

1 Aldred et al. (2019) describe the role of traffic engineers as part of a larger system of key barriers to cycling investment in the UK. Four key barriers are outlined: political barriers, resource barriers, institutional barriers, and wider stakeholder barriers. These barriers are discussed in more detail in relation to London in Chapter 7.

2 Dumbaugh et al. (2018) also found that safety is more often cited as a goal in the city's long-range transportation plan compared to congestion relief. The study found that 84% of respondents identify safety as an explicit policy goal in the long-range transportation plan of the community compared to 64% for congestion relief. The study also found that 91% of communities collect and evaluate data on traffic-related crashes, deaths, and injuries, 88% of cities have a complete streets policy or program, and 95% of cities have a bicycle master plan. Finally, 97% of cities have installed traffic-calming devices, 80% of cities conduct safety audits, and 82% of cities have guidelines for the inclusion of pedestrian infrastructure on streets, including "city-specific documents relating to the design of 'livable' or 'complete streets,' or the adoption of an existing manual on these issues, such as NACTO's [National Association of City Transportation Officials'] *Urban Streets Design Guide* or the *Manual for Living Streets*" (Dumbaugh et al., 2018, p. 10).

3 Other researchers have identified similar patterns in the built environment. According to the Center for Watershed Protection, for example, the habitat for cars takes up "as much as 65% of the total impervious cover over America's landscape [and] consists of streets, parking lots and driveways" (Frazer 2006).

4 This is not to say that this problem is not being addressed at all. As noted above, many cities have identified these issues and have included policy goals and plans to move towards Vision Zero and complete streets. However, these policies are often subsumed by bureaucratic inertia. To address climate change, we need to move much faster.

References

Aldred, R., Watson, T., Lovelace, R., & Woodcock, J. (2019). Barriers to Investing in Cycling: Stakeholder Views from England. *Transportation Research Part A: Policy and Practice*, *128*, 149–159.

Aumann, H. H., Behrangi, A., & Wang, Y. (2018). Increased Frequency of Extreme Tropical Deep Convection: AIRS Observations And Climate Model Predictions. *Geophysical Research Letters*, *45*(24), 13–530.

Benedict, M. A., & McMahon, E. T. (2002). Green Infrastructure: Smart Conservation for the 21st Century. *Renewable Resources Journal*, Autumn, 12–17.

Benedict, M. A., & McMahon, E. T. (2006). *Green Infrastructure: Smart Conservation for the 21st Century.* Sprawl Watch Clearinghouse Monograph Series. Washington, DC: The Conservation Fund.

Biophilic Cities Network. (2018). 2018 Annual Report: Connecting Cities and Nature. Last accessed 3/26/2020 from www.biophiliccities.org/annual-report.

Bliss, L. (2019). The NIMBY Principle. *CityLab*. July 26. Last accessed 3/18/2020 from www.citylab.com/equity/2019/07/nimby-vs-yimby-single-family-zoning-laws-california-housing/594373/.

Boarnet, M., & Handy, S. (2017). A Framework for Projecting the Potential Statewide Vehicle Miles Traveled (VMT) Reduction from State-Level Strategies in California. UC Davis: National Center for Sustainable Transportation. Last accessed 3/18/2020 from https://ncst.ucdavis.edu/research-product/framework-projecting-potential-statewide-vehicle-miles-traveled-vmt-reduction.

Brown, R. R. (2008). Local Institutional Development and Organizational Change for Advancing Sustainable Urban Water Futures. *Environmental Management, 41*(2), 221–233.

Brown, R. R., Keath, N., & Wong, T. H. (2009). Urban Water Management in Cities: Historical, Current and Future Regimes. *Water Science and Technology, 59*(5), 847–855.

Bruntlett, M., & Bruntlett, C. (2018). *Building the Cycling City: The Dutch Blueprint for Urban Vitality*. Washington, DC: Island Press.

Cathcart-Keays, Athlyn. (2016). Why Copenhagen is Building Parks That Can Turn Into Ponds. Citiscope. January, 21. 2016. Last accessed 8/18/2017 from http://citiscope.org/story/2016/why-copenhagen-building-parks-can-turn-ponds.

City of Copenhagen. (2012). *Cloudburst Management Plan 2012*. Copenhagen: The City of Copenhagen, Technical and Environmental Administration.

Creutzig, F. (2016). Evolving Narratives of Low-Carbon Futures in Transportation. *Transport Reviews, 36*(3), 341–360.

Danish Cyclist Federation. (2017). Copenhagen: City of Cyclists. Last accessed 3/18/2020 from www.cycling-embassy.dk/2017/07/04/copenhagen-city-cyclists-facts-figures-2017/.

Duany, A., & Talen, E. (eds.). (2013). *Landscape Urbanism and its Discontents: Dissimulating the Sustainable City*. Gabriola Island, BC, Canada: New Society Publishers.

Dumbaugh, Eric, Saha, Dibakar, Merlin, Louis, & Saginor, Jesse. (2018). Traffic Safety Practice in U.S. Cities: Survey and Focus Group Results. Report Number CSCRS-R5. Chapel Hill, NC: Florida Atlantic University, Collaborative Sciences Center for Road Safety.

Dumbaugh, Eric, Signor, Kari, Kumfer, Wes, LaJeunesse, Seth, Carter, Daniel, & Merlin, Louis. (2019). *Safe Systems: Guiding Principles and International Applications.* Report number CSCRS-R7. Chapel Hill, NC: Florida Atlantic University, Collaborative Sciences Center for Road Safety.

Ellen MacArthur Foundation, & McKinsey Center for Business and Environment. (2015). *Growth Within: A Circular Economy Vision for a Competitive Europe*. Cowes, UK: Ellen MacArthur Foundation.

Ewing, R., & Cervero, R. (2010). Travel and the Built Environment: A Meta-Analysis. *Journal of the American Planning Association, 76*(3), 265–294.

Fields, B. (2009). From Green Dots to Greenways: Planning in the Age of Climate Change in Post-Katrina New Orleans. *Journal of Urban Design, 14*(3), 325–344.

Fields, B., Thomas, J., & Wagner, J. A. (2017). Living with Water in the Era of Climate Change: Lessons From the Lafitte Greenway in Post-Katrina New Orleans. *Journal of Planning Education and Research, 37*(3), 309–321.

Flusche, D. (2010). National Household Travel Survey—Short Trips Analysis. League of American Bicyclists. January 22. Last accessed 3/18/2020 from www.bikeleague.org/content/national-household-travel-survey-short-trips-analysis.

Frazer, Lance. (2006). Paving Paradise: The Peril of Impervious Surfaces. *Environmental Health Perspectives*, January, 114(1), A21.

Gehl, J., & Svarre, B. (2013). *How to Study Public Life*. Washington, DC: Island Press.

Green, B. (2019). *The Smart Enough City: Putting Technology in its Place to Reclaim Our Urban Future*. Cambridge, MA: MIT Press.

Hankinson, M. (2018). When do Renters Behave Like Homeowners? High Rent, Price Anxiety, and NIMBYism. *American Political Science Review, 112*(3), 473–493.

Harris, L. M., Chu, E. K., & Ziervogel, G. (2018). Negotiated Resilience. *Resilience, 6*(3), 196–214.

Healey, P. (2009). City Regions and Place Development. *Regional Studies, 43*(6), 831–843.

Kelbaugh, Douglas. (2014). The Environmental Paradox of the City, Landscape Urbanism, and New Urbanism. *Consilience: The Journal of Sustainable Development*, 13(1), 1–15.

Kimble, Megan. (2019). The Fight to Make Austin Affordable. *Texas Observer.* December 6. Last accessed 3/17/2020 from www.texasobserver.org/the-fight-to-make-austin-affordable-housing/.

Kristianssen, A. C., Andersson, R., Belin, M. Å., & Nilsen, P. (2018). Swedish Vision Zero Policies for Safety–A Comparative Policy Content Analysis. *Safety Science, 103*, 260–269.

Le Corbusier. (1964). *The Radiant City*. New York: Orion Press.

Lee, A. E., & Handy, S. L. (2018). Leaving Level-of-Service Behind: The Implications of a Shift to VMT Impact Metrics. *Research in Transportation Business & Management, 29*, 14–25.

Levine, J. (2006). *Zoned Out: Regulation, Markets, and Choices in Transportation and Metropolitan Land Use*. Washington, DC: Resources for the Future Press.

Levine, Johathan, Grengs, Joe, & Merlin, Louis. (2019). *From Mobility to Accessibility: Transforming Urban Transportation and Land-Use Planning*. Ithaca, NY: Cornell University Press.

Makarewicz, C., Adkins, A., Frei, C., & Wennink, A. (2018). "A Little Bit Happy": How Performance Metrics Shortchange Pedestrian Infrastructure Funding. *Research in Transportation Business & Management, 29*, 144–156.

Matthews, T., Lo, A. Y., & Byrne, J. A. (2015). Reconceptualizing Green Infrastructure for Climate Change Adaptation: Barriers to Adoption and Drivers for Uptake by Spatial Planners. *Landscape and Urban Planning, 138*, 155–163.

Meerow, S., Newell, J. P., & Stults, M. (2016). Defining Urban Resilience: A Review. *Landscape and Urban Planning, 147*, 38–49.

National Association of City Transportation Officials. (2016). *Transit Street Design Guide*. Washington, DC: Island Press.

National Association of City Transportation Officials (NACTO). (2017). *Urban Street Stormwater Guide*. Washington, DC: Island Press.

Newman, P., & Kenworthy, J. (1999). *Sustainability and Cities: Overcoming Automobile Dependence*. Washington, DC: Island Press.

New Orleans Public Library. (1939). WPA Photograph Collection. Louisiana Division. Photo 15.8.

New York Times Editorial Board. (2019). Americans Need More Neighbors. June 15. Last accessed 1/12/2021 from www.nytimes.com/2019/06/15/opinion/sunday/minneapolis-ends-single-family-zoning.html.

Noland, R. B., & Hanson, C. S. (2013). How Does Induced Travel Affect Sustainable Transportation Policy? In *Transport Beyond Oil* (J. Renne, & B. Fields, eds): 70–85. Washington, DC: Island Press.

O'Donnell, E. C., Lamond, J. E., & Thorne, C. R. (2017). Recognising Barriers to Implementation of Blue–Green Infrastructure: A Newcastle Case Study. *Urban Water Journal, 14*(9), 964–971.

Piatkowski, D., & Marshall, W. (2018). We Count What We Care About: Advancing a Framework for Valuing Investments in Active Modes. *Research in Transportation Business & Management, 29*, 63–70.

Schlossberg, M., Millard-Ball, A., Shay, E., & Riggs, W. B. (2018). Rethinking the Street in an Era of Driverless Cars. *UrbanismNext*. University of Oregon. Last accessed 3/18/2020 from https://scholarsbank.uoregon.edu/xmlui/bitstream/handle/1794/23331/UrbanismNext_ResearchBrief_003.pdf?sequence=1.

Schmitt, Angie. (2019). Cambridge Becomes First U.S. City to Make Protected Bike Lanes Mandatory. *Streetsblog USA*. April 9. Last accessed 3/19/2020 from https://usa.streetsblog.org/2019/04/09/cambridge-becomes-first-u-s-city-to-make-protected-bike-lanes-mandatory/.

Taylor, B. D., & Hong Hwang, Y. (2020). Eighty-Five Percent Solution: Historical Look at Crowdsourcing Speed Limits and the Question of Safety. *Transportation Research Record*, 0361198120928995.

Toderian, Brent (@BrentToderian). (June 14, 2019). "If your city's transportation plan doesn't have specific and ambitious mode shift targets, and an action plan to achieve those targets, you don't have a transportation plan." Tweet.

Trancik, R. (1986). *Finding Lost Space: Theories of Urban Design*. Hoboken, NJ: John Wiley.

U.N. Habitat. (2013). Streets as Public Spaces and Drivers of Urban Prosperity. Nairobi, Kenya: UN Habitat. https://unhabitat.org/streets-as-public-spaces-and-drivers-of-urban-prosperity.

U.N. Habitat. (2016). World Cities Report 2016. *Urbanization and Development—Emerging Futures*. New York: UN Habitat.

Waldheim, C. (2006). The Landscape Urbanism Reader. New York: Princeton Architectural Press.

Winkleman, S., Deweese, J., & El-Geneidy, A. (2019). Car-Oriented Sprawl Increases Driving and GHGs in Greater Montreal. Green Resilience Strategies. Last accessed 4/1/2020 from www.greenresilience.com/montreal-sprawl.

4

ADAPTATION URBANISM

An urban resilience policy framework

Co-authored by Liliane Geerling

Addressing urban resilience tensions: building towards adaptation urbanism

As the last chapter suggests, creating operational definitions of resilience linked to key policy metrics that encourage more holistic and effective policymaking is vital to creating more resilient places. We call this type of planning adaptation urbanism. Again, adaptation urbanism is both a physical design orientation and a normative planning process. The two-part physical design construction of the term focuses on: (1) adapting urban environments to changing environmental conditions to make them safer, healthier, and more sustainable; and (2) mitigating greenhouse gas (GHG) emissions through the underlying urban design of transit-accessible, walkable, and bikeable places.

These physical landscape designs, however, are generated through a process of negotiation that helps determine who is made safer and how environmental risk is managed. As we laid out in Chapter 2, current forms of resilience planning often operate in operational silos and can result in a type of market-oriented resilience (Figure 2.2) that improves safety for some but perpetuates many negative status quo trends. Adaptation urbanism in practice is designed to create a more holistic process of engaging residents in a long-term method of rebuilding cities to make them safer for a changing climate, more energy efficient through better urbanism, and more livable and equitable for all residents. This is the adaptation urbanism resilience process (Figure 2.3) that is designed to focus policymakers and the public on a process for creating safer, desirable, more equitable, and sustainable places.

In this chapter, we unpack the meaning and process of adaptation urbanism to outline the key issues and tensions embedded in the discourse and define the specific dimensions of an adaptation urbanism-centered approach. We begin by tracing the outlines of the more integrated resilience approach and then add a specific set of indicators that delineate the key dimensions of adaptation urbanism. We break these down into conceptual indicators used to frame the planning discussion (resilience, climate mitigation, and climate adaptation) and more specific articulations of adaptation urbanism (support for sustainable transportation, compact development, green and blue infrastructure, and equity). Finally, we outline how these indicators are operationalized in case study chapters to measure the extent to which cities are planning for resilience through climate mitigation and adaptation approaches. Moreover, in terms of concrete outcomes, this chapter addresses integrating sustainable transportation to encourage compact development, retrofitting streets and public spaces with green and blue infrastructure to improve quality of life and manage water, and encouraging equitable access to more resilient areas.

From green resilience and low-carbon resilience to adaptation urbanism

In the previous chapter we outlined emerging resilience concepts and metrics related to transportation and water management. The resilience-planning ideas in these fields are closely connected, but still fragmented by funding siloes, roles, and goals related to differing conceptions about environmental management. We argue that focusing on the climate adaptation and mitigation potential of urban streets as a unified planning framework offers a potentially powerful new way of thinking and acting on urban resilience that could be used to bridge the divides between these two sectors and create an important conceptual tool for building the resilient city. The logic, as we have outlined, is direct:

> Safe/climate/spatially efficient streets combined with a green/blue/compact/affordable urban structure create the foundation for a truly resilient city.

Multiple iterations of this new type of resilience thinking are bubbling up as scholars and practitioners work to create new models for planning in the climate change era. A useful place to begin thinking about these issues is Udavardy and Winkleman's (2014) green resilience paradigm. In this framing, the benefits of climate adaptation and mitigation policies overlap in certain areas creating the potential to build synergistic responses that create both adaptation and mitigation benefits. This approach seeks to overcome one of the central barriers to local resilience planning, siloed and divided approaches that address one small part of the climate puzzle. Udavardy and Winkleman (2014) argue that:

> *Government agencies place high priority on adaptation planning, while also working on strategies and policies to reduce carbon pollution. Yet the nexus between adapting to a changing climate and reducing carbon pollution is rarely approached in an integrated fashion.*
>
> *(p. 7)*

Green resilience is designed to focus on the potential synergies between adaptation and mitigation policies in the hopes of leveraging resources from multiple agencies to address these complicated policy problems. The green resilience framework grew out of a 2014 symposium of US-based practitioners and is designed to provide a "simplified way to capture the co-benefits of an integrated approach to climate adaptation and mitigation" (Udavardy and Winkleman 2014, p. 6). In essence, the green resilience framework encourages local communities to ask two penetrating questions about their resilience policy. Udavardy and Winkleman (2014, p. 16) pointedly suggest communities should ask: "Does it cut carbon pollution while also preparing for and responding to climate impacts? How can we maximize the return on our infrastructure and climate investments—mitigation and adaptation—while also maximizing the economic, social, and environmental benefits?" (Udavardy and Winkleman 2014, p. 6).

These policy questions are designed to drive agencies to search for synergies across sectors where adaptation and mitigation actions overlap. As Udavardy and Winkleman (2014, p. 7) note, these policies represent "a continuum that can either start from the adaptation side (e.g., include GHG reduction measures in flood risk reduction projects) or from the mitigation side (e.g., enhance electricity grid resilience to climate impacts when developing renewables)." This provides important avenues for agencies across multiple sectors to begin searching for potential synergies. Taken together, these overlapping policies provide the foundation for interagency cooperation and can lead to a focus on multi-dimensional outcome measurement that is essential for effective resilience policy.

Another similar approach, low-carbon resilience (LCR), emerging from Simon Fraser University's Adaptation to Climate Change project, offers promise as well. LCR focuses on "the strategic integration of climate change adaptation and mitigation" (Harford and Raftis 2018, p. 14) by identifying co-benefits that can be achieved by systematically addressing climate adaptation and mitigation goals simultaneously at the local level. The goal, like that of green resilience, is to break down administrative silos and build pathways "to mainstream[ing]" climate resilience "into all professional and government policy and planning processes" (Harford and Raftis 2018, p. 19). One of the key mechanisms identified in the planning approach is the LCR Process Model that outlines key adaptation and mitigation project components and targets and then identifies "co-benefits and synergies as well as trade-offs and conflicts" (Harford and Raftis 2018, p. 22).

As an example of the planning process, Harford and Raftis (2018) point to the Vancouver green infrastructure and raingarden program (discussed in more depth in Chapter 10). Green infrastructure, in this iteration, is defined within an urban context as engineered assets like green roofs, natural assets like wetlands, and enhanced assets like stormwater ponds, all designed to make available "natural and naturalized areas to replace or augment the role of human-made infrastructure in water filtration, flood absorption, and other services" (Harford and Raftis 2018, p. 39). The synergistic goals, in this case, are to help improve stormwater management, add amenity value to the community, and decrease GHG emissions from the actual use and construction of the infrastructure. It is interesting to note that, in the description of benefits, Harford and Raftis (2018) do not point to the use of green infrastructure as a tool in decreasing transportation-related GHG emissions through integration of land use/transportation policy. While they do broadly point to enhanced amenity value as a way to increase walking and cycling, the missing synergies between green infrastructure and transportation climate mitigation point to a broadly underexplored area in resilience planning.

Both green resilience and low-carbon resilience provide important conceptual approaches to integrating climate adaptation and mitigation in urban policy. The tools provide specific avenues for un-siloing climate resilience planning and practice and encouraging multi-departmental coordination. While these approaches provide the conceptual foundation for rethinking administrative practices for urban climate policy, they are not explicitly targeted at urban transportation and land use planners. As we have argued throughout, addressing transportation GHG emissions and climate adaptation simultaneously offers a powerful way to steer communities towards low-carbon, climate-adapted urban places.

Adaptation urbanism synthesis

Drawing from the broader literature and the green and low-carbon resilience approaches, we crafted the adaptation urbanism normative model to evaluate existing resilience plans and help operationalize climate resilience planning at the land use/transportation policy interface. Adaptation urbanism is focused on intentionally integrating climate adaptation projects into urban fabrics to protect and enhance urbanism mitigation synergies. The policy lens is designed to help communities see the processes that are already happening with more clarity by providing a conceptual framing to help guide planners and citizens through the complex landscape of resilience planning and towards integrated approaches to connect climate mitigation and adaptation.

To help advance this discussion, we draw from the preceding literature and propose four interlinked principles that define adaptation urbanism-centered planning (Figure 4.1). These are:

1. Building towards the compact, affordable city
2. Adapting cities for people, not for cars
3. Infusing streets and public spaces with green and blue infrastructure
4. Engaging residents in the hard work of placing equity as a core goal of urban resilience.

As we have argued throughout, compact development is key to managing urban climate emissions. Compact development linked with transit and walking/biking and other micro-mobility options produces significantly lower overall GHG emissions, up to 20–50% lower emissions than more sprawling development scenarios (Creutzig 2016). This is the climate mitigation base of adaptation urbanism.

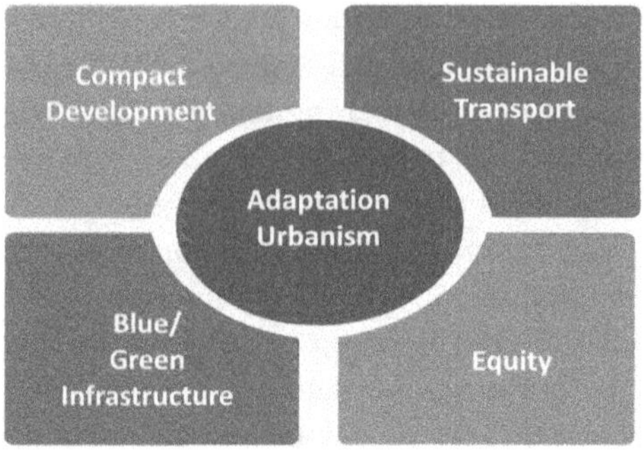

FIGURE 4.1 Adaptation urbanism principles.

While compact development linked with sustainable transport provides the foundation for managing GHG emissions, cities need to build the political capital to push for changing the transportation system and simultaneously need to manage increasing volumes of water. Strategic use of green and blue infrastructure offers the potential to help create high-amenity neighborhoods that are places people desire to live and simultaneously places that help to manage urban water issues. As the example from Copenhagen shows, these park-oriented green spaces add local amenity value and can be an important tool in managing stormwater. They help to show local communities a clear benefit for engaging in climate resilience.

Urban green and blue infrastructures, in fact, work so well in generating highly livable places, that they often create a housing price premium. As we have discussed, this creates an equity problem as increasing housing prices can push lower-income residents away and result in "climatological gentrification" (Whitehead 2013, p. 1362). The compact, green city also needs to be an affordable city where a diverse set of residents can live, work, and thrive. Resilience policy is housing policy and needs to be addressed directly. The adaptation urbanism conceptual lens is designed to push this issue to front. For urban green and blue infrastructure corridors to be equitable, they need to be coupled with affordable housing policies from the start (Smith et al. 2016; Immergluck and Balan 2018; Rigolon and Németh 2018; Fields 2019). We discuss this in more depth in Chapter 8 on New Orleans and again in Chapter 11.

Overall, more compact neighborhoods with integrated affordable housing centered around transit, walking, and bicycling are not peripheral issues to urban resilience planning. These issues are the urban base upon which all other climate adaptation and mitigation actions rest. Climate adaptation planning needs to expand beyond a focus on infrastructure hardening and elevating roadways to a deeper understanding of how cities work and who they work for.

The core principle of urban resilience planning needs to focus on adapting places for people and integrating a deeper understanding of ecological systems into the planning processes. While there are many strands to understanding people-centered adaptation, the core issue of urban resilience planning in the 21st century is adapting streets for people instead of for cars and linking these places together in ways that are significantly safer and more equitable than the current modernist paradigm permits. For 100 years, cities have been adapted for cars, generating ecological, social, and economic consequences that, with increasing demands of a changing climate, demand action. Urban resilience planning opens up a new opportunity to rethink these patterns and build communities that are better adapted to a changing climate, a climate mitigated to decrease GHG emissions, and defined by the person-scale instead of auto-scale (Gehl and Svarre 2013). These places could also be defined by improved access to opportunity for all residents, but only if there is political push to make it happen.

Adaptation urbanism provides a normative conceptual lens, a type of planning map, for envisioning resilient cities and neighborhoods that is backed up by strong data. This approach does not supplant the hard administrative work of coordinating resilience planning across departments, but rather provides four clear guiding policy principles that need to be coordinated together. Specifically, cities need to provide equitable access to compact green and blue core areas linked by transit, walking, and biking if society will be able to meet climate adaptation and mitigation goals. This is a straightforward physical representation of the resilient city that is both technologically feasible, and, simultaneously, politically challenging.

Adaptation urbanism case studies: purpose and methods

The case study analysis in the coming chapters shows both how existing technologies are being used to improve policy outcomes and how political and administrative barriers can be overcome. The case examples highlight how improved local amenities can drive political acceptance, how to overcome institutional inertia to push projects forward, and, importantly, point to key policies that can create more equitable development for all residents. The cases also point to numerous failures in leveraging climate adaptations to decrease GHG emissions and weaknesses in creating equitable development.

The case study cities (Copenhagen, Rotterdam, London, New Orleans, and Miami) were selected because of their coastal proximity and recognized status in resilience planning. They provide a cross-section of emerging urban resilience practices in coastal cities from the Global North. More research is needed to examine how these types of tools might be incorporated in "[m]ore tentative, humble and respectful ways" (Schwanen 2018, p. 3) in a Global South context.

As we have argued, new metrics need to be established to push change forward. We use a multi-tiered approach to evaluate both the resilience-planning processes and street-level projects to determine the extent of adaptation urbanism policy uptake currently occurring in the case study communities. This involves analysis of the policy implications of resilience and related plans and evaluation of the emerging landscapes of resilience themselves in the case study communities.

First, to determine how these cities are transitioning towards adaptation urbanism, we analyze resilience, climate, and selected urban plans created over the last 10–15 years to uncover the potential synergies and tensions of resilience planning (Landauer et al. 2019). Specifically, we use adaptation urbanism as a normative model to evaluate existing resilience plans to better understand how cities are planning for climate mitigation and adaptation (Butler et al. 2016). Using a structured summative content analysis framework (Hsieh and Shannon 2005; Appler and Rumbach 2016), we analyze whether this suite of resilience plans actively utilize adaptation urbanism planning concepts and the extent to which those concepts are linked to policy implementation. This approach focuses on identifying key words associated with adaptation urbanism within plans (see Appendix A) to uncover patterns of use and "discovering underlying meanings of the words or the content" (Hsieh and Shannon 2005, p. 1284). The focus is on understanding the extent of emphasis placed on adaptation urbanism concepts and provides a window into how adaptation urbanism is being conceptualized.

To help provide a more in-depth analysis of the meaning of the planning terms, we also evaluated the text more broadly in the context to adjacent plan language. We reviewed the quotes within each plan to search for broad patterns of meaning. We also interviewed a set of planning stakeholders in each case study community. The planning overviews and synthesis of these interviews are interspersed in each chapter to provide more nuanced articulations of how the plans were developed and key political, economic, and social issues associated with planning in each city.

It should be noted that our plan evaluation is not an overarching plan quality evaluation (Berke and Godschalk 2009). Emerging research from Meerow and Woodruff (2020) begins to address overarching principles of climate change plan quality. Instead, our work is a broader exploration of the underlying focus and meaning of resilience planning through the adaptation urbanism lens.

We are also interested in how resilience planners are moving from conceptual plans to designing new resilient landscapes. Specifically, we are interested in evaluating, despite the rhetorical flourishes of the plans, the key characteristics of these emerging climate resilience landscapes in the context of streets and public spaces. More succinctly, we evaluate the extent to which our case study communities are moving towards building the streets of the future or still perpetuating and expanding the streets of the past. We conducted public space analysis broadly based around Gehl and Svarre's (2013) excellent *How to Study Public Life*. We mapped and counted activities and movement in key resilience-planning project areas in each city to help link concept to practice and provide a roadmap for adaptation urbanism in the built environment. We examine spatial distribution of street space to determine how much space is currently allocated to differing modes and uses (Appendix A). To complement the public space analysis, we also examined a select set of individual streets to help uncover how green and blue infrastructures are being integrated into safe, multi-modal streets. The adaptation urbanism audit (Table 4.1) provides a simplified way to analyze projects and begin to see the core elements of adaptation urbanism in practice by outlining the green and blue infrastructure

TABLE 4.1 Adaptation urbanism audit

Green/blue street corridor elements	*Yes/no*	*Vision Zero/Safe Systems street elements*	*Yes/no*
Green medians		Brick pavement	
Street trees		Traffic calming (speed table, chicanes, etc.)	
Parks		Sidewalk	
Planters/bioswales		Continental crosswalk	
Pavement cuts into green space		Mid-block crossing treatment	
Permeable pavement		Cycle track	
Canals		Bike lane	
Rivers		Advisory bike lane	
Ponds		Protected intersection	
Water square		Roundabout	
Blue medians		Curb bulb-out	
Water boulevards		Trail/greenway	
Other:_____________		Other:_____________	

and core Vision Zero/Safe System components of streets. While much of the above analysis in our case study chapters is more technical, the adaptation urbanism audit is intentionally designed to be a simplified way to synthesize adaptation urbanism concepts down to street level. We were inspired to create this tool by reading the National Association of City Transportation Officials (NACTO) *Urban Street Stormwater Guide's* (2017) articulation of complete streets as green streets. We used their complete green streets components list as a base and layered on the additional green/blue/sustainable transport elements.

Overall, our approach is designed to link plans with places. For resilience to succeed as a vital urban planning tool for the climate change era, it must help to create safer, low-carbon *places* of meaning and value for local residents. The methodology of adaptation urbanism is designed to create an exploratory platform for analysis of this emerging resilient movement from both the conceptual level of planning and the landscape level of places.

To create more readable chapters, we have synthesized the above elements in the case study chapters. Each case study chapter includes an overview of the resilience challenges of the community, detailed analysis of the transportation and water management planning processes, and analysis of individual places and streets in the community. The approach is designed to capture both the theoretical dimensions of resilience planning in the transportation and water sectors and the emerging place dimensions of these policies. For more detailed analysis, we have included the adaptation urbanism plan analysis in Appendix A. We also provide an example of the adaptation urbanism audit in practice in Rotterdam in Appendix B.

Conclusion

The decisions on how to design our streets and public space systems may at first seem small in the face of larger problems, but these design decisions are, in fact, the base of our transportation GHG emissions and, as climate change pushes water to the forefront, the key to community climate adaptation. The case study chapters that follow present detailed portraits of how cities are beginning to take these small design decisions seriously to tackle our big problems.

References

Appler, Douglas, & Rumbach, Andrew. (2016). Building Community Resilience Through Historic Preservation. *Journal of the American Planning Association*, 82(2), 92–103.

Berke, P., & Godschalk, D. (2009). Searching for the Good Plan: A Meta-Analysis of Plan Quality Studies. *CPL Bibliography*, *23*(3), 227–240.

Butler, W. H., Deyle, R. E., & Mutnansky, C. (2016). Low-Regrets Incrementalism: Land Use Planning Adaptation to Accelerating Sea Level Rise in Florida's Coastal Communities. *Journal of Planning Education and Research*, *36*(3), 319–332.

Creutzig, F. (2016). Evolving Narratives of Low-Carbon Futures in Transportation. *Transport Reviews*, *36*(3), 341–360.

Fields, B. (2019). Post-Disaster Amenity Politics: Livability, Gentrification, and Recovery in Post-Katrina New Orleans. In *Community Livability* (F. Wagner, & R. W. Caves, eds.): 123–136. New York, NY: Routledge.

Gehl, J., & Svarre, B. (2013). *How to Study Public Life*. Washington, DC: Island Press.

Harford, D., & Raftis, C. (2018). *Low Carbon Resilience: Best Practices for Professionals*. Adaptation to Climate Change Team. Burnaby, BC, Canada: Simon Fraser University.

Hsieh, H. F., & Shannon, S. E. (2005). Three Approaches to Qualitative Content Analysis. *Qualitative Health Research*, *15*(9), 1277–1288.

Immergluck, Dan, & Balan, Tharunya. (2018). Sustainable for Whom? Green Urban Development, Environmental Gentrification, and the Atlanta Beltline. Urban Geography, 39(4), 546–562.

Landauer, M., Juhola, S., & Klein, J. (2019). The Role of Scale in Integrating Climate Change Adaptation and Mitigation in Cities. *Journal of Environmental Planning and Management*, *62*(5), 741–765.

Meerow, S., & Woodruff, S. C. (2020). Seven Principles of Strong Climate Change Planning. *Journal of the American Planning Association*, *86*(1), 39–46.

National Association of City Transportation Officials. (2017). *Urban Street Stormwater Guide*. Washington, DC: Island Press.

Rigolon, A., & Németh, J. (2018). "We're Not in the Business of Housing": Environmental Gentrification and the Nonprofitization of Green Infrastructure Projects. *Cities*, *81*, 71–80.

Schwanen, T. (2018). Towards Decolonised Knowledge About Transport. *Palgrave Communications*, *4*(1), 1–6.

Smith, G., Duda, S., Lee, J. M., & Thompson, M. (2016). Measuring the Impact of the 606: Understanding How a Large Public Investment Impacted the Surrounding Housing Market. Chicago, IL: Institute for Housing Studies at DePaul University.

Udavardy, Shana, & Winkleman, Steve. (2014). Green Resilience: Climate Adaptation and Mitigation Synergies. Center for Clean Air Policy. Last accessed 3/19/2020 from http://ccap.org/assets/CCAP-Green-Resilience-Climate-Adaptation-Mitigation-Synergies_April-2014.pdf.

Whitehead, M. (2013). Neoliberal Urban Environmentalism and the Adaptive City: Towards a Critical Urban Theory and Climate Change. *Urban Studies*, *50*(7), 1348–1367.

5

ROTTERDAM

The resilient delta city

Co-authored by Liliane Geerling

Introduction

Rotterdam has become a recognized leader in resilience planning with international news spotlighting a suite of innovative projects in the second largest city in the Netherlands (Kimmelman 2017). Rotterdam is on the Nieuwe Maas River and relies on access to the sea for the lifeblood of commerce that fuels the city, making it the largest port in Europe. At the same time, Rotterdam sits within the larger Rhine–Meuse delta, a low-lying set of tidal wetlands and river channels that opens to the North Sea. Overall, 90% of Rotterdam is below sea level. Meyer (2009, p. 432) notes this complexity when he argues that, "Urbanized deltas can be considered as areas with a double complexity: they have to deal with the complexity of the delta, as the meeting of rivers and sea, and with the complexity of urban patterns, as a condition and result of economic, cultural and social life."

Managing risk, commerce, and quality of life in this precarious position are the driving dynamics of Rotterdam's resilience planning. To address these issues, Rotterdam has enacted a series of resilience plans over the last 15 years. We analyze these resilience plans to uncover key aspects of climate adaptation and mitigation-planning policy. The plans and documents call for Rotterdam to become climate-neutral with a zero-emission transportation system by 2050. In the shorter term, the city aims to be completely climate-proof by 2025 and to decrease CO_2 emissions by almost half by 2030.

While there have been numerous and well-crafted adaptation projects started throughout the city that we highlight in this chapter, resilience-planning efforts have generally not addressed and funded climate mitigation projects in the urban transportation sector designed to decrease greenhouse gas (GHG) emissions. The decoupling of adaptation from mitigation in urban transportation resilience rhetoric and policy has, however, not prevented a number of transportation mitigation projects from moving forward outside of the resilience-planning process in the broader Dutch planning tradition of sustainability and active transportation (City of Rotterdam 2010, 2015).

As other communities look to world leaders like Rotterdam for best-practice examples (Keeton 2014; Peters 2017), it is important to conceptually tie adaptation and mitigation polices in the urban transportation sector back together into a more holistic resilience-planning framework. We highlight how Rotterdam's existing resilience-planning efforts can be seen within the broader Dutch tradition of active transportation and water planning to emphasize the broader resilience lessons of the city.

The chapter is organized in four main sections. First, we examine the coastal context of Rotterdam to understand the resilience challenges of the city. Next, we examine the Dutch transportation-planning system and how it significantly impacts resilience-planning efforts. We follow this with a review of resilience planning in Rotterdam through an analysis of resilience plans to show the challenges and opportunities posed with the adaptation urbanism transition. Finally, we discuss broader implications of the Rotterdam case for other communities and relate the findings back to the broader literature.

Rotterdam: a delta city in a world of rising seas

Situating Rotterdam as delta city is vital to understanding the resilience challenges of the city. The city is located where it is because access to the river is an economic advantage, but that access to water also requires creating a network of water defense structures. Over hundreds of years, the Netherlands has created an intricate, functional system that links coastal defenses with regional and local systems (Meyer 2009; Zevenbergen et al. 2013; Stead 2014; Fields et al. 2017). In Rotterdam, the structures start at the North Sea with the massive Maeslantkering storm surge barrier and link with other megastructures to create the full DeltaWorks defense system. These coastal structures are then paired with regional dyke systems to create a set of polder water management areas where water levels are managed through a set of closely monitored sensors that track water levels in a network of channels. The ubiquitous Dutch windmills and canals were once developed as ways to help manage these water levels and, with the addition of electric pumps today, help to stabilize water levels throughout the country. When combined with local water defense and management structures that build on the base of the Dutch canal system, these measures create a full system designed to prevent flooding to a very high level. The Dutch system is now designed to prevent up to a 1-in-100,000-year flooding event in designated areas (Deltacommissaris 2015). By contrast, US flood systems are designed to withstand a 1-in-100-year event (Fields et al. 2017).

While this chapter and book overall concentrate on the more urban neighborhood systems such as water squares, raingardens, canals, green infrastructure, and permeable pavement, these city components would afford minimal protection to

TABLE 5.1 Rotterdam water resilience system

Rotterdam resilience system: adaptation urbanism
1. DeltaWorks along the coast and inland in the Rhine–Meuse–Scheldt delta
2. Dike system along River Nieuwe Waterweg and New Meuse (sea dike)
3. Neighborhood system: polder dikes and surface water and groundwater system
a. Historic "city-beautiful" canal system as water management and public space foundation (historic green infrastructure system)
b. Addition of green streets: permeable pavement to decrease runoff pulses, filter pollutants, and act as a traffic-calming tool for neighborhood streets
c. Water squares: public space plazas that double as water retention and filtration "pools," including bioswales, raingardens, underground storage, and green roof systems

intense storms and sea level rise without the larger resilience systems in place at the regional and coastal levels. This caveat is crucial to understanding the broader Netherlands systems approach to integrated flood defense and could be a model in other coastal areas as well.[1] This type of multiple lines of defense system shows how dependent urban populations are on broader coastal and regional systems and the importance of conceptualizing flood protection as part of a broader system (Lopez 2006). This approach is conceptualized in Table 5.1.

While the large coastal defense systems are vital and increasingly focused on more naturalistic "living with water" approaches (Fields et al. 2017), managing water within urban areas has become more important as the climate has become less stable. Managing water at the urban level is, at its foundation, a spatial management challenge. Increasing volumes of water falling in storms take up a great deal of space. That water can be infiltrated into the soil, temporarily stored within the landscape, or, the most common method during the modernist era, physically drained away using the sewer system. With cloudburst events becoming more common, the sheer physical quantity of water often overwhelms drainage systems during storm events. The previous modernist solutions of expanding the sewer system to create the "drained city" (Brown et al. 2009) are running up against the massive cost and hugely disruptive nature of construction in the heart of the city. In Rotterdam, this is compounded by the lack of space in the already full subsoil, especially when gas pipes are set to be replaced with a renewable city-heating system.

Increasingly cities are looking to public spaces and then the streets as locations where water can be infiltrated or temporarily stored to avoid water from backing up into residents' homes during these intense rain events. The pressure to adapt cities to climate change to manage water is adding pressure to rethink the public policy mission of local roads and, when linked with safety, public health, and the environmental mandate to decrease GHG emissions, is creating a foundation for adaptation urbanism. Rotterdam shows the potential and tensions of this transformation process.

Rotterdam streets: moving from auto-orientation to livable streets

Despite the long history of Rotterdam as an urban settlement dating back to its founding in 1340, the city provides an instructive case for the potential of transformation as a large part of its current form was shaped by modernist planning approaches. The center of Rotterdam was destroyed in a bombing raid during World War II and then rebuilt using the latest modernist principles of the 1950s. The result was that many canals were filled in with debris from the war and replaced by large roads designed to spread development out to the suburbs. Rotterdam was to be a car city of the future along the lines of Le Corbusier, discussed in Chapter 1.

Almost 75 years later, however, these roads have not produced the type of future that most residents wanted to see. Rotterdam's downtown, like those in many car cities, was nearly deserted after office hours during the 1970s and 1980s. The city designed to hum with the energy of the future began to see the car and the spatial demands of the auto age as impediments to building a lively center becoming of a world city. Over the last 20–30 years, Rotterdam has begun to change course by focusing on new housing in the center, concentrating on the city lounge concept of improved public space. In the transportation sector, the focus has been on the insertion of separated cycle tracks and other bicycle and pedestrian facilities. Overall, the concept is to encourage green densification that improves environmental outcomes at the same time that it improves livability (Tillie et al. 2018). Water in the city has also been rethought as public spaces and increasingly roads themselves have become seen as more than just mobility mechanisms. In Rotterdam, you can see how the streets of the past are being redesigned as streets of the future. The efforts to rethink streets in Rotterdam match broader efforts in the Netherlands to rethink the transportation system.

Dutch approach to managing urban driving speed

Street space cannot be seen as a new resource for managing water, adapting and mitigating to climate change, and improving quality of life if auto-oriented streets are seen as the sole method for maintaining a functioning, modern city. The Dutch have proved that high-quality-of-life, economically thriving cities can be created on the base of a truly multi-modal street system. Despite the widespread perception that Dutch streets have always been this way, the history of the last 50 years, particularly in Rotterdam, shows that it took large political pressure and a massive public *push* to create this multi-modal system. The urban base of Dutch resilience is built on this transformed role of city streets brought about through sustained political pressure.

For example, streets in the Netherlands are now some of the safest in the world, but this was not always the case. The Dutch transportation-planning system from the 1950s to 1970s was based on the foundation of the US-style system of increasing speed and flow of cars in urban areas. Canals throughout the country were filled in and buildings were demolished to expand roadway width to increase the "flow" of vehicles. In Rotterdam, for example, Schiekade, a main street in the heart of the city, had its central canal filled with debris from World War II and was transformed into a commuting artery. Instead of accommodating water in the core as an amenity, water was pushed away and the new lifeblood of the modernist city, cars, were given preeminence in public space.

The core of the city was envisioned along the lines of a biological analogy where cars were pumped through the city to maintain the life and energy of the modern city. The result was that the former pedestrian and bicycle-filled streets began to be filled with high-speed cars. Water was hidden away and replaced with the exhaust of automobility. The result, sadly in Rotterdam and around the Netherlands, was a spike in road fatalities that brought Dutch and US transportation fatality rates to similar levels in the early 1970s (Evans 2014).

This increase in fatalities and the oil embargo helped to push the Dutch to reconsider transportation-planning priorities (Feddes and de Lange 2019). Beginning in the mid-1970s, the Dutch began to explore how to create more livable streets through traffic calming and strategic use of bicycle facilities. Pilot programs were conducted in Tilburg, The Hague, and Delft (Bruntlett and Bruntlett 2018). The lessons from these pilots and broader work in slow-speed neighborhood networks helped to form the foundation of a new transportation-planning system referred to as Sustainable Safety. This approach, similar to the Swedish safety model Vision Zero, focuses on designing roadways that limit severe and fatal crashes through a safe systems approach.

While there are multiple elements to this approach, one of the core elements is managing speed in urban areas. The Dutch approach acknowledges the obvious limits of human physiology when confronted with fast-moving vehicles: higher-speed crashes between cars and humans result in increased fatalities. The Dutch method to improve safety is either to separate vulnerable road users (pedestrians and cyclists) on higher-speed roads above about 20 mph (30 km/hour) or significantly traffic-calm neighborhood roads to prevent high-speed traffic (Furth 2012). The Dutch have created a systematic way of analyzing speed and appropriate facilities based on traffic volume (average daily traffic) and speed. The approach focuses on setting a safe speed given the landscape conditions. In practice in urban areas, this translates to "the requirement that where motorized traffic mixes with vulnerable slow traffic, the speed of motorized traffic needs to be reduced" (Wegman and Aarts 2006, p. 133). While not every street in the Netherlands matches this format exactly (Weijermars and Wegman 2011), most of the streets in the entire country now adhere to the basic underlying principle: never mix vulnerable road users with high-speed traffic.

The core of the Dutch system for neighborhood areas is limiting the speed of auto traffic through physical, traffic-calming tactics. The goal is to make neighborhood streets where cars literally are prevented from driving above 30 km/hour because crashes above this speed threshold result in far higher numbers of severe and fatal injuries. This speed broadly matches the physical limits that vulnerable road users can withstand in a crash with an automobile.

These 30-km zones have gradually been implemented across the country, accounting for about 15% of all urban road length in 1998 and increasing to about 70% of all urban road length in 2007 (SWOV 2018). The growth of these 30-km zones has resulted in significant improvements in safety. Analysis of a selected set of 30-km roads shows that decreasing speeds from 50 to 30 km resulted in a 22% decrease in injury crashes (SWOV 2018).

These 30-km zones utilize a set of visual and physical cues to create low-speed neighborhood streets. First, there is a transition zone that tells drivers that they are entering a slow zone. Speed tables and pavement changes are often used to send this message to drivers. As drivers continue down the street, the message is repeated with significant traffic calming and tight lane widths to limit auto speeds. Chicanes, additional speed tables, and curb bulb-outs are also often used. In addition to slowing speed, these areas can be enhanced with green infrastructure to absorb rain pulses to decrease the flooding potential of streets. Permeable pavement can also more easily be integrated into this type of slow-speed neighborhood street environments, offering an opportunity to link Sustainable Safety/Vision Zero goals with climate adaptation and mitigation.

Not all 30-km zones are, however, created equal (SWOV 2018). Rotterdam, for example, is not known as a leader in active transportation planning in the Netherlands (Wagenbuur 2011). Despite recent efforts to improve bicycling accessibility with provision of cycle tracks in higher-speed areas in the center of the city, Rotterdam has a modernist base of streets and culture of car use that is difficult to dislodge. From a worldwide perspective, Rotterdam has an enviable bicycle mode share of 31%, but the city is well behind other larger Dutch cities in terms of bicycle mode share. Amsterdam (bicycle mode share of 48%) and Utrecht (bicycle mode share of 51%), for example, are world leaders (Sutton 2017). The difference is that, while Rotterdam has an increasing network of protected cycle tracks and has experienced a 60% increase in bicyclist use from 2006 to 2016 (Wagenbuur 2017), many streets in 30-km zones are not significantly traffic-calmed and are also lined with extensive, cheap car parking. Where the positive climate transportation choice in Amsterdam discussed in Chapter 1 is the bicycle because it is faster and cheaper, the car has maintained its place in Rotterdam because of spatial subsidies that make the car competitive. While the combination of walking, bicycling, and transit now accounts for approximately 60% of all trips in Rotterdam, the streets are much more geared to the car than in many other larger Dutch cities. The result is that, while Rotterdam has significantly improved its bicycle infrastructure, the city has been left behind by many of its Dutch companion cities in terms of advancing a truly resilient transportation system that is both adapted to and mitigates climate change.

New goals advanced in the city's planning documents aim to change this. The city is beginning to weave green infrastructure together in street designs to help slow traffic and improve the water management potential of the urban landscape. Rotterdam is planning to significantly expand the use of the 30-km zones in the city in the coming years to help improve livability and safety in the city center. Right now, about half the traffic moving along one of the key roads in the center, Coolsingel, is through traffic moving to other areas of the city. Rotterdam is aiming to use 30-km zones in the center to discourage this through traffic and enhance livability to create a "city lounge" feeling in the center city (Nieuws van vandaag 2019).

To help achieve successful implementation of these goals, high-quality 30-km zones that "repeat the message" through the entire length of the street segment are important. We first heard this described this way by Edwin Koster of the Fiesterdond Zwolle. He was taking our group of US students on a tour and showed us a 30-km street and pointed out that some 30-km streets did not have consistent traffic-calming throughout the entire street segment. Drivers would respond by increasing speeds after they initially slowed. He suggested that "repeating the message" with traffic calming is really at the core of good 30-km design. Without repeated reminders in the physical form of traffic calming, drivers will speed up and decrease the safety and livability of the road (SWOV 2018).

Repeating the design message offers an opportunity to add green infrastructure in the form of green curb bulb-outs, bioswales, planters, and other elements that can serve the dual functions of slowing traffic and acting as "mini-sponges" to better manage water. The changes to create highly livable, safe neighborhood streets can be relatively inexpensive. The suite of changes to retrofit neighborhood streets to basic 30-km zones, for example, costs about 29,350 Euros (about $32,000) per km (CROW 2018) but can be even less on new roadways or when utilized as part of a larger resurfacing project. A full suite of green infrastructure changes can add to initial cost but can often be compensated for through decreased water management costs. When all of this comes together, neighborhood streets can be transformed into access corridors that double as amenities, places for living with water that are safer, more attractive, and better adapted to the climate of the future (Fields et al. 2017).

While Rotterdam has not been seen as a leader in the area of fostering these types of slow-speed neighborhood streets, many of its current streets represent great examples of streets transformed. The image of Molenwaterweg (Figure 5.1), for example, shows all of this coming together: a neighborhood slow street with local shops and housing, green infrastructure, and enhanced safety. The street actually translates as the mill waterway and highlights the canal system of the neighborhood and the mills that pumped the excess water of the Cool neighborhood to the Schie waterway.

Overall, the streets in the area tend to be narrow and include multiple functions (Table 5.2). For example, on Molenwaterweg, the place functions of the street in the form of café seating and sidewalks are afforded approximately the same space (20.5 ft: 6.2 m) as the road lane and parking functions (19 ft: 5.8 m) of the street.

This balanced approach to marrying movement and place in the streetscape is also increasingly seen in the area as a larger system of traffic-calmed streets adjacent to Rotterdam Centraal has been developed over the last few years. Molenwaterweg connects to a set of water boulevards with water in the center, green space and trees on both sides of a canal, and, finally, slow-speed streets on

FIGURE 5.1 Molenwaterweg.

TABLE 5.2 Molenwaterweg (Mill Waterway) street dimensions

Street sections	*Width*
Sidewalk	7.5 ft (2.3 m)
Parking	7 ft (2 m)
One-way road	12 ft (3.6 m)
Café seating	9.5 ft (3 m)
Sidewalk	3.5 ft (1 m)

either side of the canal. Water boulevards are a ubiquitous street typology in the Netherlands that help to create a high quality of life in Dutch cities by joining the movement, place, and water management functions of streets together in blue and green corridors. This central Dutch street typology has, however, mostly gone unnoticed as a potentially transformative resilience innovation.[2] The streets around Rotterdam Centraal show how these functions come together to create a template for adaptation urbanism.

Just a few streets away along the water boulevards is another green resilient street, Schepenstraat. Schepenstraat was recently redesigned in a partnership between the City of Rotterdam and local neighbors. The City of Rotterdam planned to address subsidence in the area by raising the street, with the unfortunate effect of severely impacting the mature trees in the area. The street design also left in place the limited traffic calming of the original street design, with the result being large amounts of cut-through traffic that often ignored the 30-km speed of the street. Neighborhood residents looked at the City's plan and thought they

FIGURE 5.2 Schepenstraat.

could do better. Neighborhood residents used the City's new Right to Challenge provision to formally work with the City to create a plan for the area that better fit neighborhood needs.

The Right to Challenge provision (City of Rotterdam 2020) allows neighborhood residents to petition the City to create a new design for a project provided that the new design is the same cost as the City's original design and there is broad neighborhood support for the new plan. The neighborhood residents must do the work to create the improved plan in coordination with the City.

The results on Schepenstraat (opened in summer 2019) have been impressive. The new design added green space to the street, saved some of the mature trees and incorporated a set of new trees that were transplanted into the neighborhood from the City's "tree orphanage," added raised pedestrian crossings, added bicycle parking, and incorporated improved drainage and rain barrels to the area (Figure 5.2). All of these changes helped to create a more resilient street that better addresses water and flooding issues and simultaneously helps to traffic-calm the area to encourage safe walking and bicycling. The new design is a near-perfect example of adaptation urbanism where climate adaptation concerns have been woven together with climate mitigation street designs that privilege active transportation and livability. The Schepenstraat Right to Challenge development was recognized as a featured project in the 2019 Yearbook Landscape Architecture and Urban Design in The Netherlands.

While this type of citizen-led effort requires immense commitment and a design-savvy populace, the idea of setting out adaptation urbanism goals for municipal streets and then coordinating designs with the local residents is a powerful concept that could be applied more broadly. To ensure equitability, this type of process would require that areas that do not have a cadre of professionals living in the area receive additional support in creating designs that matched their neighborhood's concerns. Templates of potential designs could be created to address local context and then be used as a base for working with neighborhoods. By setting the outlines of the project along broad adaptation urbanism principles, streets around the city could be transformed to be greener, safer, and, overall, more resilient.

The new street design of Schepenstraat, linked with the transforming streets and water boulevards around Rotterdam Centraal, provides safer active transportation access to transit and trains, creating an integrated bike–train combination that is vital to a truly resilient transportation system (Bruntlett and Bruntlett 2018).[3] In total, the area includes a broad set of key adaptation urbanism features (Appendix B) and creates a template for what resilient streets can become. In addition, Rotterdam has announced 233 million euros-worth of green space projects to be constructed in the core of the city to help address the need for revitalization and green space following the coronavirus. According to the City of Rotterdam, "The corona crisis shows us that, especially in a city, public space is essential for the quality of life and living" (NU.nl 2020). The plan calls for major greening of public squares and the redevelopment of the traffic circle of Hofplein into a people-centered space with added greenery. Overall, the story behind how Rotterdam is transforming their streets and the challenges and opportunities of this change process can provide important lessons for other more car-oriented cities to see what is possible.

The emergence of Rotterdam as a world leader in resilience

As the above discussion shows, Rotterdam is piloting a new way of integrating open space, street space, and water management. While the street space transformation has been more difficult because of the highly car-dependent transportation system put in place after World War II, the public space transformations designed to live with water have been more advanced and have pushed Rotterdam into the international discussion of world leaders in resilience.

From a water management perspective, the process of integrating these sectors in Rotterdam is ongoing and is being influenced by a series of water plans from the national to the local level (Stead 2014). As the limits of structural water planning and more detailed information on the potential impacts of climate change became known in the early 2000s (Woltjer and Al 2007), the Netherlands more broadly and the city of Rotterdam specifically began to reconceptualize water planning focusing on augmenting structural flood control with more green and blue infrastructure designed to live with water. In the city of Rotterdam, a set of strategic development plans were crafted during this period (Table 5.3).[4] The policy focus of the plans shows the changing conceptualization of water, risk, and resilience in the emerging climate change era. The initial suite of plans through 2007 did not address resilience in a substantive way, but plans crafted during the second half of the time period begin to integrate substantial resilience concepts in policy language (Stead 2014).

Rotterdam started to work on more integrated water quality as well as quantity issues with the first Waterplan in 2001. This first plan is significant because the city

TABLE 5.3 Rotterdam resilience plans

Resilience-planning timeline	*Date*
Pre-resilience base: bicycle urbanism and water planning	1970s–2000
Waterplan I	2001
Rotterdam Waterstad 2035	2005
Waterplan II	2007
Rotterdam climate-proof progamme	2008
Rotterdam adaptation strategy	2013
Water-sensitive Rotterdam	2015
Rotterdam resilience strategy	2016

started to invest in extra water storage capacity with projects like the Zuiderpark and in improving the surface water quality with projects like the Bergse Plassen. In addition, older sewers began to be refurbished and temporary rainwater storage concepts began to emerge.

In 2005, the urban water management issues were more fully connected to the urban-planning agenda with the Rotterdam Waterstad 2035 plan. To produce Waterstad 2035 a more diverse set of stakeholders was brought together for the first time: municipal employees from the engineering, urban planning, water management, and development departments, together with people from the water boards and advisory firms. Waterstad 2035 was primarily used to encourage the city government to look differently at the water management issues and see these as an opportunity to innovate green and enhance livability of the city.

Many of the concepts of Waterstad 2035 were implemented in the second Waterplan in 2007. This plan was designed to begin to rethink the role of water in Rotterdam and work towards creating an attractive, water-proof city. It made a direct link between water as an opportunity for the spatial development of Rotterdam for the first time. This plan, while mentioning the increasing pressures of climate change, did not utilize a resilience framework. There were no mentions of resilience, mitigation, or adaptation in the plan. This matches Stead's (2014) analysis which suggests that resilience planning in a climate context in Rotterdam is a fairly new phenomenon.

Rotterdam planning began to change with the Rotterdam Climate Proof Progamme in 2008. This plan was the first that began to make climate policy a central feature of local planning efforts. The plan was designed to make Rotterdam's inhabitants fully resilient to climate change impacts by 2025. Extending this concept further was the Rotterdam Adaptation Strategy in 2013 which focused on integrating the attractive, water city concepts of the 2007 Waterplan with the newer, resilience concepts. Policy development and planning at regional and national level have supported and strengthened Rotterdam's approach. Deeper analysis of Rotterdam's resilience plans can be found in Appendix B.

Piloting the transition: Benthemplein Water Square

The result of this set of plans was a suite of innovative, demonstration rainwater storage projects. Probably the most widely known project that emerged as a result of the second Waterplan is the Benthemplein water square (Figure 5.3). The water square was a design process led by Rotterdam-based De Urbanisten in coordination with the local community. The water square, completed in 2013, can be understood as a twofold strategy. It enhances public open space and improves water storage capacity. It also generates opportunities to create environmental quality and identity in public spaces in the neighborhood.

Most of the time the water square is dry and is used as a recreational space. When it rains, three basins collect rainwater: two shallower basins for the immediate surroundings receive water whenever it rains and one deeper basin receives water only in heavy rainfall events. After a rain event, the water of the two shallower basins flows into an underground infiltration device and from here gradually seeps back into groundwater. This helps decrease the strain from the main sewer in times of heavy rainfall and prevents overflows, but also helps to keep the groundwater balance in both dry and wet periods. This helps to keep the city trees and plants in good condition and to reduce urban heat island effect. The water from the deeper basin flows back into the open water system of the city after a maximum of 36 hours to ensure public health. Overall, the water square can hold about 450,000 gallons of water (1.7 million liters) and cost EUR 4.5 million (C40 Cities 2014).

In addition to improved water quantity and quality management, the water square helps to educate residents about the importance of water in the community and simultaneously builds a community amenity. After heavy rainfalls the basin fills and is eventually cleaned out after water levels fall, opening up the space again for recreation. The water square also includes open stainless-steel gutters, a water wall, and a rain well, which gush the rain water visibly on to the square. The square is

FIGURE 5.3 Benthemplein water square.

monitored by cameras as well as underground IT systems. Because of the extra technology and clean-up after rain events, the maintenance costs are higher than those of an ordinary square. Although the design was made by using participatory planning, some residents are still unaware of the water storage purpose of the square and trash from school students sometimes clogs the gutters, limiting the effectiveness of the water square. These lessons suggest that park management and potential design changes may be necessary as this type of pilot project is implemented on a larger scale.

Emergent resilience plans

Rotterdam resilience projects have begun to move from demonstration projects like the Benthemplein Water Square towards an emphasis on smaller-scale, less expensive, bottom-up projects to address climate change adaptation. These projects are designed to build climate awareness among the diverse population in the city and enhance coalitions between the city government, housing corporations, water boards, local companies, and local inhabitants. These types of projects are the focus of Water Sensitive Rotterdam (WSR) which started in 2015. WSR was designed to be not just another governmental strategy, but a real city movement. WSR focuses on rainwater as a valuable resource which should be locally used whenever and wherever possible to enhance the attractiveness of the city, maintain ecological processes, and ensure adequate drainage to protect the city from flooding. The WSR strategy is to implement small-scale rainwater retention measures on a larger scale to increase the "sponginess" of the city as a whole, while at the same time adding quality to public space. Monitoring, intensive collaboration with scientists, and the development of cost-benefit analysis are essential for WSR.

The WSR process coincided with the growth of the Rockefeller Foundation's 100 Resilient City Program. This program asked the City of Rotterdam to produce the Rotterdam Resilience Strategy in 2016. This strategy focuses on both spatial adaptation and flood risk management in Rotterdam and overall resilience for the city inhabitants. These large goals are paired with efforts to enhance social resilience and broader economic and potential cyber-attacks on city infrastructure. The six themes for the plan are: social cohesion and education, energy transition, climate adaptation, cyber use and security, critical infrastructure, and changing urban governance. These themes are then translated to broad goals for Rotterdam and finally to a set of 68 policy action steps. These action steps include building on a number of existing projects or programs, like the Roadmap Next Economy, WSR, and the program WE–Society, but most are new or starting projects. Funding is not secured and needs to be found for many projects. The overall goal of the Rotterdam Resilience Strategy is to begin to move innovative projects and procedures towards standard practice across the city.[5]

An example that is part of the more bottom-up approach is the ZoHo raingarden. The raingarden is part of the European subsidy program to make the Agniesebuurt and Zomerhofkwartier climate adaptive and part of the broader

FIGURE 5.4 ZoHo raingarden.

Rotterdam Weatherwise initiative. The project repurposed a short street segment near Rotterdam Centraal Station into a raingarden and walking/cycling path. Rain barrels were also added to the project to capture rainwater from an adjacent, unused elevated railway (Hofbogen). The rain barrels (designed and developed by Studio Bas Sala) form the letters ZoHo and have become an icon for the area and a key part of the revitalization plan for the area (Figure 5.4). A built-in smart solar-powered system monitors the weather forecast via the internet. If a heavy shower is approaching, the system releases the water from the barrels and creates buffer space for the coming rain shower. During long periods of drought, the water is precisely retained to provide water to the surrounding greenery in the raingarden.

Discussion: Rotterdam resilience planning and the seeds of adaptation urbanism

Over the last 10 years, Rotterdam has made significant progress towards articulating and pilot-testing a set of resilience-planning projects designed to improve water management and improve livability. These efforts build on a rich Dutch tradition of water management and planning that are keys to understanding resilience planning in a delta city. This resilience base has been augmented with a series of innovative projects that extend the living-with-water concept into the heart of the city and into the mainstream of city planning and project selection.

While Rotterdam's resilience planning has begun to be integrated into the bureaucratic fabric of water and open space planning in the city, the transportation sector has been only minimally impacted by the resilience movement. As the outline of key projects above indicates, resilience planning in Rotterdam has successfully focused on reconceptualizing public space to help manage water, but these efforts have not been well integrated with transportation sector-planning efforts.

As noted previously, Rotterdam has a strong climate mitigation-planning framework and has significantly improved active transportation and transit opportunities within a broader network of urban revitalization projects. It is important, however, to understand that resilience planning has not been the impetus to the transportation changes in Rotterdam but has instead been operating on a parallel track. The rhetorical absence of urban transportation climate mitigation-planning projects from the broader resilience-planning narrative in Rotterdam speaks more to narrow use of resilience as a term rather than any substantive failure to seriously engage in climate mitigation planning.

For example, planning in the broader ZoHo area of Rotterdam currently includes a number of transportation-planning efforts designed to decrease carbon emissions through integration with a refurbished and well-connected train network at the Centraal Station. These transportation-specific projects appear to be moving forward independently of resilience-planning efforts. The area, with its water square and water boulevards, revitalized housing, well-connected and improving active transportation systems, and linkage to European and regional rail, is truly a model of what an operationalized adaptation urbanism framework could resemble at a neighborhood level. This is the template of what a safe/climate/spatially efficient transportation system can look like within the broader confines of a green, blue, dense city. The metrics of success are all there for Rotterdam, but the planning that produced this was not purely within the resilience sphere.

In examining planning documents, we did not uncover any substantial tension between these types of climate mitigation projects and broader adaptation goals. New projects like the Benthemplein Watersquare focus on repurposing underutilized spaces for adaptation and improved quality of life rather than purely focusing on open space protection. This is probably due to the established spatial planning principles designed to integrate new adaptation projects within the existing urban fabric. This, again, points to the adaptation urbanism potential for the area and highlights the importance of broader planning regimes as a base for this type of resilience planning. Communities without this type of integrated planning system may be challenged to replicate the climate adaptation and mitigation components without more focused inclusion in overarching resilience-planning processes.

For these reasons, the rhetorical absence of transportation climate mitigation as a central planning component of resilience plans is significant. As previously discussed, resilience planning is increasingly being used as a key defining feature of planning in the climate change era. Communities like Rotterdam are rightly held up as exemplars of resilience planning to be emulated through best-practice policy dissemination. While Rotterdam itself is planning for both climate adaptation and mitigation through distinct policy subsystems, many other communities that might seek to employ the Rotterdam resilience-planning model may not have a strong transportation mitigation-planning policy sphere to engage. Replication of the Rotterdam resilience approach without the deeper Dutch tradition of active transportation planning would only address half of the policy problem.

Conclusion

This chapter highlights Rotterdam's extensive resilience-planning efforts over the last decade and highlights the impressive efforts to integrate water into public and open space planning. These climate adaptation efforts form the core of most of the City's policy actions and have resulted in a suite of innovative projects to enhance livability and water management within the urban core. While these efforts are impressive, our analysis also found that Rotterdam's resilience plans had limited emphasis on climate mitigation from the transportation sector. While mitigation activities appear to be progressing in other policy subsystems like the port and housing, the lack of emphasis on transportation within the planning documents represents a missed communication opportunity to discuss the rich Dutch policy contributions to transit and active transportation and appears to be an important potential blind spot that could limit other communities as they seek to replicate Rotterdam's resilience system.

For resilience planning to truly address the core concerns of the climate change era (increased climate risk and the need to decarbonize urban systems), resilience plans should be framed as a planning tool to address transportation with both climate adaptation and mitigation as twin aims, not as separate policy silos. Efforts to integrate the transportation sector into the broader resilience-planning movement to rethink water, GHG emissions, and quality of life could significantly accelerate Rotterdam's efforts to meet ambitious climate-planning goals.

Notes

1 The Dutch system consists of three layers of safety: the first layer of vital infrastructure to keep the unwanted water out, a second layer of spatial design measures that focus on water sensitivity and as final layer and of last resort, evacuation routes.

2 Water boulevards are truly the quintessential Dutch street typology with a canal in the center and roads on either side of the canal. There are two basic types of water boulevards. The first focuses on the hard-scraped canals seen in Amsterdam and many other Dutch cities. The second type of water boulevard is the more naturalistic green-buffered, city-beautiful canal system seen in Rotterdam. I heard the term water boulevards used by a Dutch student, but the term, to our knowledge, is not widely used in the Netherlands. The concept was used in the London-based Landscape Institute's How to Prevent Flooding Competition in 2015. One of the short-listed finalists by Baharash Architecture creates a well-crafted template of the water boulevard idea for London. The short film (Landscape Institute 2015) defines water boulevards as places "which mitigate[s] the risks of flooding while also creating healthy places for people to live, work, and visit. The project integrates green infrastructure and water-sensitive urban design into our streets." The concept of water boulevards offers an important resilient street type that could be extended from the Dutch landscape to help address water management, transportation, and quality of life in coastal cities around the world.

3 The potential of this combination of modes is highlighted by the fact that currently 11% of all trips over 15 km (9 miles) in the Netherlands are train trips and 43% of train trips are accessed by bicycling (Jonkeren et al. 2019). With the shift to 100% renewable energy for the train system recently completed by the Dutch national rail service (NS) and the plans to expand high-frequency rail transport on key lines between Dutch cities, the potential for a fully integrated zero-GHG emission transportation system is emerging (Railjournal.com 2017; Bruntlett and Bruntlett 2018, p. 160).

4 Rotterdam also developed the Weather Wise plan in 2019, but this is not included in the analysis.

5 While our emphasis focuses on the public space and street projects, there is a great deal of other work across multiple other resilience sectors. Resilience in Rotterdam is clearly being conceptualized as a multi-sector planning tool.

References

Brown, R. R., Keath, N., & Wong, T. H. (2009). Urban Water Management in Cities: Historical, Current and Future Regimes. *Water Science and Technology*, *59*(5), 847–855.

Bruntlett, M., & Bruntlett, C. (2018). *Building the Cycling City: The Dutch Blueprint For Urban Vitality*. Washington, DC: Island Press.

C40 Cities. (2014). Benthemplein Water Square: An Innovative Way to Prevent Urban Flooding in Rotterdam. August 27. Last accessed 4/3/2020 from www.c40.org/case_studies/benthemplein-water-square-an-innovative-way-to-prevent-urban-flooding-in-rotterdam.

City of Rotterdam. (2010). *Rotterdam Climate Proof 2010*. Rotterdam: Rotterdam Climate Initiative.

City of Rotterdam. (2015). Rotterdam 2015–2018 Programme on Sustainability and Climate Change. Rotterdam: City of Rotterdam. Last accessed 16/1/2020 from: www.scribd.com/document/362256661/Rotterdam-Programme-on-Sustainaibilty-and-Climate-Change-2015-2018.

City of Rotterdam. (2020). Right to Challenge. Last accessed 3/10/2020 from www.rotterdam.nl/wonen-leven/right-to-challenge/.

CROW. (2018). 30km Zones Fact Sheet: What are the Considerations for and Against 30km Zones? Last accessed 3/12/2020 from www.swov.nl/en/facts-figures/factsheet/30-kmh-zones.

Deltacommissaris. (2015). Delta Programme 2015: The Decision to Keep the Netherlands Safe and Livable. Ministerie van Infrastructuur en Milieu. Report. The Hague, Netherlands: Deltacommissaris.

Evans, L. (2014). Traffic Fatality Reductions: United States Compared with 25 Other Countries. *American Journal of Public Health*, *104*(8), 1501–1507.

Feddes, F., & de Lange, M. (2019). *Bike City Amsterdam: How Amsterdam Became the Cycling Capital of the World*. Amsterdam: Nieuw Amsterdam.

Fields, B., Thomas, J., & Wagner, J. A. (2017). Living with Water in the Era of Climate Change: Lessons from the Lafitte Greenway in Post-Katrina New Orleans. *Journal of Planning Education and Research*, *37*(3), 309–321.

Furth, P. G. (2012). Bicycling Infrastructure for Mass Cycling: A Trans-Atlantic Comparison. In *City Cycling* (J. R. Pucher, & R. Buehler, eds.). Cambridge, MA: MIT Press.

Jonkeren, O., Kager, R., Harms, L., & te Brömmelstroet, M. (2019). The Bicycle–Train Travellers in the Netherlands: Personal Profiles and Travel Choices. *Transportation*, 1–22.

Keeton, Rachel. (2014). Rotterdam Has a Plan to Disseminate Its Climate Change Expertise to the World. *NextCity*. April 7. Last accessed 9/18/2017 from https://nextcity.org/daily/entry/rotterdam-has-a-plan-to-disseminate-its-climate-change-expertise-to-the-wor.

Kimmelman, M. (2017). The Dutch Have Solutions to Rising Seas. The World is Watching. *The New York Times*, June 15.

Landscape Institute. (2015). How to Prevent Flooding Film Ideas Competition: Water Boulevards. February 24. Last accessed 6/15/2020 from www.youtube.com/watch?v=qCw2xV9TZ4s.

Lopez, J. A. (2006). The Multiple Lines of Defense Strategy to Sustain Coastal Louisiana. Metairie, LA: Lake Pontchartrain Basin Foundation. Last accessed 1/5/2015 from www.SaveOurLake.org/.

Meyer, H. (2009). Reinventing the Dutch Delta: Complexity and Conflicts. *Built Environment,* 28(4), 432–451.

Nieuws van Vandaag. (2019). Vaker Groen Licht voor Fietsers en meer 30 km-Zones voor Automobilisten in Rotterdam. April 16. Last accessed 2/11/2020 from https://komieuitrotterdamdan.nu/2019/04/16/vaker-groen-licht-voor-fietsers-en-meer-30-km-zones-voor-automobilisten-in-rotterdam/.

NU.nl. (2020). College wil 233 Miljoen Investeren in Zeven Stadsparken in Rotterdam. Last accessed 6/24/2020 from www.nu.nl/rotterdam/6058654/college-wil-233-miljoen-investeren-in-zeven-stadsparken-in-rotterdam.html.

Peters, Adele. (2017). This Neighborhood is Fighting Floods by Welcoming It. *Fast Co.* Last accessed 8/18/2017 from www.fastcompany.com/3068730/this-new-orleans-neighborhood-is-fighting-flooding-by-welcoming-it

Railjournal.com. (2017). December Launch for Dutch High-Frequency City-Services. March 23. Last accessed 3/19/2020 from www.railjournal.com/passenger/main-line/december-launch-for-dutch-high-frequency-inter-city-services/.

Stead, Dominik. (2014). Urban Planning, Water Management and Climate Change Strategies: Adaptation, Mitigation and Resilience Narratives in the Netherlands. *International Journal of Sustainable Development & World Ecology*, 21(1), 15–27.

Sutton, Mark. (2017). Netherlands Further Builds on Cycling's Modal Share, Hitting 51% in Utrecht. *Cycling Industry News*. October 26. Last accessed 3/11/2020 from https://cyclingindustry.news/netherlands-further-builds-on-cyclings-modal-share-hitting-51-in-utrecht/.

SWOV. (2018). *30 km/h Zones*. SWOV Fact Sheet. May. The Hague: SWOV.

Tillie, N., Borsboom-van Beurden, J., Doepel, D., & Aarts, M. (2018). Exploring a Stakeholder Based Urban Densification and Greening Agenda for Rotterdam Inner City—Accelerating the Transition to a Liveable Low Carbon City. *Sustainability*, *10*(6), 1927.

Wagenbuur, Mark. (2011). Rotterdam Remedies a Lower Cycling Rate. *Bicycle Dutch*. March 24. Last accessed 3/11/2020 from https://bicycledutch.wordpress.com/2011/03/24/rotterdam-remedies-a-lower-cycling-rate/.

Wagenbuur, Mark. (2017). Riding in Rotterdam. *Bicycle Dutch*. January 17. Last accessed 3/11/2020 from https://bicycledutch.wordpress.com/2017/01/17/riding-in-the-rotterdam-rain/.

Wegman, F. C., & Aarts, L. T. (2006). Advancing Sustainable Safety: National Road Safety Outlook for 2005–2020. Leidschendam, NL: SWOV Institute for Road Safety Research.

Weijermars, W., & Wegman, F. (2011). Ten Years of Sustainable Safety in the Netherlands: An Assessment. *Transportation Research Record, 2213*(1), 1–8.

Woltjer, J., & Al, N. (2007). Integrating Water Management and Spatial Planning: Strategies Based on the Dutch Experience. *Journal of the American Planning Association*, *73*(2), 211–222.

Zevenbergen, Chris, Van Herk, Sebastian, Rijke, Jeroen, Kabat, Pavel, Bloemen, Pieter, Ashley, Richard, Speers, Andrew, Gersonius, Berry, & Veerbeek, William. (2013). Taming Global Flood Disasters. Lessons Learned from Dutch Experience. *Natural Hazards*, 65(3), 1217–1225.

6

COPENHAGEN CLIMATE INNOVATION

Building on the base

Introduction

> The point of Tåsinge Plads is that it works when it's raining, but, more importantly, it works when it's not raining.
>
> *René Sommer Lindsay, former Project Lead Tåsinge Plads Climate Resilience Project (interview with the author: Lindsay 2018)*

Copenhagen has long been recognized as world leader in active transportation and is quickly building a reputation as policy leader in resilience policy. After a serious cloudburst flooding incident in 2011 where nearly 6 inches (150 mm) of rain fell in about 2 hours, the city began to seriously consider how to address the 30% more rain projected because of the changing climate. The city has undertaken a focused effort to pilot innovative projects and build a base of knowledge that can be used in an ambitious set of 300 climate adaptation projects designed to make the city safer for the changing climate and, importantly, improve neighborhood quality of life. As the opening quote from René Sommer Lindsay suggests, climate adaptation is both about managing the extremes of climate and improving everyday landscape for people.

Copenhagen's path towards climate resilience provides important guidance for other cities just starting out on the path to integrating climate adaptation and mitigation into their municipal planning. Copenhagen's resilience vision is built on top of decades of comprehensive active transportation and transit planning focused on decreasing greenhouse gas (GHG) emissions (climate mitigation). Public space and street projects designed to address water are being layered on top of the existing and expanding active transportation network to help create a template for "sponge cities" (Colville-Andersen 2018, p. 229). Unlike in Rotterdam, where urban resilience plans have focused almost exclusively on climate adaptation with active transportation moving along in a parallel policy silo, resilience planning in Copenhagen has much more explicitly linked climate adaptation and mitigation together to create a robust resilience architecture through projects specifically targeted at its streets and public spaces. The resilience-planning template of Copenhagen is still a work in progress with a suburban driving culture and potential political backlash threatening progress (Henderson and Gulsrud 2019), but the innovative projects and broad linkages to financing made available through the series of resilience plans offer an important window into what is possible when innovation is piloted and resilience is pushed into the mainstream.

The chapter is organized in three main sections. We begin by examining the background for Copenhagen's resilience challenge. This is followed by discussion on the evolution of Copenhagen's street-planning approach and connections to resilience planning. Finally, we discuss the implications of the Copenhagen case. Deeper analysis of Copenhagen's resilience plans can be found in Appendix A.

Copenhagen resilience challenge: transformation on the edge of the Baltic

Copenhagen is known today as an economic powerhouse with attractive neighborhoods and new towers gleaming on the waterfront next to some of the best restaurants in the world. These amenities sit next to the old harbor that, because of investments in its sewer system, is now swimmable with floating pools dotting the inner-city core (O'Sullivan 2016). Residents head down to the waterfront on their bikes and jump into the cold blue waters and return home along streets edged by cycle tracks. This Copenhagen, however, was not the Copenhagen of just a few decades ago when the harbor area was rimmed with failing industries, plans for large-scale highways proliferated, the water quality was poor, and the streets were filled with auto exhaust. In other words, as Mikael Colville-Andersen (2018, p. 64) points out, "Copenhagen wasn't always Copenhagen." Copenhagen has rather been transformed into a greener, more thriving version of itself through conscious policy experimentation and long-term push for change. The transformation of Copenhagen tells a story of what cities can be if they aim high and provides an important foundation to understand the challenges and potential that will be needed to transform cities towards greater resilience.

Copenhagen sits on the edge of the Baltic Sea and has traditionally been a crossroads for trade and industry. During the 1970s, however, the city's old port and industrial sectors on the waterfront began to decline. This left the city, like many other older port and industrial towns, in a difficult economic situation. The city created an innovative model of revitalization focused around repurposing older industrial land into new housing and business clusters and then using proceeds from the sales to fund investment in a new metro system to link the city together.

The city's transformation over the last quarter-century from, as Katz and Noring (2017) argue, "an ailing manufacturing city to one of the wealthiest cities in the world" provides an important case study showing how innovative city management focused on "strategic zoning, land transfers, and revenue-generating mechanisms" (p. 4) can push a city forward to deep change.

While this chapter focuses on Copenhagen's resilience planning, it is important to situate the city in the broader economic transformation context, particularly in terms of funding for resilience projects. In the same way that the fairly wealthy, livable Copenhagen of today was created through transformation, the Copenhagen of enhanced resilience, transit, and bicycles was not the Copenhagen of the 1970s. The street spaces of Copenhagen in the 1970s were often stark and bare and focused on moving as many vehicles as possible with public spaces filled with cars.

Vestiges of that unadorned Copenhagen still exist in many of the streetscapes of the city. For a city known for its sustainability and green orientation, one of the surprising aspects of the current Copenhagen cityscape is the lack of trees and greenery in the street right of way. Outside of the small urban core, many of the main arterial streets were made wide for the automobile in the 1950s and 1960s and often lack trees. Most of these streets have now been retrofitted with raised cycle tracks and act as functional movement corridors (more on this story later in the chapter), but they still often lack urban trees. While the streetscapes can be slightly gray, parks and connected green spaces are spread throughout the city because of the Finger Plan that focuses development around a set of green wedges that extend around the "fingers" of development of the city using green infrastructure to steer development (Beatley 2012, p. 13). Instead of a single green belt, the green fingers provide corridors interspersed throughout the city that provide access to green space throughout the city (Ministry of the Environment, Denmark 2015). While this 1948 plan focused on maintaining green space, it also focused on developing a radial road network that was supposed to be augmented with large highway developments throughout the city. While many of the larger highway developments were pushed back through concerted activism (Cathcart-Keays 2016a), many of the larger radial roadways still remain. This combination of lush green in the connected parks and a harsher street environment provides both the foundation for Copenhagen's reputation as a green city and an opportunity to enhance resilience through the addition of green streets that extend the park setting into the heart of the city.

Copenhagen is a city that has repositioned itself as an economic and resilience leader by turning disused industrial space into public places, linking the city with a metro system, adding a comprehensive protected bicycle network, all while transforming lost spaces into valued amenity places (Trancik 1986). This process is ongoing and is moving from public spaces into the heart of the city's streets. We tell one slice of the story of the Copenhagen transformation story through a set of resilience-planning cases below.

The rise of resilience planning in Copenhagen: negotiating the adaptation/mitigation divide

In the summer of 2011, Copenhagen had already begun to seriously consider the impact of climate change and was beginning to focus on how to make the city more resilient to a changing environment. The city was finalizing the Copenhagen Adaptation Plan and beginning to establish key priorities for adapting the city to climate change. On July 2, 2011, the city was hit with a massive storm, a cloudburst that dumped about 6 inches (15 cm) of rain on to the city in about 2 hours. City streets and basements were inundated, and the resulting damages, as we have discussed, were calculated to reach about $800 million (City of Copenhagen 2012). Like after many disasters, the event caused a rethinking of the city's relationship to the environment, in this case its relationship to water.

Unlike in many cities, however, the disaster led to more than just a surface-level reassessment of environmental conditions. In Copenhagen, the flooding proved to be a catalytic event that has led to a deep commitment to action, particularly in terms of adapting the city to flooding. The flooding was one key element that helped to spur project commitments in the 2012 Cloudburst Management Plan and put greater emphasis on climate change more broadly in the Copenhagen 2025 Climate Plan, which includes the goal of being the first carbon-neutral capital city by 2025. The goals of these plans include both adapting the city to a changing climate and mitigating GHG emissions. These dual goals operate at different governmental levels and through different pots of money and bureaucracies. Marrying the two climate policy goals of adaptation and mitigation has proven to be a complex challenge in Copenhagen.

Landauer et al. (2018) provide an in-depth analysis of the Copenhagen Adaptation Plan and the 2025 Climate Plan in a broader comparative analysis of resilience planning in Copenhagen and Helsinki. The authors center their analysis on the difficulty of incorporating both adaptation and mitigation measures in resilience planning at the local level. In Copenhagen they focus on examining policy efforts towards water management and energy efficiency of buildings. They find that, while the goals of adaptation and mitigation could be synergistic, they are often not woven together at the local policy level.

The reason for the disconnect identified by Landauer et al. (2018, p. 2) is differences in policy objectives in bureaucratic silos and because of perceived "competing uses of physical space" to accomplish mitigation and adaptation policy objectives. To accomplish resilience goals, multiple governmental agencies must work together across traditional boundaries and often in the same physical spaces. For example, the utility company, water agency, and transportation department may be working in the same area on projects designed to emphasize differing aspects of climate adaptation and mitigation. These agencies often come into conflict as they seek to carry out the narrower objective and can often miss synergistic opportunities because of the traditional bureaucratic structures, goals, or simple lack of communication. Landauer et al. (2018, pp. 19 and 20) conclude that, "Overall, urban policy-making and planning processes need to better account for the inter-relationships between adaptation and mitigation," particularly in "dealing with 'non-climate' policies, such as urban mobility policy, to share responsibility and increase collaboration."

We provide more comprehensive analysis of resilience plans in Copenhagen in Appendix A, but the tensions between mitigation and adaptation are significant barriers towards implementing integrated resilience policy at the local level. We delve deeper into the interaction of urban mobility, public space, and water management in the section below. Despite the tensions, we find that project-level work in Copenhagen in the area of streets and public spaces is beginning to create more synergistic solutions and suggest that one of the reasons for this is the preexisting relationship already established in the area of sustainable mobility. In Copenhagen, sustainable mobility has been seen as a significant municipal goal for many years and climate adaptation is now being "layered" on top of the preexisting bureaucratic structures. The result is much more integrated resilience planning that, despite the tensions, aims to create synergistic projects focused on adaptation and mitigation.

Resilience planning at the project level: from instant *hygge* to living with water

In Chapter 3, we introduced Copenhagen's first major effort to address cloudbursts, Tåsinge Plads. This project transformed a wide asphalt lost space into a green oasis in the city designed to better manage water, add a community amenity, and make the city neighborhood more livable. In this section, we examine the elements of this project and show how the tensions between adaptation and mitigation have been negotiated at the project level.

In 2012, Tåsinge Plads was a small square surrounded by a large asphalt parking area in a fairly non-descript neighborhood on the edge of the Østerbro area of Copenhagen. The blocks around Tåsinge Plads were filled with parked cars and known to flood during heavy rain events. At the same time, the city was attempting to reinvest in areas to help spur revitalization. Both of these aims came together in the Tåsinge Plads water square project where the dual aims of improved water management and revitalization came together in a multi-year planning effort for the area.

Former City Project Manager for Tåsinge Plads revitalization effort, René Sommer Lindsay, describes the project as building on a strong citizen participation model where local residents were engaged in the goal of improving the water storage capacity of the square and enhancing the quality of life for residents. Multiple meetings were held both in traditional sites and actually in the small existing square. These events included an "instant *hygge*" cultural project designed to engage residents in a coffee conversation during a temporary art exhibit focused in the square. The *hygge* concept broadly means cozy or fun, but has a much deeper meaning for the Danish in terms of connection to place and community. Whatever the term, the idea of connecting the project to the heart of local culture is a key aspect of building more engagement.

In terms of water management, the central driving challenge behind the project was the need to address the 30% more rain expected because of climate change and the rise of cloudburst events. The planning process focused on repurposing some of the asphalt and building a set of water catchment features that would allow infiltration, water storage, and more traditional stormwater drainage. In many ways, this was a spatial challenge of figuring out where to put the extra water in a dense urban neighborhood. This matches Landauer et al.'s (2018) conception of competing uses of physical space discussed above. The goal of both the technical and communication strategy was to focus attention on this spatial policy question of what to do with the 30% more rainfall expected because of climate change.

The project team chose a planning framework for articulating the pressing needs and goals of the project, the 10–10–10 concept. In this framing, the project's goal was to identify where the 30% excess water would physically go in the neighborhood. In the 10–10–10 framing, the goal was that 10% of the increasing volume of rainwater would be infiltrated into new green space, 10% would be stored within bioswales and water storage tanks at the new water square, and 10% would use the traditional stormwater drainage system. These figures are rough estimates from a technical perspective, but proved to be a good framing device for the aims of the project and the need to communicate the spatial demands of water to area residents. Overall, the completed project can prevent 7,000 m^2 (7,655 square yards) of rainwater from entering the sewer system (City of Copenhagen 2015).

Former City Project Manager Lindsay argues that resilience planning needs to focus not just on the technical components of planning from an engineering perspective, but also on communicating those technical dimensions of projects to the broader community to generate support and ownership of the project. He says that his "interest in citizen participation and storytelling" led him to use the 10–10–10 concept to help create "a shared goal of things that are possible…Visions need to be communicable…and then you put the 10–10–10 and that meant that you have some visions that are easy to understand and easier to collaborate" (Lindsay 2018).

One of the easy-to-understand, but challenging elements of the project was that accommodating more water or encouraging more cyclists in the area would put pressure on one of the dominant land uses in the area, car parking. At the beginning of the planning process, residents expressed a desire to increase parking spaces through the new design. Lindsay says that,

> At the beginning people wanted more street trees… and more parking… Basically people out there liked it quiet and with a few more trees and more parking. We wanted to push the agenda [for decreasing parking] but we couldn't do it without their approval.
>
> *(Lindsay 2018)*

In this particular project, one of the key constraints in the planning process was that the same number of parking spaces needed to be maintained. This was an unusual constraint for central Copenhagen where active transportation projects often supplanted street parking, but a set of particular rules in this area prevented decreasing the number of parking spaces. Through repurposing the large roadway space, Lindsay and his team were able to create a design that maintained the same number of parking spaces for the area and accommodated the expansion of Tåsinge Plads as a water square and green space.

The parking constraint does, however, help to show what is possible even in a dense area with parking demands. Much of the space used for the new park really was "extra" street space, simply paved edges of streets and roads that could be reclaimed without impacting traffic flows or parking. The project did, however, focus on managing car speed through narrowing lanes. This proved popular with area residents. Lindsay argued that, "We also concluded that almost everyone in the area wouldn't mind if they went 20mph. They don't mind if they drive slow" (Lindsay 2018). By communicating the spatial demands of water management and the potential to slow traffic in the neighborhood, the project planners were able to create a popular project and meet important climate adaptation and mitigation goals.

On the funding side, the Tåsinge Plads project, like other Copenhagen projects, produced a business case showing, as Lindsay says, "how much money a traditional project would cost and then shows how the new project saves money and water" (Lindsay 2018). This emphasis on cost and potential savings of living with water projects provides an important rationale for moving these new resilience projects forward. While there are always difficulties with silo thinking or, as Lindsay describes it, "the bureaucracy of boxes" (Lindsay 2018), Tåsinge Plads provides an excellent example of how projects can work through complex sets of citizen and government demands and still produce a cost-effective, highly livable project. Overall, the Tåsinge Plads project cost about $2.5 million, but prevented much greater sewerage costs in the future.

Resilience planning isn't just a technical exercise at the project level, but requires rethinking the bureaucracy and building a new narrative about city goals within administrative silos. Tåsinge Plads is part of a broader set of projects in the immediate Østerbro area referred to as the Climate Quarter. The Climate Quarter combines a number of street, building, and public space projects together under a single planning umbrella designed to showcase resilience developments in the area. By placing a number of projects together under a single planning name, officials were able to communicate the significance of resilience and help pull multiple streams of funding together. There was separate funding, for example, for climate adaptation from the city and utility company, urban revitalization funding from the city, and climate mitigation funding dedicated to rehabilitating buildings. Lindsay maintains that the Climate Quarter moniker helped to link these projects and leverage additional resources and attention that might have been missing without the climate district framing. He argues, "The Climate Quarter was just a website, but it became a story…about pulling these pots of money to work together to support each other." More broadly, Lindsay points out that "[h]aving the concept of the Climate Quarter was really helpful because all of the people who were managing the money had a common story…about how all of these things were connected" (Lindsay 2018).

The Tåsinge Plads and the broader Climate Quarter have acted as pilot projects designed to provide a proof of concept for funding and other technical components as well as providing a clear image for residents of what living with water could look like. Morten Kabell, the former CEO of Copenhagenize Design Company and current co-CEO of the European Cyclists' Federation, argues that Tåsinge Plads has become

> a prototype of how Copenhagen will change over the next 18 to 20 years… As part of these projects there's planning [for] a lot more greenery in streets and squares on roads to make sure that water can be soaked up and can be used on the surface creating a better urban life… Tåsinge Square was a prototype and was a way to see how this can this be done with local engagement with local involvement, but as one of more than 300 projects that Copenhagen has tasked itself to carry out over the next 18 years.
>
> *(Kabell 2018)*

The lessons learned from Tåsinge Plads and the Climate Quarter help to show how adaptation and mitigation can be integrated to create more synergistic solutions to address some of the challenges identified by Landauer et al. (2018). Specifically, the Tåsinge Plads case shows how communication strategies and pilot initiatives can be used to build both institutional and community project momentum. This momentum allows for greater community buy-in for project goals and helps to build dialogue across agencies that can increase the likelihood for project success. The work is still complex and difficult, but the lessons of the case appear to indicate that, at least in Copenhagen, complex resilience goals can be woven together.

In addition, the project shows how tensions over spatial demands on urban transportation projects can be addressed. In this case, there were significant tensions over how to maintain on-street parking and how to manage wide neighborhood streets. The project shows how these spatial tensions can be addressed through repurposing existing street space in creative ways that generate space for adaptation water squares like Tåsinge Plads and, importantly, allow for traffic calming that helps to increase safety and accessibility for active transportation to act as an important element of climate mitigation.

In the following section, we examine specifically how street spaces have changed over the last 50 years to create a multi-modal system in Copenhagen and how these changes are increasingly linked to the broader resilience-planning agenda. We'll include an examination of another project in Climate Quarter, the St. Kjelds traffic circle redesign, that further shows how adaptation and mitigation are being brought together in Copenhagen streets.

Copenhagen: a world leader in active transportation

Copenhagen is today known as one of the premier bicycle cities in the world with 62% of all trips to work or school within the inner city by bicycle (Henderson and Gulsrud 2019, p. 6). This version of Copenhagen, however, only exists because of push by local residents and a commitment to innovation and practical change by the city (O'Sullivan 2016). In the early 1960s, Copenhagen was rushing towards modernity by trying to add space for car lanes and parking. While the city continued to expand roads and was still a long way from creating the intricate public space and protected bicycle system of today, a key turning point in the push back against the car took place in the center of the city with the pedestrianization of Strøget. In 1962, the city pushed through a pedestrian plan that limited car traffic for 1.1 km (0.7 miles) on the street through the heart of the city. Despite repeated protestations by the business community that the plan would ruin economic development, the plan actually helped add life, energy, and commerce back to the heart of the city. Pedestrian traffic grew by 35% just in the first year after the conversion (Gehl and Svarre 2013, p. 151) and the street is still today a showcase of pedestrian vitality.

There is often a latent demand for active transportation that public space conversions tap into. In Copenhagen, systematic studies of public spaces led by Jan Gehl have repeatedly shown the positive impact of these types of public space transformations. In fact, within the urban design world, "Copenhagenize" is a term that

> is often used to describe the results developed from systematic data-driven urban improvements. To "Copenhagenize" has become the description of a process as well as a term to describe a particular way of thinking and planning with regard to people and life in the city.
>
> *(Gehl and Svarre, p. 157)*

This process takes public life seriously and tracks the use of public space by people walking and biking to determine how to improve the experience of place to push for wider change across the city.

During the 1980s and 1990s, Copenhagen began to take this model of data-driven public life seriously and push back on the car in significant ways, each step establishing a momentum for the next step. The city began to limit parking in the center through a 2–3% decrease per year in parking spaces, replacing parking with walking and bicycling facilities. The changes each year were small, but the cumulative impact has been large. Repeated studies of public life in Copenhagen have shown "a direct connection between the number of car-free square meters and the extent of staying activities in the city" (Gehl and Svarre 2013, p. 129), where people spend time in the public spaces of the city. In this way, reductions in car parking and overall road space for cars are matched by an increase in city amenities that make the city more livable.

FIGURE 6.1 An interlude: skateboarding and streets as places of movement and culture.

Balancing the movement and place functions of streets often involves negotiating tensions about access to place, particularly for groups that have traditionally been excluded from using city space. In many cities, the function of streets and public spaces is being reinterpreted/challenged by skateboarders who seek to reenvision the cityscape as places of self-expression. Skateboarding and other micro-mobility modes are an increasing presence on streets for transportation (Fang and Handy 2019) and also for the sheer fun of exploring the city's built environment. On a recent trip to Copenhagen, I was able to sit down with James Thoem of Copenhagenize Design Company who by day works to improve streets for active transportation and in his spare time skates the city's streets. Skaters, he says, seek to stretch the use of streets and use it for a purpose it was "not engineered for. [Skaters] appreciate these spaces in way that others might not...[They] appreciate it in a way that is beyond car flow." This sense of exploring the streets as "architectural spaces for performing" speaks to new ways of understanding streets as spaces of movement and places of culture and freedom. When the demands of the movement function of cars are lessened, the freedom function of streets can begin to be brought forward. For Thoem, the idea of climate adaptation can also be used to help provide new spots that can be skated when it is dry and used for water when it rains. This vision requires rethinking green infrastructure and stretching it in places to accommodate the urban street culture of skating by inserting some paved locations into the climate adaptation design vocabulary. Resilient streets and public spaces should accommodate different uses and users. The skaters of

Copenhagen speak to the potential to create places where unique cultures of freedom can be expressed and performed. We'll revisit this idea again in the New Orleans chapter where the brass bands of the city challenge the pure movement function of streets (Chapter 8).

While on-street parking continues to be a significant issue in Copenhagen in many neighborhoods, most of the larger surface-level parking in the city center has been removed. For example, Israel Plads, a major central square adjacent to the Nørreport Station, was fully transformed from a surface-level parking lot into a community amenity in 2014. Surface parking was pushed below ground, providing space in the center for the Torvehallerne Market on one side and a park, skating spot, and water features on the other side of the square. This transformation provides a template for reconnecting the city and shows how multiple groups of residents including skaters can help to enliven city spaces (Figure 6.1).

The pedestrianization of Strøget, reductions in city center parking, and public space revitalization projects would, on their own, be noteworthy, but the dramatic transformation of street space to accommodate safe cycling and decrease car use makes the Copenhagen story central to urban resilience planners. Copenhagen, as we have argued, was a city in the 1960s and 1970s with high levels of car use and, sadly, high levels of fatalities. The fatality rate in the transportation sector was, for example, higher in Denmark in the 1970s than the United States (Evans 2014).

Denmark and Copenhagen in particular, however, chose a radically different path from the United States in terms of transportation safety. Rather than continuing to enhance speed in urban areas, the Danes began to move towards road design reforms and speed management and have achieved significant safety improvements. Evans (2014, p. 1506) notes that if the United States could match the reductions achieved in countries like Denmark "20,000 fewer Americans would be killed annually and almost a million injuries prevented."

One specific area where these safety improvements can be seen is in the area of active transportation. Investments in active transportation infrastructure in Copenhagen have significantly increased the number of cyclists, decreased the number of fatalities and serious injuries, and improved public health. Copenhagen invested 2 billion kroners ($317 million) in active transportation infrastructure from 2006 to 2016 (Colville-Andersen 2018, p. 165). The result of this and prior investments has been a large increase in cycle use and a decrease in injuries and fatalities (Table 6.1). From 1995 to 2018, for example, the number of kilometers of cycle tracks increased from 293 to 382 (30% increase). Cycle tracks represent the core of the bicycle infrastructure system in Copenhagen and account for 59% of bicycle infrastructure tracked by the Bicycle Account. The cycle track system is augmented with green cycle routes and bike superhighways (36% of the system). Bike lanes, on the other hand, only account for about 5% of the total bicycle infrastructure system.

The result of creating a protected system of bicycle infrastructure is increasing usage and safety. Reported bicycle use for work and school trips in the larger

TABLE 6.1 Copenhagen (CPH) bicycle transportation data

Key Copenhagen bicycle statistics	*1995*	*2000*	*2004*	*2010*	*2016*	*2018*
Bike lane length	Not reported	10 km (6.2 miles)	14 km (8.7 miles)	23 km (14.3 miles)	33 km (20.5 miles)	33 km (20.5 miles)
Cycle track length	293 km (182.1 miles)	307 km (190.8 miles)	329 km (204.4 miles)	359 km (223.1 miles)	375 km (233.1 miles)	382 km (237.4 miles)
Green cycle routes	41 km (25.5 miles)	43 km (26.7 miles)	37 km (23.0 miles)	42 km (26.1 miles)	61 km (37.9 miles)	63 km (39.1 miles)
Bike superhighways	Not reported	Not reported	Not reported	Not reported	52 km (32.3 miles)	167 km (103.8 miles)
Percent CPH residents biking to work/school	31% (to work)	34% (to work)	36% (to work)	35%	41%	49%
Percent CPH residents reporting feeling safe bicycling	51%	57%	58%	67%	76%	77%
Bicycle serious injuries	231	168	124	91	94	81 (2017)

Copenhagen area has increased from 31% in 1995 to 49% in 2018. While cyclist numbers have increased significantly, the risk of a cycling fatality has decreased by 23% during the last decade (City of Copenhagen 2017a, p. 10). Serious injuries have also decreased from 231 in 1995 to 81 in 2017 (65% decrease). This is matched by perceptions of safety by Copenhagen bicyclists. In 1995, 51% of Copenhageners reported feeling safe on a bicycle. By 2018, that figure had increased to 77%. At the same time, the result of these investments was improved health outcomes for residents with public health benefits estimated to be $270 million per year (Colville-Andersen 2018, p. 167).

The City of Copenhagen includes these types of public health community benefits along with travel time and emission calculations in assessing the overall cost and benefits of investments in bicycle versus auto infrastructure. Gossling and Choi (2015, p. 112) note that analysis of the cost–benefit analysis (CBA) findings broadly shows that that "the cost of a km driven by car is more than six times higher than the cost of a km cycled" (at €.50 per kilometer driven) despite using "imperfect and conservative" estimates in the analysis framework. From a policy perspective, Gossling and Choi (2015, p. 111) further note that Copenhagen appears to be "the only example of a city where comparative, comprehensive (externality-focused) CBA assessments have been used to guide and implement policy." This model of comparing costs and benefits between different modes appears to be a promising area of policy innovation and may offer important administrative leverage in changing funding priorities.

The bicycle investments in Copenhagen also spread accessibility benefits across multiple age groups in the community. The result of a much safer system has been that vulnerable road users such as children and older residents feel safe to use the system. For example, the active transportation mode share of trips to school in 2016 was 70% in Copenhagen (City of Copenhagen 2017a, p. 11). To contrast the success in Copenhagen, the percentage of kids walking and biking to school in the United States is less than 15% (Safe Routes to School National Partnership 2011). When you see kids moving freely in a city, you know that car traffic has been significantly tamed and speeds are slow. Parents feel that the city is safe and kids are free to explore. Active transportation use by vulnerable populations should be a key metric for a successful transportation system and is the type of data-driven public life indicator (Gehl and Svarre 2013) that cities should begin to track.

Copenhagen is building on this type of success in transforming its public spaces for use by a wide swathe of the population and aiming to use active transportation and transit as a central component of its plan to be carbon-neutral by 2025. The goal is to increase this to 50% for all metropolitan commute trips by 2025 (Henderson and Gulsrud 2019, p. 23) to help meet climate mitigation goals and transform Copenhagen into a carbon-neutral city.

While the current share of bicycle commute trips is laudable, there is a divide between central Copenhagen and the outer suburbs that may threaten the ability to meet the transportation goals. In Central Copenhagen, only 30% of residents own a car and only 34% of trips within the city are by car (Henderson and Gulsrud 2019,

p. 6). If you travel to Copenhagen, however, you will notice that the streets are still filled with cars during the day. Despite the comparatively wide cycle tracks and the dense network of pedestrian and transit infrastructure, the bulk of the right of way for streets is still given over to car traffic (Colville-Andersen 2018). Car travel in Copenhagen is literally driven by "suburban cars [that] have swarmed through the city" (Henderson and Gulsrud 2019, p. 7) during the day. You can feel this invasion during the day and watch the city return to a slower, car-light pace at night as the cars return to the suburbs.

Henderson and Gulsrud (2019, p. 5) examine the fight over street space as a central component of the "politics of mobility" in Copenhagen. They examine differing political movements and their policies regarding active transportation in the city. At the core, they argue that the lack of tolling and pricing and fairly inexpensive parking has encouraged cross-city commuting and car use by suburbanites. The coming political battles over the harbor tunnel and expansion of the beltway around Copenhagen will provide a significant test of Copenhagen's ability to meet larger climate mitigation goals. We will return to the question of whether Copenhagen's model is politically sustainable, but, for now, it is useful to situate the successes of Copenhagen within the broader political battles that happen in cities around the world. Negotiating the spatial politics of urban climate change policy in city streets will be a continuing challenge.

Designing success: the physical infrastructure of transportation climate resilience

While Copenhagen is facing political challenges that potentially threaten to temper its active transportation policy success, the basic template for the positive safety and high active transportation mode share is fairly straightforward. Copenhagen's success is the result of building active transportation infrastructure that is comfortable, convenient, and safe. The two most-cited reasons for bicycling by Copenhagen cyclists are that it is the fastest and easiest mode of transportation. The eco-friendliness of cycling is cited by only 7% of Copenhagen cyclists as a reason for using the bicycle (City of Copenhagen 2017b, p. 5). Sustainable transportation success is led by convenience compared to other modes and not by playing to eco-consciousness (Colville-Andersen 2018).

Underlying the convenience of the Copenhagen bicycle transportation system is a high safety record. In many ways, the Danish active transportation system mirrors the Dutch system pretty closely with a focus on traffic-calmed residential streets and fully separated facilities on higher-speed streets (discussed in Chapter 5).

Colville-Andersen (2018) succinctly lays out how the Danish planning system works. He argues that the Danish best practices for active transportation infrastructure are based on four basic road typologies that should be used based on speed and volume of car traffic. This system is not technically complicated. In planning any urban road, a traffic engineer should look at the design speed of a road and the number of vehicles using the roadway. From these two variables, one of four design templates is matched to existing conditions to create a safe system. At lower speeds and traffic volumes (below 30 km/19 mph), cars and bicycles can share the same space if there is traffic calming in place. For slightly higher speeds (around 40 km/25 mph), bike lanes could be used. As speeds and traffic volumes get higher, full separation of bicycles and cars is required. At speeds at 50–60 km (31–37 mph), curb-separated cycle tracks are used. Finally, at the highest speeds (70–130 km/43–80 mph), bicycle facilities should be separated by a median from road traffic.

This template of separation of vulnerable road users from higher-speed cars creates a safer road system because it is focused on the physical limits of vulnerable users rather than the dictates of car flow and speed. Vulnerable road users can only withstand a certain amount of force in a crash and survive. While each individual crash is unique in some aspects, research suggests that vulnerable road users have only a 1 in 10 chance of surviving a crash at speeds at or above 64 km (40 mph). Conversely, vulnerable road users have a 9 in 10 chance of survival at speeds of 32 km (20 mph) or less (Vision Zero Network n.d.). Because crashes at speeds at or above about 50 km result in a significantly higher fatality rate for vulnerable road users, pedestrians and bicyclists need to be separated from cars on roads with these speeds. When you build a system based on separation of vulnerable road users at these thresholds, you create a safer system. When you ignore the limits of human physiology and favor urban space for car speed and flow, the result is a far less safe system for vulnerable road users. It is a policy choice.

In Copenhagen, the policy choice over the last 30 years has focused on safety over speed. The city has built a solid system of traffic-calmed streets augmented with curb-separated cycle tracks and a small component of bike lanes (Colville-Andersen 2018, p. 180). This type of urban road template in place in both Denmark and the Netherlands is among the safest in the world (WHO 2018). Urban speeds are generally slow on roads that are shared with vulnerable road users and, when speeds are higher, vulnerable road users are separated. This approach matches, as the World Health Organization suggests, "best practice" where "[e]ffective speed management is, as such, central to most road safety intervention strategies" (WHO 2018, p. 8).

While in many places in the world best practices of speed management are ignored, the difference in Copenhagen is that they have acted to make building the safe street design standard practice. These designs are not complex and are often straightforwardly functional. The key has been to create a full active transportation system that is direct, convenient, and safe. As Robert Weetman (2018) notes, "What we need to copy from Copenhagen is the decision to put lots of *good enough* and *direct* routes in place fairly quickly."

The Copenhagen model of functional, data-driven bicycle planning is key to building a resilient street network. It has helped to normalize bicycling as a mode of transport and make the low-GHG choice the easy and safe choice. As Morten Kabell points out (Kabell 2018):

> "For us the bicycle is not something special. As I usually say, I'm not a bicyclist. I'm just a Copenhagener who rides his bike every single day of the year...because that is the main mode of transport...It's part of resilience. It's part of making sure that Copenhagen can go carbon neutral in 7 years' time."

A deeper examination of the design characteristics of Copenhagen's bicycle transportation system helps to pinpoint how climate goals are being actively integrated within the base of a resilient transportation system. As we have discussed, there are three central elements of the bicycle transportation system: protected cycle tracks, traffic-calmed residential streets, and the emerging bicycle superhighway and green route system. Examples of the integration of these three elements help to show how this convenient, safe active transportation system works in practice and how green infrastructure elements are being added to help link the climate mitigation and adaptation potential of streets.

Cycle tracks as resilient infrastructure

As we have pointed out, Copenhagen is widely known for its raised cycle track system that separates cyclists from higher-speed traffic and makes for a pleasant, easy, and safe movement experience. Operating on the same level as sidewalks and distinguished by asphalt paving, cycle tracks have been carved into the wide modernist streets that Copenhagen built in the 1950s and 1960s. In large measure, the space for cycle tracks was acquired by removing car parking on the edges of the larger roads. The system is highly efficient at moving people and creates a safe place for bicycle movement. Colville-Andersen (2018, p. 180) describes the raised cycle track system as the "gold standard" of Copenhagen bicycle infrastructure and it forms the backbone for inter-neighborhood trips in the city. The key component to remember here is that space was acquired for this system by "taking" parking and excess capacity from the roadway. This was a conscious and contentious policy choice, but it has been at the core of the success of the Copenhagen system. In many ways, this is what linking safety and spatial efficiency looks like in practice.

This can be observed on Nørrebrogade, one of the leading connector streets into central Copenhagen. The auto road space was narrowed, and cycle tracks were placed on the edges of the road. This has proven to be a spatially efficient and effective way to move large numbers of people into the city center. Nørrebrogade is among the busiest cycle streets in the world, with over 48,400 cyclists using the cycle tracks on an average day. This is almost a 500% increase from 1978 (City of Copenhagen 2017a, p. 5). The gradual conversion of the street to make it more attractive to cyclists, pedestrians, and transit riders has led to increasing numbers of active transportation and transit riders and a decrease in car traffic, and resulted in improvements to safety outcomes. Pedestrian use has increased 60%, bus travel speed on the corridor has increased by 10%, and car traffic has declined by over 60% on this corridor and by 10% in the overall neighborhood (Copenhagenize 2013a). The result is 19,000 fewer car trips moving through the neighborhood

FIGURE 6.2 Bülowsvej bioswale cycle track.

TABLE 6.2 Mode use change central Copenhagen 1970–2016

Mode	*1970*	*2016*
Cars	351,133	252,600
Bikes	100,071	265,700
Total	451,204	518,300

and a 45% decrease in crashes (Copenhagenize 2013b). Importantly, the area still acts as a commuting corridor and a home to local businesses, but it now generates lower GHG emissions, and is safer, quieter and, generally, a more pleasant place. Overall, more people are actually entering the core area of Copenhagen now as compared to the 1970s, but the way they are moving has changed from cars to bicycles (Table 6.2). This type of system moves more people, more quickly and safely, and uses less city space than the auto-centric alternative. This is a template for a low-carbon transportation system.

Copenhagen is also beginning to integrate cycle track with green infrastructure. The new cycle track on Bülowsvej just outside of the city center shows how bioswales, linear paths of green infrastructure, can be integrated with the bicycle system to add micro-green space and a network of mini-sponges to the urban street grid (Figure 6.2). The project is currently only about three blocks long but shows how green infrastructure can be married to cycle tracks to create a transportation system that manages water and GHG emissions, and adds to the livability of local neighborhoods. As we discussed in Chapter 3, a successful resilient transportation should be safe/climate/space-efficient. The cycle tracks of Copenhagen meet all the criteria for a successful resilient transportation system. They move resilience from a concept to a design template.

Residential street resilient design template

While the sidewalk-level cycle tracks are the most obvious infrastructure success story of Copenhagen, the system depends on access from residential streets to provide a continuous active transportation network. The infrastructure on residential streets is more subtle and focuses on slowing car traffic to allow safe mixing of cyclists with cars at speeds below 30 km (19 mph). The example in Figure 6.3 shows a fully traffic-calmed residential street with the full suite of infrastructure treatments designed to slow traffic down to speeds of 20 km (12 mph).

The elements visible in the image are: a cycle track on the very edge of the image on a higher-speed street, a cobbled transition zone, mini-green planters to limit the width of the road, car parking between the planters, sidewalks on either side of the street, a speed hump, signage to indicate a kids' play street, bollards to limit the speed of cars on a turn, another speed hump, and a chicane further down the street that doubles as a kids' play area. This suite of micro-level resilient infrastructure tools makes it clear that this is a slow-speed street and, importantly, uses multiple physical design elements to continue to "remind" the driver that speeds are slow. As we discussed in the previous chapter, these physical reminders are vital to ensuring that drivers continue at slow speeds for the extent of the neighborhood street. These design elements are the bicycle and pedestrian infrastructure of the 20/30-km street and make this type of safe system function. They are also the base

FIGURE 6.3 Skovgaardsgade Copenhagen.

of neighborhood transportation resilience. While many of the residential streets of Copenhagen are not this well traffic-calmed, the city recently passed a Vision Zero ordinance that should help to further institutionalize these types of treatments on a wider set of neighborhood streets. Measuring the extent of these type of high-quality traffic-calmed streets could be a useful addition to the data-driven bicycle planning being pioneered by the Copenhagen Bicycle Account.

One of the best examples of the new slow-speed neighborhood streets can be found in the Climate Quarter at Sankt Kjelds Plads. Sankt Kjelds Plads is about two to three blocks away from Tåsinge Plads and functioned as just another non-descript traffic circle until it was transformed into a traffic-calmed urban forest in 2019. Streets leading away from the traffic circle have had significant green infrastructure added to soak up water and improve the public space for the neighborhood. One of the intersecting streets was closed to car traffic and had cycle tracks added through the now dense green forest section of the traffic circle (Figure 6.4). Overall, the traffic circle now provides excellent access to pedestrians, cyclists, and transit users through the street network, and still allows local car traffic into a slow-speed network of local streets. This type of conversion project opens significant potential for rethinking streets as water management, public space, and active transportation systems. The integration of these systems in a single urban space speaks to the potential of a new way to plan for resilient streets.

FIGURE 6.4 Sankt Kjelds Plads before (May 2017) and after (June 2019).

Green routes to resilient transportation: bicycle highways

The final major component of the Copenhagen active transportation system is a network of bicycle superhighways (*supercylisters*) and green cycle routes (*gronne cykelruter*) that are designed to link the city with a continuous separated network of bicycle facilities that have limited at-grade intersections. Currently, 483 km (300 miles) of bicycle superhighways are planned for the Copenhagen region with secure financing in place for the first 200 km (124 miles) (Colville-Andersen 2018, p. 194).

While the name bicyle highways may make these facilities seem more akin to their congested car cousins, they are in fact mostly wide trails that link through extended park-like corridors. The comparison to car infrastructure can, however, be instructive when it comes to cost and water management. Copenhagenize Design Company (2017) notes that,

> The five new Cycle Super Highways have cost 154 million DKK (€20.7 million), while the same road length for motorist highways would cost 17.71 billion DKK (€2.38 billion). Municipalities expect an increase of 1.5–2 million bicycle users with the new routes running.

These spaces also allow for the inclusion of green infrastructure and extended green space networks throughout the city that can be used to manage water.

A better name might be taken from one of the most complete bicycle superhighway sections in Copenhagen, the Green Route. Copenhagen has almost 64 km (40 miles) of these more natural, park-like green routes, with plans for an additional 48 km (30 miles) in the works (Here and Now CIC 2017). These routes provide a great example, showing how active transportation and water management functions can be tied together. The Nørrebro section weaves through the city along an abandoned rail line that has been converted into a rails-to-trail linear, green park with a wide cycle trail. The 10-km (6.2 mile) section links the Red Square Park in Nørrebro across the city to Copenhagen Unviersity's Frederiksberg campus. Along the section, a wide green space provides a park-like setting for most of the route and acts as a recreational amenity and important pervious water management feature. On a sunny day, movement and place converge, with the park packed with families and cyclists moving slowly but steadily to work or school or the grocery store. The green route becomes the neighborhood green park.

Resilient streets and public spaces: the connection between climate adaptation and mitigation

A new project in Hans Tavsens Park, just off the Green Route, provides probably the most complete example of the linkage between water management and public space/active transportation planning. The project, in the planning stages now with a completion date of 2021, aims to address cloudburst stormwater by using the park space and street space as temporary water storage during intense rain events. Project manager Tine Langsted Krogstrup of the landscape arrchitecture and urban planning firm SLA is helping to lead the project. She notes that the project is a joint endeavor between the City of Copenahgen and the utliity company. The utility company, she says, is focused on climate adaptation to address the projected increase in cloudbust events. The city shares this interest, but is also focused on using water as a community amenity. Langsted Krogstrup argues that this is "where this gets to be more than adaptation" and more about "making city nature" in a way that can be "be sensed and measured" (Krogstrup 2019).

The goal is to use the park and the street as a linked water management system as the terrain-based approach is far cheaper than adding capacity through gray infrastructure systems. The streets leading away from the park, Hans Tavsens Gade and Korsgade, are being planned to take the water and move it towards the lakes below. To accomplish this, the street segments at the bottom of the watershed are being lowered 80 cm (31.5 inches). All of this is being done within a cost-constrained planning framework where green infrastructure components can only be added, as Langsted Krogstrup notes, "as long as it is cheaper than the traditional pipe solution." The full cost estimate for the project is $21.5 million (145 million kroners), with the city portion being $8 million (54 mllion kroners).

To accomplish these tasks, SLA is holding a series of public participation sessions with area residents designed to integrate neighborhood concerns into the larger project goals. Much of the discussion is around communicating the technical project issues to residents and helping them understand both the potential and constraints of the project. To help accomplish this, project team members have taken to discussing water managmenet in terms of water stored in Olympic-sized pools rather than in liters. By showing residents that seven Olympic-sized swimming pools worth of water can be stored in the project, residents can grasp the scope of the water management dimensions of the project more easily. Storytelling, again, becomes a key component of resilience planning.

The project also includes maintaining an existing cycle track linkage from the Green Route through Hans Tavsens Park and into the neighborhood streets of Hans Tavsens Gade and Korsgade (Figure 6.5). The plans for the cycle track involve managing bike speed in congested areas around a school and similar elements that might be used in slower-speed neighborhood streets. Small chicanes, green infrastructure, and other elements are designed to subtly slow bicycle movement in congested corridors. The full system links the Green Route through a newly created water amenity zone and on the larger bicycle network of the city. It is important to understand that the adaptation planning is happening within a mature bicycle system.

The overall project is focused on managing water on top of this preexisting base of active transportation. While the project is funded through climate adaptation planning, Langsted Krogstrup notes that there is "always a lot of focus on bikes in Copenhagen" and the new adaptation elements are being planned to keep "up what's [already] there for the bikes." The bicycle infrastructure is the climate

FIGURE 6.5 Hans Tavsens Park design.

mitigation component of the project, but it is not even seen as the core element of the project. It is rather something that is just expected to be planned for within standard operating procedure in Copenhgen.

The Hans Tavsens Park plan, for example, won the prestigious Nordic Built Cities Challenge Award in 2016, but the project description focuses almost exclusively on the climate adaptation elements of the project (Nordic Innovation 2016). The plan submitted for the competition is a *tour de force* of urban climate adaptation focusing on using green and blue infrastructure to manage, clean, and create a sense of water in the community. While climate adaptation, urban nature, and placemaking components of the plan are called out as central elements, climate mitigation as a design element is not mentioned in the plan. Climate mitigation is, however, a well-established planning component embedded deeper in the plan through the focus on linkages for active transportation and transit. Vulnerable road users are the primary focus of the traffic-planning component of the plan with an emphasis on safety and "good, coherent bicycle and pedestrian connection" (SLA 2016, p. 25). The multi-modal base of Copenhagen's transportation network is just assumed and built right into the whole project without the need for special mention. Climate mitigation isn't called out for special focus in the plan because it is expected and normal and what you would expect from any good Copenhagen project.

This is a key point in understanding resilient street planning and implications for policy transfer. Resilient streets need to be both climate-adapted and climate-mitigated. In Copenhagen, active transportation is an almost unstated part of the base of mainstream project work and, therefore, doesn't need to be called out for special treatment in resilience projects. In non-mature active transportation cities, however, resilience projects often focus on climate adaptation to the exclusion of climate mitgation because they are not part of the scope of resilience projects. Policy transfer of best practices of resilient street typologies from best-practice leaders like Copenhagen needs to focus on planning from the base of active transportation climate mitigation up to the addition of climate adaptation. As best-practice projects like the Hans Tavsens Park project are replicated in other cities, it is vital that the climate mitigation components of resilience projects are not left behind the hardened walls of adaptation-centered resilience.

Implications for policy

As Colville-Andersen (2018, p. 64) argues earlier in the chapter, "Copenhagen wasn't always Copenhagen." Through data-driven planning focused on improving public life (Gehl and Svarre 2013), Copenhagen has rebuilt itself from the edge of financial ruin into a new resilient city. The focused interventions in the city's transportation and public space system have centered on decreasing car speed and space and adding connected and protected walking and bicycling infrastructure. The changes to the transportation system are technically simple, but transformative in terms of climate mitigation, safety, and public life. This base of active transportation and placemaking is at the core of resilience planning efforts to make Copenhagen carbon-neutral by 2025. With a suite of 300 adaptation projects being layered on top of this base, the city has the potential to show how the modern city can be transformed to become a beacon for the emerging resilient city.

The key resilience-planning lesson from Copenhagen is that climate adaptation and mitigation need to be pursued simultaneously to reach these lofty goals. In Copenhagen, active transportation enhanced through community placemaking is the base of a resilient street system and the key to meeting climate mitigation goals. Climate adaptation in the form of managing water in streets and public spaces is built on top of this base and extends the placemaking potential of street and public space projects. In Copenhagen, climate adaptation and mitigation are closely tied to urban placemaking and create a powerful template for city transformation into climate-adapted, mitigated, and livable neighborhoods.

Policy transfer of resilience best practices from Copenhagen should include both the base of the safe active transportation system and the newly adapted green water squares and streets. Policy transfer of the climate adaptation components without the base of active transportation is only half of the resilience equation. Policy transfer of the base of active transportation and placemaking-centered adaptation creates places for people and places of low GHG emissions. These are the types of places that people want to call home and the types of places that people will work towards. Resilience in Copenhagen is not so much about what the city has lost, but more about what it is gaining.

A final, more hidden component of the Copenhagen system is that social housing is expected to be part of the planning process. The social equity of affordable housing is, proverbially, baked into the project through social housing provision. As new green amenities are added to neighborhoods to enhance resilience and housing prices are pushed upwards, much more focus needs to be placed on the continued provision of social housing in cities like Copenhagen and, in cities without a strong structural system of social housing, a targeted approach to expansion of affordable housing needs to become a key resilience-planning focus.

References

Beatley, T. (2012). Introduction: Why Study European Cities? In *Green Cities of Europe* (T. Betley, ed.). Washington, DC: Island Press.

Cathcart-Keays, A. (2016a). Story of Cities# 36: How Copenhagen Rejected 1960s Modernist 'Utopia'. *The Guardian*. May 5.

City of Copenhagen. (2012). Cloudburst Management Plan 2012. Copenhagen: City of Copenhagen, Technical and Environmental Administration.

City of Copenhagen. (2015). Tåsinge Plads: A Green Oasis in the Climate Resilient Neighbourhood. A Place Where Rainwater Sets the Scene for Play and Social Interaction. Copenhagen: City of Copenhagen, Technical and Environmental Administration.

City of Copenhagen. (2017a). Copenhagen—City Of Cyclists Bicycle: The Bicycle Account 2016. Copenhagen: City of Copenhagen, Technical and Environmental Administration Mobility.

City of Copenhagen. (2017b). City of Cyclists: Facts and Figures 2017. Copenhagen: City of Copenhagen, Technical and Environmental Administration.

Colville-Andersen, M. (2018). *Copenhagenize: The Definitive Guide to Global Bicycle Urbanism*. Washington, DC: Island Press.

Copenhagenize. (2013a). Norrerbrogade—A Car-Free(ish) Success. Last accessed 3/24/2020 from www.copenhagenize.com/2013/02/nrrebrogade-car-freeish-success.html.

Copenhagenize. (2013b). Closing Streets to Cars for Good. Last accessed 3/24/2020 from www.copenhagenize.com/2013/03/closing-streets-to-cars-for-good.html.

Copenhagenize Design Company. (2017). Bike Superhighways in Copenhagen Capital Region. Last accessed 3/24/2020 from www.copenhagenize.com/2017/06/bicycle-superhighways-in-copenhagen.html.

Evans, L. (2014). Traffic Fatality Reductions: United States Compared with 25 Other Countries. *American Journal of Public Health, 104*(8), 1501–1507.

Fang, K., & Handy, S. (2019). Skateboarding for Transportation: Exploring the Factors Behind an Unconventional Mode Choice Among University Skateboard Commuters. *Transportation, 46*(1), 263–283.

Gehl, J., & Svarre, B. (2013). *How to Study Public Life*. Washington, DC; Island Press.

Gössling, S., & Choi, A. (2015). Transport Transitions in Copenhagen: Comparing the Cost of Cars and Bicycles. *Ecological Economics,* 113, May, 106–113.

Henderson, J., & Gulsrud, N. M. (2019). *Street Fights in Copenhagen: Bicycle and Car Politics in a Green Mobility City*. London: Routledge.

HERE+NOW CIC. (2017). Active Travel & Greening Case Studies. Prepared on Behalf of the Central Scotland Green Network Trust (CSGNT). April. Last accessed 12/5/2019 from www.thehereandnow.org.uk/green-active-travel-case-studies.

Kabell, Morten. (2018). Interview with author. November 2.

Katz, B., & Noring, L. (2017). The Copenhagen City and Port Development Corporation: A Model for Regenerating Cities. Centennial Scholar Initiative at Brookings.

Krogstrup, Tinne Langsted. (2019). Interview with author. June 21.

Landauer, M., Juhola, S., & Klein, J. (2018). The Role of Scale in Integrating Climate Change Adaptation and Mitigation in Cities. *Journal of Environmental Planning and Management*. Published online April 3.

Lindsay, Renne Sommer. (2018). Interview with author. October 7.

Ministry of the Environment, Denmark. (2015). The Finger Plan: A Strategy for the Development of the Greater Copenhagen Area. Last accessed 3/19/2020 from https://danishbusinessauthority.dk/sites/default/files/fp-eng_31_13052015.pdf.

Nordic Innovation. (2016). The Soul of Norrebro. Last accessed 3/20/2020 from www.nordicinnovation.org/programs/soul-norrebro.

O'Sullivan, F. (2016). Even Copenhagen Makes Mistakes. *NextCity*. February 1. Last accessed 3/20/2020 from https://nextcity.org/features/view/copenhagen-affordable-housing-sustainable-cities-model.

Safe Routes to School National Partnership. (2011). What is Safe Routes to School? Background and Statistics. June 14. Last accessed 3/24/2020 from www.saferoutespartnership.org/sites/default/files/pdf/What-is-SRST-factsheet-REVISED-06–14-11-w-footnotes.pdf.

SLA. (2016). The Soul of Norrebro: Hans Tavsens Park, Blagard School and Korsgade Nordic Built Cities Challenge. Last accessed 3/24/2020 from www.nordicinnovation.org/sites/default/files/inline-images/Soul%20of%20Norrebro_booklet.pdf.

Trancik, R. (1986). *Finding Lost Space: Theories of Urban Design*. John Wiley.

Vision Zero Network. (n.d.) National Speed Fatality Map Highlights Tragic Losses. Last accessed 3/4/2020 from https://visionzeronetwork.org/resources/speed-fatality-map.

Weetman, Robert. (2018). Amsterdam vs. Copenhagen Part 3. Nicer Cities, Livable Places. Last accessed 03/24/2020 from https://robertweetman.wordpress.com/2018/02/15/amsterdam-vs-copenhagen-part-3/.

World Health Organization. (2018). Global Status Report on Road Safety 2018. Last accessed 1/31/2020 from www.who.int/violence_injury_prevention/road_safety_status/2018/en/.

7

LONDON

From regional resilience to healthy streets

Introduction

The birth of contemporary town planning can be traced to London to combat the challenges of the industrial revolution. Ebenezer Howard's Garden Cities, built as railway suburbs in the early 1900s north of London, sought to capture the benefits of nature and city life while eliminating pollution and other detractors of urban slums (Hall 2014). Established in 1899 by Howard, the Town and Country Planning Association is active today with programs to promote sustainable development, climate resilience, green infrastructure, affordable housing, and healthy placemaking–all of which are ideals echoed throughout the book.

Over a century later, London remains an innovator in promoting regional planning efforts to encourage a sustainable future. In 2020, metropolitan London was home to over 9.3 million residents with forecasts to grow to 11 million by 2050. Accommodating significant population growth while addressing ambitious city and national goals to reduce carbon emissions is one of the fundamental challenges of the Greater London Authority (GLA). Central to their strategy is transforming the transportation system managed by Transport for London (TfL).

TfL accounts for the largest share of the GLA's annual budget. In 2019, the TfL budget accounted for 63% (£10.7 billion: $14.5 billion) of GLA's £17 billion ($23 billion) annual budget. TfL is one of the largest multi-modal transportation agencies in the world, managing 9,300 buses and 270 Tube stations across the 402-km (250-mile) London Underground network, the Docklands light rail system, six commuter rail lines known as the London Overground, London Trams, and helps to set the strategic vision for the roadway network across the region. To put the size and scale of TfL into perspective, the agency has 28,000 permanent employees. TfL employs three times more people than the transit agency in Los Angeles even though London and Los Angeles County have similar populations.

The GLA has been a progressive agency engaging in regional planning to promote climate resilience. The recent London Environment Strategy (Mayor of London 2018a) sets forth policies and plans to grow to 11 million residents by 2050 and protect air quality, promote green infrastructure, address climate change mitigation and adaptation, encourage clean energy, handle waste, promote ambient noise, and promote a low-carbon circular economy.

One of the key features of the GLA environment plan is to become a zero-carbon city by the year 2050. This goal is within the framework of achieving the 2015 Paris Agreement to limit average global temperature rise to 1.5°C above pre-industrial levels. To become a zero-carbon city, the Mayor's Transport Strategy (Mayor of London 2018b) targets a goal of 80% of all journeys to be made by foot, cycle, or public transport by the year 2041. To achieve these goals, significant changes to the status quo transportation-planning system need to be implemented. London has begun to move towards taking the first steps in building a new resilient mobility system, but the paradigm shift necessary to achieve the targeted goals must confront bureaucratic inertia in the form of auto-centric street guidance and deep institutional reluctance to broaden transport goals and roles.

This chapter examines how London has been grappling with these issues at the regional and local scales. In relation to the four key adaptation urbanism principles outlined in Chapter 4, the resilience-associated plans of London from 2010 to 2018 made limited steps towards sustainable transport, compact development, green infrastructure inclusion in streets, and improving equity (see Appendix A). More recent plans emerging late in 2018 to the present appear to be beginning to address these issues more systematically. Promising new developments like the application of the Healthy Streets Approach are gaining global attention for envisioning how streets are designed, managed, and used around a holistic set of goals to promote public, community, and environmental health. This includes promoting green infrastructure as a key tool to improve local environments. This is coupled with promising trends in the water management sector that are beginning to promote blue–green approaches to water. While these two trends have not clearly combined yet, there is the potential to link new sustainable transport and water management advances together to create green, safe, healthy streets that are both climate-mitigated and adapted.

The next section outlines the key resilience challenges for London related to transportation and water management. This is followed by a discussion of one of the signature efforts to change London streets, the Mini-Hollands program that was designed to create a Dutch-style bicycle infrastructure system to reduce car dependence in the outer suburbs of the region. The current approaches to address climate change and transport efficiency (the Mayor's Strategy: Mayor of London 2018b) and more holistic efforts to address street design and function efforts to improve public health and walking and bicycling (the Healthy Streets Approach) are examined in the next section. The final section of this chapter discusses how London can "mind the gap" by incorporating more green and blue infrastructure goals into the Healthy Streets Approach towards the adaptation urbanism framework highlighted throughout this book.

London resilience context: London as water city

The Clash's apocalyptic anthem "London Calling" defined the punk/post-punk movement of the late 1970s, and surprisingly also outlined significant concerns about Thames River flooding. Mick Jones from The Clash explained that the song's lyrics were inspired by a London *Evening Standard* headline about a potential catastrophic Thames flooding event. The headline felt like "just another example of how everything was coming undone" (Myers 2013). That feeling of impending catastrophe echoes in the current climate change era.

While the Thames Barrier (opened in 1982) has helped to decrease immediate concerns about flooding, London is still particularly challenged by surface flooding and rising sea levels from climate change. Tidal, river, and surface flooding all threaten London (Greater London Authority 2014). The Environment Agency of the UK keeps an at-risk list of potential problem areas for flooding and has identified as at risk

> the Houses of Parliament, Whitehall, City Hall, Canary Wharf, Westminster Abbey, the Tower of London, Kew Gardens, the O2 Arena, 51 railway stations, 35 Underground stations, eight power stations, more than 1,000 electricity substations, 400 schools, 16 hospitals and over half a million of Greater London's roughly 3.3 million homes—not to mention 1.5 million of its people.
>
> *(Hill 2015)*

While key issues revolve around needed changes to the Thames Barrier and other river flood control measures, the focus of this chapter is on how streets can better be used to control surface flooding and act to decrease greenhouse gas (GHG) emissions which are driving the larger climate crisis. Surface flooding issues, as we have discussed, are exacerbated by impervious surfaces that propel rainwater into often limited sewer systems. As cloudburst events are expected to increase with climate change, impervious surfaces like streets can act to significantly increase risk of flooding.

Researchers in the UK have been at the forefront of reenvisioning how public space can be used to better address flooding and improve local quality of life. The Blue Green Cities Research Project (2013–2016) included nine UK universities led by the University of Nottingham focused on examining how blue–green infrastructure could be better integrated to help improve urban resilience. The project focus was on how the Blue–Green City could "recreate a naturally oriented water cycle while contributing to the amenity of the city by bringing water management and green infrastructure together" (Wright and Thorne 2014). This matches the living-with-water ethos developing in the Netherlands.

The Blue–Green Cities research project was quickly followed by the Urban Flood Resilience (UFR) research project (2016–2020), again with a multi-university partnership. The project was focused on key policies "to make urban flood resilience achievable nationally, by making transformative change possible through adoption of the whole systems approach to urban flood and water management" (Urban Flood Resilience Project Team 2018, p. 5).

O'Donnell et al. (2017) provide a comprehensive overview of the broad aims of the project and emerging research. One of the key aspects of the research was to examine the socio-political-technical elements that can advance or hinder use of blue–green cities concepts like green infrastructure, sustainable urban drainage systems (SuDS), or sponge cities (O'Donnell et al. 2017). In a survey of water professionals, O'Donnell et al. (2017, p. 3) found that 89% of the respondents reported that there was "a reluctance to support novel/new approaches to flood and water management and change practices, typically from traditional hard-engineering grey solutions towards more sustainable Blue–Green strategies." The power of the status quo was the largest reported barrier to blue–green adoption.

Addressing this barrier is challenging because the basic components of the water management bureaucratic state do not easily bend to new, innovative components. Decades of bureaucratic practice and standards stand in the way of change and result in institutional "inertia" (Potter and Vilcan 2020, p. 14) that often limits incorporation of synergistic benefits and broader resilience thinking. One of the most interesting elements of the research project focuses on how to overcome these types of technical, administrative, and public perception hurdles to blue–green projects. O'Donnell et al. (2017, p. 5) point to the Learning and Action Alliance (LAA) as a promising framework to enable "stakeholders to progress from siloed-thinking and knowledge preservation towards an integrated approach that promotes knowledge sharing and inclusivity to deliver urban flood resilience" (O'Donnell et al. 2017, p. 5). The approach focuses on bringing city, professional, and other community stakeholders together "to collaborate and co-produce a city vision for flood and urban water management" (p. 3). LAAs are "a response to increasingly louder calls for integrated solutions to 'wicked problems'; communal problems that cannot be solved by science or traditional top-down governance alone, and are beyond the remit of individual stakeholders or organisations" (O'Donnell et al. 2017, p. 40). While LAAs have been used in the water management sector, the approach appears promising and could be an important platform for adaptation urbanism planning that requires cross-sector collaboration and innovative partnership building across water management and transportation sectors.

Applications of these types of blue–green projects are beginning in London. The GLA (2016) created the London Sustainable Drainage Action Plan. The goals of the plan are to begin to see rainwater "as a valuable resource rather than a waste product" that can be implemented through a "roll back [of] the tide of impermeable surfaces" designed to create "'sustainable drainage' systems that mimic the ways that nature manages rainwater and add to the services provided by our existing drains and sewers" (p. 2). A series of five small pilot projects have been undertaken across the city (Greater London Authority n.d.). One of the projects, the Alma Road project, is centered in a couple of blocks in Enfield with the goal of decreasing flooding and "slowing traffic ensuring increased safety for pedestrians" (Susdrain 2017). While the plan begins to reenvision transport and water management goals of the city, the project contains limited traffic-calming elements and bicycle enhancements. Difficult hurdles of bureaucratic inertia and cross-sector collaboration still need to be addressed, particularly in the realm of street management. Later in the chapter we will discuss the potential of the London Healthy Streets Approach as a potential mechanism to help overcome these hurdles and integrate green infrastructure more directly into street designs.

London streets: from dark asphalt to healthy green

London's complex transportation needs are built on, as singer David Byrne (2009) notes in a travelogue of bicycling conditions, "a maze of smaller" streets, high-street commercial areas, and larger transportation arteries like the City Road and other streets converted to arterial roadways. These streets have been, up until very recently, focused mostly on car transportation. Street environments have been fairly hostile spaces for active transportation.

Over the last decade, significant efforts have been made to increase walking and bicycling in the heart of the British capital. New street templates with significant traffic calming and a pedestrian feel are beginning to develop. Exmouth Market in Islington, for example, has developed over the last 20 years as a slow-speed, pedestrian-scaled street with "a European feel, everyone outside" (Parham 2013, p. 203). More and more London streets are beginning to feel like places to stay rather than simply move through, but, as in other places, concerns about gentrification and housing displacement often follow these amenity-led street projects (Parham 2013). In terms of bicycle adoption, the introduction of the Santander bike share system and the promotion of cycle superhighways, and adjacent quietways of varying quality (Kersley 2019) have been catalysts to change in the city. The result of these programs has been an improvement in the cycling mode share from 1.2% in 2000 (Pucher et al. 2012) to 2.5% in 2018 (Transport for London 2019).

While these figures only show a modest change and do not place London in the forefront of leading world cycling cities, the changes have been considerable, particularly in certain neighborhoods, with bicycle commuters into central London outnumbering car commuters (BBC 2016). While bicycling numbers are on the rise, London has always had a high share of walking and transit trips. For example, when walking (25%), public transport (35.5%), and bicycling (2.5%) are added together, 62.5% of trips in 2018 were from sustainable modes (Transport for London 2019, p. 10).

While these changes have increased active transport use, safety has continued to be a significant problem. People walking and cycling cumulatively accounted for 62% of all fatalities from the transportation sector in 2018 (Transport for London 2019, p. 136). While walking fatalities declined from 73 to 57 in 2018, the walking safety issue is still a key issue for London to address as over half of all transport fatalities were pedestrians. London does, however, appear to be heading in the right direction. In 2018, London had zero child road fatalities and overall fatalities were down 37% over the baseline 2005–2009 period (Transport for London 2019, p. 133). London is also pursuing a Vision Zero strategy with the goal of eliminating transportation fatalities and serious injuries by 2041 (Transport for London 2019, p. 18).

In terms of cycling specifically, London has begun to expand its bicycle infrastructure with the goal of 24% of London residents living within easy access of high-quality cycling infrastructure by 2024. In 2018, the percentage of residents with access to high-quality infrastructure was 11.5% (Transport for London 2019, p. 118). While London has begun to build some excellent new separated facilities, the new bicycle infrastructure often ends abruptly and/or is based on shared-lane designs that place bicyclists with large buses. The current London bicycling system as a whole does not broadly match best practices from the Netherlands or Denmark where vulnerable road users are separated in higher-speed or higher-volume roadways.

In many ways, London has given over the overwhelming majority of the road space to cars even though they account for only 37% of all trips. Pedestrians and transit riders fight for space with bicyclists at the margins of streets while these sustainable modes account for 62.5% of all trips. In fact, calculations by TfL show that separated cycle tracks are five times more efficient at moving people than traditional road lanes (Anderson 2017). Spatial allocation of street space does not match current patterns of transport use in London and helps to contribute to the high share of walking and cycling fatalities. If London can begin to allocate space more efficiently to sustainable modes, the potential for healthy, safe, and sustainable transport is high. This new space can then also be used to address flooding with insertions of green infrastructure that have the synergistic benefits of decreasing urban heat island impacts, enhancing neighborhood amenity values, and slowing traffic to safer speeds.

In response to the coronavirus pandemic, London appears to be reexamining the potential of street space to be repurposed for these broader benefits. TfL unveiled the Streetspace for London program in May of 2020. The program aims to create a large zone in the center of London with limited car access and extended space for pedestrians and an expansion of the cycleway network from 160 km (99 miles) to 190 km (118 miles). London's Mayor Sadiq Khan says, "London's road to recovery cannot be clogged with cars" (Warren 2020).

While these plans appear to be pushing London forward to better integrate sustainable transport, significant barriers have traditionally limited street space conversions, particularly for cycling. Many of the same types of conceptual and institutional barriers that have hindered blue–green infrastructure development have acted to limit best-practice bicycle infrastructure in London. Aldred et al. (2019a), for example, lay out key barriers to cycling uptake in the UK more broadly and London in particular. The authors find that there are four key barriers to improving cycling infrastructure in the UK: political barriers, resource-related barriers, institutional barriers, and wider stakeholder barriers. While leadership and additional resources are important, more subtle political and institutional barriers appear to be particularly problematic. Aldred et al. (2019a, p. 152) argue that the "importance of 'car culture' within the planning and policy field" appears to be a significant barrier. This can be manifest in different ways, but often the underlying rules of how projects are judged for funding are biased towards cars and make investments "difficult to prove for a cycling scheme" (p. 154). This creates an embedded "car-centric paradigm" (p. 154) that limits cycling-funding opportunities. These barriers are further cemented by traffic-engineering standards that rely on traffic flow as the only legitimate metric for evaluating transportation projects. These political, institutional, and funding barriers are amplified by hostile stakeholder views of cycling projects. Aldred et al. (2019a , p. 156) argue that this "complex web of interacting factors appears to be blocking the investment needed to 'get England cycling'." The transportation bureaucratic state is a strong barrier to creating a more resilient transportation system.

Mini-Hollands program

One of the more illustrative cases where these varying factors came into play was the Mini-Hollands program pushed by then-Mayor Boris Johnson. The Mini-Hollands pilot focused on providing £100 million ($136 million) to three outer boroughs (Enfield, Kingston, and Waltham Forest) where only 1% of trips were made by cycling. The vision of this project was to use Dutch best-practice cycling concepts to transform these areas with cycle tracks and "quietways" which would restrict automobile movements along the "high street" (i.e., main commercial corridor) of the suburb.

While the aim of the program was to "to make these boroughs as cycle-friendly as their Dutch equivalents" (Mayor of London n.d.), the program ran into concerted political resistance and initially transformed only a small number of streets in each pilot area. In the borough of Waltham Forest, hundreds of people lined up to protest the street conversion projects when they were proposed in 2015 (Hill 2015). In a separate protest, one of the more theatrical demonstrators carried a "coffin marked 'R.I.P. Walthamstow Village'" which "was carried solemnly through Orford Road" (Davis 2015). While the protestors represented a sizable group of merchants and car owners, 50% of households in the area do not own cars (Landor Links 2019). Equitable distribution of street space is challenging and often contested.

Despite these protests, a series of street changes were implemented that improved walking and cycling conditions in the pilot areas and gradually began to create the base of a larger active transportation system. While not achieving Dutch-level infrastructure standards, the projects significantly improved safety and comfort in the pilot areas. For example, the Waltham Forest Mini-Holland added additional bike parking, conducted cyclist training, and added 22 km (14 miles) of semi-protected or protected routes across the area (Loakes 2018). In addition, a number of green, modal filters were added to streets to prevent what the British call "rat running" or cut-through traffic. While the program aimed to emulate Dutch cycling conditions, the Mini-Hollands program did very little to integrate Dutch water management practices into the streetscape beyond these small green additions.

In terms of the impact of the program on active transportation, Aldred et al. (2019b) examined the impact of new active transport treatments on usage levels in each of the pilot communities. The team surveyed residents immediately adjacent to the treatments and those further away from the infrastructure changes. Those in the "high-dose" areas with multiple infrastructure changes were 24% more likely to have cycled in the last week and were estimated to have increased walking and cycling by 41 minutes per week. Despite these changes, reported car use had not significantly decreased after 1 year of the intervention, but, overall, the authors suggest that "large-scale interventions with ambitious area-based components can lead to uptake in active travel, even over only a year, with the programmes only partly implemented" (p. 158).

In Waltham Forest, the site of the flamboyant protests, Orford Road has been transformed into a comfortable, slow-speed street where families stroll along a vibrant commercial strip (Figure 7.1). We conducted a place analysis of road design and use patterns of the Orford Road area in the summer of 2019 (see Appendix A for more details). The main Orford Road design changes focused on a two-block-long commercial section of the road that was converted to one-way traffic with expanded sidewalks. The street is closed to cars from 10 a.m. to 10 p.m. The treatment area varies a bit in terms of layout, but the main travel lane is approximately 2.3 m (7.5 ft) wide with a 0.6-m (2-ft) brick buffer on each side. The sidewalks are 2 m (6.5 ft) on each side with some café seating and other sidewalk

FIGURE 7.1 Orford Road Mini-Holland.

space added in some areas. There were some flowers and planters installed and a street closure at Eden Road added a new public space (Walthamstow Village Square), but, overall, there were minimal green infrastructure components added to the street. In terms of social use, at 11 a.m. in early July 2019, 15 families with baby carriages moved through the area over a 15-minute period. One bus and several bicyclists moved through the narrow street during this time as well. The new public square was well used, and the street was calm, pleasant, and full of life. Business occupancy is now higher than prior to the treatment (Loakes 2018).

Leading away from the intervention site, Orford Road converted back to a more standard British street design with dark asphalt, two-way travel and no on-street parking (17 ft: 5.2 m). Cars were double-parked along the street and on to the sidewalks. While some quietways bicycle routes came close to the area (the Lea Bridge Road is just blocks away), there was limited traffic calming on most streets with a few traffic humps and the occasional traffic diverter that limited car entry.

Continuing several blocks from Orford Road, Hoe Street has been redeveloped with a four-block-long raised cycle track on each side of the street. The cycle tracks are 5.5 ft (1.7 m) wide with bricked road tables at side streets. The cycle tracks continue along Hoe Street towards Walthamstow Central Station, but abruptly end in small bike lanes. In many ways, this segment represents the current state of the Mini-Hollands: short-length facilities of high quality that end in auto-oriented streets of the past. The question is whether the legacy of the Mini-Hollands program will spur change in these other streets or, instead, result in small bubbles of improved neighborhoods with limited connections.

Overall, the Waltham Forest Mini-Holland had some strong infrastructure elements but was not linked to best-practice infrastructure beyond the small area confines of the projects. While there were limited green infrastructure components in the projects, they were enough to result in a very different feel for the intervention areas compared to adjacent streets. Connecting a series of streets together with these types of treatments could begin to alter transport patterns in the outer boroughs of London and help to transform streets into healthier places. The addition of green infrastructure to these types of treatments could then improve water management and address heat island impacts to create climate-adapted neighborhoods for people. The Mini-Holland project felt like a small, but important, step towards adaptation urbanism design.

Transport for London: the Mayor's Transport Strategy and Healthy Streets

Programs like the Mini-Hollands program are guided by coordination between local boroughs and TfL. TfL is one of the largest and most powerful multi-modal transportation agencies in the world. In most cities across the globe, transportation agencies are fragmented by mode. Streets are governed by engineering and public works agencies, public transport is operated by transit agencies, taxis and transportation network companies are governed by separate agencies. As an extreme example, the San Francisco Bay area has more than 20 different public transit providers serving the nine-county area (MTC 2020). TfL has brought all modes, including the responsibility for streets, taxis, and the London Underground, into a single agency.

This coordinated approach extends to efforts to decrease congestion and pollution in London. In 2003, London became the second major city after Singapore to enact a congestion charging scheme. Rates in 2020 for the congestion charge included £11.50 ($15.62) to drive within the zone in Central London between 7 a.m. and 6 p.m., Monday–Friday. Moreover, if the vehicle does not meet the Ultra-Low Emission Zone standards, higher tolls are applied, which can range up to £100 ($136) for trucks and buses.

Benefits of the toll include reduced traffic, fewer emissions, fuel savings, and increased safety. According to C40 Cities, the congestion charge resulted in a 20% drop in traffic equating to 75,000 fewer vehicles. This has been attributed to reducing congestion by 30%. The study found that most people shifted to public transport and cycling. In addition, traffic fatalities decreased and pollution levels have fallen dramatically with particulate matter (PM10) falling by 15% and CO_2 emissions falling by 16% (C40 Cities, 2011).

Mayor's Transport Strategy

TfL takes policy leadership from the GLA and the Mayor of London. A key focus of the 2018 Mayor's Transport Strategy is to increase the sustainable transport mode share from 62.5% to 80% by 2041. To accomplish this goal, proposals to encourage more spatially efficient modes like transit, walking, and cycling over less spatially efficient modes like private cars have been brought forward. The Mayor's Transport Strategy (Mayor of London 2018b, p. 20) notes, "A shift from car use to these more space-efficient means of travel also provides the only long-term solution to the congestion challenges that threaten London's status as an efficient, well-functioning city." As we have argued throughout, spatial efficiency policies open up the opportunity for applying the principles of adaptation urbanism and incorporating green and blue infrastructure elements into the street design.

The Transport Strategy outlines a plan for creating a good public transport experience and connecting new homes and jobs through smart growth principles. This includes utilizing new rail corridors (known as Crossrail 2) and transit-oriented development to construct 200,000 new homes and 200,000 new jobs. However, the plan notes,

> To reach its full potential and optimise the places it serves, Crossrail 2 will need to be complemented by a network of streets that enable and encourage walking and cycling and deliver a reliable and clean bus and freight network. *(p. 247)*

This integrated view of transport relates to perhaps the most innovative aspect of the strategy, which is a focus on the Healthy Streets Approach.

Healthy Streets Approach

Key to achieving London's zero-emissions climate goal is a strategy to reenvision streets as healthy places. Lucy Saunders, creator of the Healthy Streets Approach, notes that a shift to focus on individual and community health was a way to reframe debates away from mode-specific thinking. The Healthy Streets Approach is a £2.3 billion ($3.12 billion) plan designed to shift the conversation towards a broader focus on improved public health as a key goal of transport policy. Instead of singular modal focus, the goal became improving community health and access to destinations. By placing health and safety as the core goals of the program, London has built an important way to work across policy silos.

The Healthy Streets Approach was first articulated in the 2014 *Improving the Health of Londoners : Transport Action Plan.* This document laid out the connection between health and transport and defined the whole-street approach to transport planning. The whole-street approach attempts to define the broad characteristics of streets that make them attractive and healthy places or, on the contrary, uninviting and unhealthy spaces. Integration of green infrastructure and promotion of SuDS were included as key components of creating these new green places. The goal was to create healthy places, low-carbon places that would encourage active transport and improve air quality in London.

Overall, the Healthy Streets Approach seeks to measure how the street functions, how people feel about the street, and how people use the street. This holistic evaluation of streets moves beyond simple car-based transport metrics and seeks to evaluate streets as key components of healthy places. This is a huge advance in policy metrics, moving from a narrow transport system of measurement to much more complete social and place-based metrics.

Multiple sets of data are measured to evaluate these key street factors. The ten Healthy Streets Indicators are the foundation of the Healthy Streets Approach. The indicators set out the vision for how streets should look and feel if they are healthy, inclusive environments. To deliver this vision it is essential to integrate transportation planning, urban design, placemaking, and land use into a health framework. These indicators are used to annually track the changes in how streets function and how they are used by people at 1,520 randomly selected locations. This same method is used to evaluate specific locations using before-and-after surveys where changes are implemented. In addition, a Healthy Streets Check for Designers is used to assess new designs for engineering projects through a spreadsheet that links street characteristics directly to the ten indicators (Transport for London 2019). This tool incentivizes designers to prioritize the allocation of street space in ways that meet basic human needs, e.g., minimum footpath widths, removing known sources of road danger and incorporating sustainable green infrastructure measures.

Green infrastructure is also expected to become a more central component of the street environment. TfL (2019, pp. 129 and 130) notes that:

> The Mayor aims for London to be a National Park City where more than half of its area is green, where the natural environment is protected and the network of green infrastructure is managed to benefit all Londoners. Within this context, protecting and enhancing green infrastructure on transport land will help to improve the natural environment and contribute to London's overall resilience to climate change.

The Healthy Streets Approach offers a genuinely innovative way to reframe transportation policy discussions from a purely movement-oriented focus on car throughput to a multi-dimensional analysis of the characteristics of healthy, safe, thriving places. This approach reframes the discussion about street design away from mode silos and technical language inherent in most transportation agencies towards clear indicators and everyday accessible language designed to engage a wider range of stakeholders. The Healthy Streets Approach is intended to look beyond the siloed approach of most transport agencies towards streets designed for the health of the community.

This approach puts healthy streets first as the goal rather than advancing a specific mode like car travel or even the bicycle, as was the public framing of the Mini-Hollands program. Balderson (2019, p. 17) notes that the

> Mini-Hollands put the emphasis on cycling but the focus now is on the more holistic Healthy Streets approach. Pedestrians and buses are a vital part of the picture and this has to be reflected in everything we do, from public communications to scheme design.

The Healthy Streets Approach reframes community planning conversations around how to create streets that promote health, while at the same time promoting streets that foster sustainable transport. This in turn supports and promotes equitable outcomes for all members of the community.

Mind the gap: towards adaptation urbanism

London has made tremendous strides in promoting regional resilience and sustainability. In 2018, the Mayor of London released a new set of plans (see Appendix A for a summary of prior plans leading up to 2018) aimed at significant environmental goals to ensure that London becomes a zero-carbon city by 2050. A central strategy towards this goal is to shift 80% of trips to walking, cycling, and transit by the year 2041. To achieve this goal, TfL is promoting the Healthy Streets Approach outlined above.

However, reviews of planning documents and background analysis revealed some limitations that illustrate an important gap in the adaptation urbanism framework. As outlined in Chapter 4, adaptation urbanism's principles seek to integrate compact development, sustainable transport, blue/green infrastructure, and equity at the street scale. While the Healthy Streets Approach goes a long way towards achieving adaptation urbanism principles, improving water management through the use of green infrastructure in street settings appears to be a difficult hurdle. As we discussed earlier in the chapter, complex rules often govern water management and including green infrastructure in street projects appears to be a complicated challenge. While we found multiple examples of streets in our other case study cities where active transport and green infrastructure were being woven together, we found few examples in London at present. Examples from other cities, especially Copenhagen and Rotterdam, illustrate that the inclusion of water management into streetscapes can both better adapt streets to a changing climate to manage water and urban heat island impacts and slow traffic and encourage active transport to decrease GHG emissions. While the Alma Road project and increasing use of SuDS in Hackney and Southwark appear promising, there do not appear to be a large number of implemented street projects that integrate green infrastructure and traffic calming currently in use across the London region. The vison appears to be emerging, but the projects have not yet bubbled to the surface. Bridging the gap between the current state of practice in London towards fully embracing adaptation urbanism at the street scale is possible. Planning guidance in London is evolving fast and new plans in line with the Healthy Streets Approach could help to change this. The Healthy Streets Approach specifically calls for the inclusion of more green infrastructure and SuDs into streetscapes. This model could be applied across all of London's boroughs to create healthy, green, slow-speed streets, but systematic adoption will require changing underlying administrative cultures in both the water and transport sectors.

References

Aldred, R., Watson, T., Lovelace, R., & Woodcock, J. (2019a). Barriers to Investing in Cycling: Stakeholder Views from England. *Transportation Research Part A: Policy and Practice, 128*, 149–159.

Aldred, R., Croft, J., & Goodman, A. (2019b). Impacts of an Active Travel Intervention with a Cycling Focus in a Suburban Context: One-Year Findings from an Evaluation of London's In-Progress Mini-Hollands Programme. *Transportation Research Part A: Policy and Practice, 123*, 147–169.

Anderson, M. (2017). London's Protected Bike Lanes Move People 5 Times More Efficiently Than Car Lanes. *Streetsblog*. November 29. Last accessed 07/13/2020 from https://usa.streetsblog.org/2017/11/29/londons-protected-bike-lanes-move-people-5-times-more-efficiently-than-car-lanes/.

Balderson, K. (2018). Lessons Learnt From Mini-Holland. In *Enjoy Waltham Forest Walking and Cycling Account 2017/18*. Transport for London. Last accessed 6/21/2020 from www.enjoywalthamforest.co.uk/wp-content/uploads/2019/01/Final-Walking-Cycling-Account-201718.pdf.

BBC. (2016). Cyclists in Central London Set 'to Outnumber Car Drivers'. February 3. Last accessed 6/20/2020 from www.bbc.com/news/uk-england-london-35475318.

Byrne, D. (2009). *Bicycle Diaries*. New York: Viking.

C40 Cities. (2011). London's Congestion Charge Cuts CO_2 Emissions by 16%. November 3. Last accessed 6/7/2020 from www.c40.org/case_studies/londons-congestion-charge-cuts-co2-emissions-by-16.

Davis, B. (2015). Grand Opening of Mini Holland Scheme Dominated by Angry Protestors. *The Guardian East London and West Essex*. September 15. Last accessed 6/19/2020 from www.guardian-series.co.uk/news/13720251.grand-opening-mini-holland-scheme-dominated-angry-protestors/.

Greater London Authority. (n.d.). Lessons Learned from the Five SuDS Projects. Last accessed 6/19/2020 from www.london.gov.uk/what-we-do/environment/climate-change/surface-water/lessons-learned-five-suds-projects.

Greater London Authority. (2014). Flood Risks in London: Summary of Findings. London: GLA. Last accessed 6/17/2020 from www.london.gov.uk/sites/default/files/gla_migrate_files_destination/14–04-07-Flood%20risk%20slide%20pack%20-%20FINAL_0.pdf.

Greater London Authority. (2018). London Sustainable Drainage Action Plan. Last accessed 6/18/2020 from www.london.gov.uk/sites/default/files/lsdap_december_2016.pdf.

Hall, P. (2014). *Cities of Tomorrow: An Intellectual History of Urban Planning and Design Since 1880*. Hoboken, NJ: John Wiley.

Hill, D. (2015a). Beyond the Thames Barrier: How Safe is London from Another Major Flood? *The Guardian*. February 19. Last accessed 6/17/2020 from www.theguardian.com/cities/2015/feb/19/thames-barrier-how-safe-london-major-flood-at-risk.

Hill, D. (2015b). Waltham Forest 'Mini-Holland' Row: Politics, Protests and House Prices. *The Guardian*. Last accessed 6/19/2020 from www.theguardian.com/uk-news/davehillblog/2015/nov/07/waltham-forest-mini-holland-row-politics-protests-and-house-prices.

Kersley, A. (2019). London's Cycling Quietways are a Mess. And They're About to get a Whole Lot Messier. *City Metric*. November 12. Last accessed 6/20/2020 from www.citymetric.com/transport/london-s-cycling-quietways-are-mess-and-they-re-about-get-whole-lot-messier-4848.

Landor Links. (2019). *Livable Neighborhoods 2019*. London: City Monitor.

Loakes, C. (2018). Foreword. In *Enjoy Waltham Forest Walking and Cycling Account 2017/18*. Transport for London. Last accessed 6/21/2020 from www.enjoywalthamforest.co.uk/wp-content/uploads/2019/01/Final-Walking-Cycling-Account-201718.pdf.

Mayor of London. (n.d.). Transforming Cycling in Outer Boroughs: Mini-Hollands Programme. Last accessed 6/20/2020 from www.london.gov.uk/what-we-do/transport/cycling-and-walking/transforming-cycling-outer-boroughs-mini-hollands-programme.

Mayor of London. (2018a). *London Environment Strategy: Executive Summary*. London: Greater London Authority. Last accessed 6/7/2020 from www.london.gov.uk/sites/default/files/les_executive_summary_0.pdf.

Mayor of London. (2018b). *Mayor's Transport Strategy*. London: Greater London Authority. Last accessed 6/7/2020 from www.london.gov.uk/sites/default/files/mayors-transport-strategy-2018.pdf.

Metropolitan Transportation Commission (MTC). (2020). Transit Operators. Last accessed 6/7/2020 from https://mtc.ca.gov/about-mtc/what-mtc/partner-agencies/transit-operators.

Myers, M. (2013). Anatomy of a Song: The Sound of Going to Pieces. *Wall Street Journal*. August 30. D.4.

O'Donnell, E. C., Lamond, J. E., & Thorne, C. R. (2017). Recognising Barriers to Implementation of Blue–Green Infrastructure: A Newcastle Case Study. *Urban Water Journal*, *14*(9), 964–971.

Parham, S. (2013). *Market Place: Food Quarters, Design and Urban Renewal in London*. Newcastle upon Tyne: Cambridge Scholars Publishing.

Potter, K., & Vilcan, T. (2020). Managing Urban Flood Resilience Through the English Planning System: Insights from the 'SuDS-face'. *Philosophical Transactions of the Royal Society A*, *378*(2168), 20190206.

Pucher, J., Lanversin, E., Suzuki, T., & Whitelegg, J. (2012). Cycling in Megacities: London, Paris, New York, and Tokyo. In *City Cycling* (J. Pucher, & R. Buehler, eds.): 319–345. Cambridge, MA: MIT Press.

Susdrain. (2017). Alma Road, Rain Gardens, London. *Case Studies.* Last accessed 6/20/2020 from www.susdrain.org/case-studies/pdfs/alma_road_rain_gardens_london.pdf.

Transport for London. (2014). *Improving the Health of Londoners: Transport Action Plan.* London: Transport for London. Last accessed 1/12/2021 from http://content.tfl.gov.uk/improving-the-health-of-londoners-transport-action-plan.pdf.

Transport for London. (2019). Travel in London Report 12. Last accessed 6/19/2020 from http://content.tfl.gov.uk/travel-in-london-report-12.pdf.

Urban Flood Resilience Project Team. (2018). Mid-Project Progress Report: Achieving Urban Flood Resilience in an Uncertain Future. EPSRC-Funded Research Consortium. Last accessed 6/18/2020 from www.urbanfloodresilience.ac.uk/documents/midproject report-v8.pdf.

Warren, H. (2020). How London Transport is Preparing for Life After Lockdown. *Bloomberg*. June 9. Last accessed 6/19/2020 from www.bloomberg.com/graphics/2020-london-cycling-streetspace/.

Wright, N. G., & Thorne, C. (2014). Delivering and Evaluating Multiple Flood Risk Benefits in Blue–Green Cities. *11th International Conference on Hydroinformatics HIC 2014, New York City, USA*. Last accessed 6/18/2020 from https://academicworks.cuny.edu/cgi/viewcontent.cgi?article=1337&context=cc_conf_hic.

8

NEW ORLEANS

When bouncing back is not enough

Co-authored by Tara Tolford

Introduction

As a delta city (Meyer 2009; Campanella 2010; Fields et al. 2017), New Orleans' history shows the tensions of attempting to control and exploit the rich resources of the Mississippi River, Lake Pontchartrain, and bayous that define the region, all while minimizing the vulnerability of the water landscape. In the words of geographer Peirce Lewis (2003, p. 19), New Orleans is the "impossible but inevitable city" where the access to water is both necessary for its existence and simultaneously a threat to its continued viability.

New Orleans' history of addressing water as both a resource and a hazard (Colten 2005, p. 17) broadly matches approaches of other delta cities to control nature. The early flooding disasters and disease outbreaks of the 18th and 19th centuries were thought to be conquered by the technological developments of the early 20th century. New Orleans built higher levees, pioneered using massive pumps to move water away, buried many of the canals that crisscrossed the city, and used that space to add new roadways to spur population growth in the low-lying areas now open to development. While New Orleans' lakefront parks provided access to water, most of the rest of the city was now hidden from water behind a vast levee and flood wall system. New Orleans was an archetypal "drained city" (Brown et al. 2009), outlined in Chapter 3, where water was buried, and the space taken over by the car to push development to the periphery. As the catastrophe[1] of Hurricane Katrina in 2005 showed, the drained-city model did not fully address environmental vulnerability and, in fact, may have encouraged development in more environmentally tenuous areas (Lewis 2003).

As the limits of the drained-city model became apparent, new resilience-based approaches have begun to emerge that focus on creating more integrated systems of living with water that link green infrastructure systems and larger structural water control systems. The concept is that areas most susceptible to environmental risk can be transformed into green and blue corridors that act to help manage water during flooding events and provide important new amenities to the communities during daily use. This approach, as we have seen in Rotterdam with the Benthemplein Water Square and in Copenhagen with Tåsinge Plads, has focused on targeted use of new green and blue amenities added to communities to enhance resilience and improve quality of life.

While new resilience-based approaches can be integrated to better manage environmental risk, significant equity challenges emerge when green infrastructure projects interface with communities that have high levels of poverty. Adding green infrastructure to a community enhances safety and adds a new community amenity to neighborhoods, both significant elements that can put pressure on housing prices (Fields 2019). This could create the setting for climatological gentrification (Whitehead 2013) where wealthier residents inhabit the safest most amenity-rich locations and lower-income residents are suborned to the lower-lying remnants of developed land.

In New Orleans, climatological gentrification is a preexisting condition. New Orleans' development history shows how lower-income, mostly black residents of the city were pushed into the lowest-lying, least amenity-rich areas (Colten 2002) and, after Katrina, how redevelopment systematically favored richer, whiter areas (Brand and Baxter 2020). Preexisting equity and racial challenges must be addressed for resilience to meaningfully act as a mechanism for bouncing forward rather than acting as an instrument that supports a deeply inequitable status quo (Shaw 2012). Layering climate change on top of the preexisting social vulnerabilities provides a stark challenge to resilience planners and cautionary narrative about the potential limits of resilience rhetoric (Laska 2012).

In this chapter, we address these challenges by analyzing the planning activity that followed Hurricane Katrina in relation to transportation and water management policy. We begin by laying out the broad resilience challenges of New Orleans and place these in context to historic city development. We then trace how resilience concepts were embedded in the planning documents of post-Katrina New Orleans. Finally, we examine transportation and water management policy shifts and specific projects to uncover key tensions in resilience planning. Overall, New Orleans resilience planning has successfully planned a series of innovative pilot projects in park and open spaces throughout the city but has not yet moved towards systematically incorporating these elements within the street spaces of the city. Resilience-planning efforts have also not consistently addressed the deeply inequitable foundations of New Orleans' socio-economic system that continue to lock generations in poverty. Resilience planning is deeply political and can address or perpetuate these circumstances. We conclude by pointing out the need for resilience planners to directly address affordable housing issues as a core resilience concern to help address access to the emerging resilient landscape.

Background: Robert Moses meets the drained city

Technology may be neutral in the abstract, but the application of technology and who benefits and who doesn't have important political implications (Green 2019). In New Orleans, water management and transportation technologies have been implemented in ways that have helped to shape a highly racialized, unequal landscape. Specifically, new water and transportation technologies have allowed New Orleans to grow into more environmentally sensitive areas and cemented racial disparities. Colten (2002), for example, analyzes the extension of sewerage and drainage in the city from 1900 to 1930. He finds that, while drainage and sewerage systems were extended to largely black sections of the city for public health reasons, racialized real estate practices helped to push black populations into the least desirable land areas. Colten (2002) argues that restrictive covenants helped to lock in or, in Colten's language, "fossilized prevailing racial settlement patterns" (p. 251) with the end result being that "low-value land associated with environmental problems [was turned] over to minority populations" (p. 253). It is within this context of racialized environmental risk that the drained city grew.[2]

As engineering technology advanced further into the 20th century, environmental challenges in New Orleans were seemingly conquered: levees were raised, pumping stations built, and the back-swamp areas drained to encourage development as the threat of flooding was decreased (Colten 2005). Existing canals and waterways were shunted into pipes and culverts underground and paved over to create broader streets. Lewis (2003, p. 80) succinctly captures the zeitgeist of 20th-century New Orleans where new highways "convert[ed] swamps into a vast new opportunity for suburbanization." This was the drained city where, as Brown et al. (2009, p. 852) describe, "stormwater was largely viewed as a nuisance" to be moved away as quickly as possible "to facilitate the rapid urban expansion of cities."

While the new drainage and sewerage systems opened potential land for development, transportation infrastructure was added to help provide fast access to these new areas. A key component of the New Orleans transportation system, the Pontchartrain Expressway, sits on top of concealed remnants of the 19th-century New Basin Canal. The expressway buried New Orleans' past and opened a new era of auto-oriented development, filling in more low-lying areas and spreading out into the backswamps at lower development densities.

The Pontchartrain Expressway and the broader expressway template for New Orleans were laid out by Robert Moses on one of his many consulting projects.[3] The 1946 Arterial Plan for New Orleans was commissioned by the State of Louisiana Department of Highways. It created a template of high-speed roads that would encircle the French Quarter and downtown to provide access to the new suburbs in the reclaimed swamps. While some parts of Moses' plan, particularly the French Quarter Expressway section, were fought back by the local preservation community (Baumbach and Borah 1980), a number of other neighborhoods were ripped apart to build high-speed roads to someplace else. This predominantly impacted lower-income, mostly black, residents of New Orleans.

One particular example shows the disregard for existing residents. Moses, in discussing the expansion of a road through Louis Armstrong's old Perdido Street neighborhood argued that "a number of buildings of comparatively little value" needed to be secured to construct the surface-level road that would become Loyola Avenue. This area was the first landscape of jazz where Armstrong and others had developed their craft and helped push New Orleans' most famous cultural export out into the world. The streets of this neighborhood and many other New Orleans neighborhoods were spaces, not just movement, but places where the rich cultural traditions of New Orleans flourished. Through the eyes of Moses, this was a place that needed to be wiped away for the future growth of the Central Business District (Fields 2005). This same planning process took place along Claiborne Avenue where the black business district and its oak-lined avenue were torn apart to construct Interstate 10 through the heart of the city.

While tracking historic development dynamics are complicated and Moses' vision was mediated through development planning throughout the 1950s and early 1960s (Baumbach and Borah 1980), the outcome for New Orleans was not the gleaming new modern city that Moses had envisioned, but rather a city where the population declined from approximately 627,000 residents in 1960 to 483,000 in 2000. This 40-year period saw the growth of intense concentrated poverty and perpetuated a legacy of unequal risk to flooding in a type of slow-motion disaster (Brand and Baxter 2020). In New Orleans, the drained city was created through a deeply inequitable, racialized process.

RHYTHMIC INFRASTRUCTURE

We have argued that truly resilient streets have both movement and place functions. In most cities, the place function of the street is often hidden and abstract, but in New Orleans it is activated and experienced. This is probably most easily seen in terms of its multiple parading traditions (Heard 1997). New Orleans' streets represent a unique form of mediation between movement and culture where place is formed and reformed from street to street through the advancing parade. From second-line parades on Sunday afternoons to Mardi Gras krewes big and small, there is a sense that streets can be places of meaning with shared histories. As Tom Piazza notes (2005, p. 105),

> There is nothing better than standing out there, among friends known and unknown, appreciating the pure thereness and nowness of the moment, which you experienced last year and hope to experience again next year, a thereness and nowness that hovers above the street level of contingency and passing time, and connects you back to a place that is the ground of being itself.

New Orleans challenges us to dig deeper into the meaning of resilient streets and adds a rhythmic infrastructure as a core cultural element of resilience. Freedom to dance and sing and celebrate and remember are central elements of resilient streets. While the parade culture opens the place potential of streets, the strict dictates of the auto-purpose of the street often push up against it. Brass bands and second lines repeatedly fight for street space against police enforcement of the movement function of streets. "Takin' it to the streets," as Regis (1999, p.472) argues, is brass band chant about both struggle and "transformation."

The deeper potential of New Orleans' streets speaks to actualizing the brass band chant. As Wagner (2006, p. 105) argues,

> This idea of the "street as a place" is evident on an everyday basis in New Orleans ...The creole urbanism of New Orleans holds the promise of an alternative, and yet unrealized, modernism that is opposed to the dominant mode of life in the United States.

This unrealized vision begins with unleashing the freedom of streets as places, places of movement, and deep down, streets as a movement of places from neighborhood to neighborhood. When the streets are clogged with cars, the echoes of this form of freedom are hard to hear. When movement and place merge, streets become permitted for a different type of freedom.

The Katrina disaster and the rise of resilience planning

The "inherited geographies" (Lewis 2003, p. 37) of New Orleans' past provide a key vantage point for understanding community resilience. Resilience planning does not operate on a clean slate after a disaster (Fields 2009; Wagner and Frisch 2009). Instead, coastal disasters highlight the weakest spots in water and socio-political systems. In 2005, the storm surge of Hurricane Katrina showed the underlying weaknesses of relying on a purely structural flood defense system and unequal environmental and social risk as the city's flood infrastructure crumbled, resulting in 767 fatalities in Orleans Parish and 1,145 fatalities in the state of Louisiana as a whole (Markwell and Ratard 2014). In addition to the human cost of the flooding, 80% of the structures in New Orleans were damaged by the flooding.

The resulting recovery process was complicated, contentious, and both successful in reviving portions of the economy and highly uneven and inequitable in its impact on the city's large low-income population (Gotham and Greenberg 2014; Brand and Baxter 2020). While some areas of the city have been repopulated and begun to thrive with new businesses, many other areas of the city remain locked in a process of decline. Fifteen years after Katrina, New Orleans population stands at approximately 390,000 residents, about 90,000 fewer than before Katrina and over 230,000 fewer than New Orleans at the height of its population in 1960.

In the immediate aftermath of the storm, a succession of overlapping neighborhood and citywide planning processes were undertaken, designed to demonstrate neighborhood needs, secure recovery funding, and prioritize where those funds would be spent (Nelson et al. 2007). The immediate recovery process was synthesized through the Office of Recovery and Development Administration (ORDA) into a set of targeted projects around the city. Many of these projects were implemented and many languished for lack of dedicated funding, lack of political push, or both.

From a policy perspective, many of the key concepts embedded in these plans were ultimately uploaded into the comprehensive *Plan for the 21st Century: New Orleans 2030*, adopted in 2010 (Goody Clancy 2010) and followed by a complementary new comprehensive zoning ordinance. Like many of the post-Katrina plans, the comprehensive plan and zoning ordinances outlined a vision for a more walkable, livable city, emphasizing compact and mixed-use development patterns in support of retaining the urban character of historic neighborhoods and promoting strategic increases in density in select locations (Fields 2019).

While the full story of the catastrophe and recovery planning is beyond the scope of this chapter, we analyze how resilience became a key and contested framework and, specifically, how water management and transportation were integrated into the recovery agenda. In many ways, the story of the unequal recovery of New Orleans shows both intense individual and collective resilience and the limits of resilience planning in practice.

Resilience in post-disaster planning: bouncing back or bouncing forward?

In post-Katrina New Orleans, resilience emerged as a term, a guiding concept, a meme, and a threat (Kang 2018). In the immediate aftermath of Katrina, New Orleans was a deeply inequitable community scarred by concentrated poverty, the result of generations of racialized political and land use choices. In this setting, a view of resilience that privileged the bouncing-back ethos would privilege reconstructing a highly inequitable social and economic system. Brand and Baxter (2020) capture the underlying tensions of the resilience dialogue and question whether resilience can effectively guide an equitable recovery if it is divorced from the deeper social justice questions of rebuilding. They argue that,

> For many, this future landscape was imagined as resilient, green and sustainable, socially just and equal. Yet policy makers and urban designers who raised questions about how, why, and where resettlement *should* take place in the wake of Katrina often excluded the deeply unequal and settled patterns of a

> racial state, geographies developed, and resisted over different racial formations and political economies of urban development across the city's history.
>
> *(Brand and Baxter 2020, p. 218)*

In the intense moments after a disaster, the seemingly abstract, philosophical questions about the meaning of resilience are tested. The distinctions between bouncing back and bouncing forward (Shaw 2012) are made manifest in the land use and infrastructure decisions that politically determine who is directly allowed to rebuild where and, often more subtly, encouraged to stay. In New Orleans after Hurricane Katrina, one of the strongest tests of the meaning and practice of resilience came in relation to use of green space in city-rebuilding efforts.

In the immediate aftermath of the flooding, one of the seemingly straightforward policy responses proposed to guide recovery was to encourage rebuilding in the higher-ground areas of the city and the creation of green space in lower-lying areas to help limit flooding. This could be an important response to help the community bounce forward to a safer land use pattern, but only if there was an equitable process of engagement to help determine who benefits. As we have already discussed, however, these higher-ground areas were historically afforded to the wealthier (and whiter) population due to an intensely racialized process of infrastructure and land use decision making. The population, then, that would most be impacted by the hazard mitigation policy of abandoning lower-lying areas would be the predominantly lower-income, back-of-town communities that had already suffered through the racialized land use decisions.

These same residents also came to the rebuilding process with a deep awareness that the political process had often been rigged against their interests. The Robert Moses of the world had for generations devalued minority communities and pushed these residents away from amenities to the edges of safety. For resilience planning to be seen as anything other than a land grab, deep, meaningful engagement needed to be undertaken to begin to build the trust necessary to undertake equitable rebuilding. The starting line for post-disaster resilience planning is not the day after the disaster, but instead the decades of lived experience and personal histories that precede it.

Deep, meaningful engagement with impacted populations was not, however, the initial process undertaken in the immediate, chaotic moments after the disaster. With most of the city living in exile, expert-driven, often economically powerful political players were brought together to reenvision the city's future (Nelson et al. 2007; Olshansky et al. 2008; Wagner and Frisch 2009). It is during these initial planning processes[4] that proposals emerged to encourage development of the higher-ground areas of the city and develop a network of connected parks and green spaces in the lowest-lying areas of the city. These so-called "green dots" became flashpoints for a traumatized community as the *Times-Picayune* newspaper published a conceptual map of the proposed locations for these new green areas which lay directly on top of existing communities.

Lamb (2020) provides a detailed account of the planning process that developed the multiple iterations of the green dot maps and examines key resilience policy lessons that flow from the experience. Because of the long history of environmental racism in the city, conceptual proposals to use green infrastructure to help manage flood risk that focused on resettling mostly African-American neighborhoods created intense controversy. Lamb (2020) refers to this type of process as a form of "greenlining" where areas of perceived environmental risk would be turned into park space with the end result being "a radical realignment of the city's population" (pp. 78 and 79).

The story of environmental risk, safety, and hazard mitigation is also more complex than the simplistic green dot maps would suggest. Flood safety in a coastal environment is determined through an interplay of natural wetlands that act to buffer storm surge, structural flood protection systems like levees, internal systems of pumps and drainage combined with green and blue infrastructure systems, and land use decisions that can enhance or diminish risk. These are complex systems that interface with human populations that have varying degrees of resources to cope with environmental risk. A simple green dot on top of some of the lowest-lying areas tells one story of risk, but it is really this complex network of structural and natural systems that interface with human populations that determines who is made safe and who is more exposed to risk.

While the green dot planning narrative is multi-faceted with numerous groups and planning processes impacting the political landscape, the final perception that emerged in impacted neighborhoods was that the green space proposals were indeed efforts to promote greenlining and not to substantively engage with the more complex coastal safety dialogue.[5] This perception and the larger distrust of the process and motives of planning teams effectively scuttled the larger green space adaptation proposals.

The story of the green dots on one level speaks to a lost resilience or design moment (Wagner and Frisch 2009) where New Orleans could have been remade as a safer, more inclusive community. The resilience implications are, however, far deeper. The green dots case speaks to the hard-political complications of resilience practice in deeply inequitable communities. The central challenge of resilience practice in a post-disaster setting is to create a process of engagement with the community (or often communities) in crafting visions and plans designed to help bounce forward in relation to climate adaptation, mitigation, and, probably most importantly for impacted communities, equitable outcomes. The technical infrastructure elements of climate adaptation and mitigation are important and difficult, but the process helps to determine political acceptance and equity results. In this context, resilience planning is a central political process, a "negotiated resilience" (Harris et al. 2018, p. 202), that helps to determine the relative safety of impacted populations. Who is made safe is a political choice and resilience planning is a political process.

Overall, the result of the green dot planning experience is summarized by Lamb (2020, pp. 84 and 85):

> More than a decade after the initial controversy surrounding the green dot map, the episode still looms large in discussions about water management in New Orleans. The swift and overwhelmingly negative response…decisively ended official discussions of large-scale reshuffling of land uses to make way for stormwater-absorbing green space … the green dot map episode [was seen] as having created an atmosphere of suspicion and distrust, against post-Katrina planning generally and against green infrastructure specifically.

Bouncing back: the drained city as the model for Katrina recovery

With this overarching equity background in mind, we shift to a more detailed analysis of water and transportation resilience planning and how they interact with these broader concerns. In post-Katrina New Orleans, the drained city and resilient, water-sensitive city ideologies were both pursued. With the failure of the green dot experience, the first set of water management projects to emerge after Katrina doubled down on the drained city ideology seeking to bounce back to the preexisting approach of focusing solely on structural approaches of enhanced levee defense systems and internal drainage systems.

In the aftermath of the catastrophe, the United States Army Corps of Engineers significantly enhanced levee protection for New Orleans and the broader south-eastern area of Louisiana. The system is now more robust, but still limited in terms of protecting against the largest and most powerful storms that could be projected to hit New Orleans in the future. While the city has fitfully "recovered" from Katrina, the impending climate crisis with rising sea levels and the threat of stronger storms presents an existential threat to New Orleans and southern Louisiana (Frank 2019; Schleifstein 2019).

It is within this complicated context that internal water management within the city of New Orleans should be seen. As we discussed above, New Orleans needs stronger coastal defenses, enhanced wetlands to act as storm surge buffers, and improved water management within this larger, multiple-lines-of-defense system (Lopez 2006). In the urban context, New Orleans has worked to address water issues by investing in massive gray infrastructure projects with bigger pipes and pumps to move water once it falls within the levee system. Larger structural systems are important considering the threat profile of New Orleans but have been seen as the sole mechanism for managing water by many key city agencies.

While the first set of official federal and city projects sought to bounce back to the preexisting water management philosophy, a parallel track of planning sought to bring broader resilience issues to the forefront. One of the most significant planning processes to emerge after Katrina was the Dutch Dialogues started in 2008. The Dutch Dialogues were led by the New Orleans-based planning and landscape architecture firm Waggonner and Ball, in partnership with the American Planning Association and the Royal Netherlands Embassy. Drawing on the experience of the Dutch to live with water, the dialogues brought together local and international experts to promote interdisciplinary communication and a transformative visioning process for a future where water is incorporated into the landscape rather than walled away. The Dutch Dialogue planning efforts were expanded in 2009 with a more in-depth examination of potential locations for pilot projects and more detailed discussions of the living-with-water ethos. In the end, the Dutch Dialogues process produced a wealth of valuable, practical, and visionary proposals for refocusing the city on its water heritage. Instead of proposing shifting existing populations out of lower-lying areas, the plans focused on reusing parks, canals, and street space as key public assets for achieving the vision for a livable, delta city.

The broad visions that emerged from the Dutch Dialogues were greatly expanded in the Greater New Orleans Urban Water Plan (Waggonner and Ball Architects 2013). The plan, completed in 2013, was both visionary and technical, expansive and highly specific, and represented a groundbreaking effort designed to position New Orleans as a national and global leader in resilience and water planning. The plan was awarded the American Planning Association's National Planning Excellence Award for Environmental Planning in 2015, significantly impacted public awareness of and dialogue about water management, wrangled ideological buy-in from recalcitrant partners like the Sewerage and Water Board, and spurred local government interest and internal action. The city government under then-Mayor Mitch Landrieu embraced this vision, establishing the city's Office of Resilience. The interdisciplinary staff of the office were tasked with implementation of policy and projects, resulting in the Resilient New Orleans Strategy in 2015. The Resilience Strategy resulted in a $141 million National Disaster Resilience Competition grant from the US Department of Housing and Urban Development (HUD) in 2016 to build the Gentilly Resilience District (GRD: discussed below), Federal Emergency Management Agency (FEMA) Hazard Mitigation Grant Program awards,[6] and new ordinances establishing stormwater management standards and requirements for new development in 2018. Each of the projects, programs, and ideas in these later documents is firmly rooted in the Urban Water Plan's vision.[7]

Green and resilient and equitable? The Lafitte Greenway

While efforts to adapt New Orleans to changing climate move forward in the water sector, efforts to rethink the transportation system and decrease greenhouse gas (GHG) emissions have also begun to gain traction in the post-Katrina era. In much the same way as in the water sector, initial efforts sought to bounce back to the preexisting system by rebuilding the road network as it was prior to the storm (Fields et al. 2017). As post-Katrina planning processes moved forward, however, there was a considerable push to rethink the purpose and meaning of street and public spaces.

One of the key resilience projects to emerge after Katrina designed to rethink transportation and public space was the Lafitte Greenway. The Lafitte Greenway grew out of citizen efforts to create a more sustainable vision for the city to expand green space into the heart of the city (Fields 2009). As discussed above, adding green space became a contentious issue after Katrina as early efforts to reconsider the city's overall footprint by replacing damaged housing with "green dots" were met with determined resistance.

While greenspacing existing neighborhoods became the proverbial third rail of post-Katrina planning in New Orleans, the Lafitte Greenway project generated a mostly positive reception as the project did not involve repurposing existing housing stock, but instead sought to repurpose existing (and underutilized) open space in the city. In 2005 before Katrina, the Lafitte corridor was an abandoned 3-mile (4.8-km) linear space that was historically home to the Old Basin Canal and a rail network. The canal was filled in in the 1930s and the rail line was decommissioned just before the storm. On the eve of Katrina, the corridor sat empty and forlorn, a lost space (Trancik 1986) in the heart of the city.

Through significant push from local advocates like the Friends of the Lafitte Greenway, Bike Easy, and receptivity among city staff, the Greenway was placed in line for recovery funds during the post-Katrina planning processes and has been developed into a linear green space that links MidCity to the back end of the French Quarter (Fields 2009). The Greenway was also central to rethinking the role of water in the city. As part of the Dutch Dialogues and then the Urban Water Plan, the Greenway area was reimagined as a new living-with-water amenity with the Old Basin Canal being resurrected as a key water asset for the new resilient city (Fields et al. 2015).

As we discussed above, many of the visionary water-planning elements that emerged from post-Katrina New Orleans have been slow to materialize. The broader water elements of the Lafitte Greenway have not been implemented. Currently only smaller-scale water and green infrastructure projects have been implemented adjacent to the Greenway.

The linear corridor has, however, become a key linkage in the bicycle system of the city. The Greenway project is just one of a number of other advances in the bicycle transportation system. Prior to Hurricane Katrina, New Orleans did not have any on-street bicycle facilities and had a small trail network around parks and along the Mississippi River. New Orleans moved from just 3 miles (4.8 km) of bicycle facilities in 2005 to 119 miles (191.5 km) of bicycle facilities in 2017 (Zaccaro and Atherton 2017). New Orleans now consistently ranks among the top ten major US cities for bike mode share over the last decade.[8] These strong numbers are reflected in use along the Lafitte Greenway. The University of New Orleans Transportation Institute has tracked the growth of bicycling at the Greenway location and has found a 27% increase in use from approximately 750 average daily users in 2016 to over 950 in 2019. In terms of place activation, the Greenway transformed a vacant space to a place with over 950 users moving along the linear green spine through the heart of New Orleans.

The Greenway, in fact, has been so successful at signaling revival that multiple new commercial and housing developments now line the corridor. These new trail-oriented developments (TrOD) are designed to use the lure of the park-like setting to spur more compact development that is linked with active transportation options

(Fields 2009). While the TrOD concept is designed to decrease GHG emissions by linking more compact development with active transportation options, the enhanced amenity value (Crompton 2001) of the linear park can put pressure on affordable housing, creating a potential green gentrification cycle.

The gentrification potential of amenity-centered greenways has proven to be an issue in other US cities such as Atlanta with the Beltline Trail (Immergluck and Balan 2018) and Chicago with the 606 Trail (Smith et al. 2016). Rigolon and Németh (2018, p. 71) note that, without a clear focus on affordable housing, large green infrastructure projects like the 606 Trail can result in a process of environmental gentrification where "the influx of wealthy residents to historically disenfranchised neighborhoods due to new green spaces" increases housing cost and potential displacement of existing residents. This process appears to be occurring along the Lafitte Greenway with the new, higher-end housing options pushing housing values upward. While this is a sign of an improving market and, on some levels, a major achievement considering the depths of the Katrina disaster, managing the displacement impact of greenway projects is vital to ensure equitable access to the new, green community.

Post-Katrina planning often failed to directly prepare for the housing affordability impacts of new resilience projects. In an analysis of Lafitte Greenway planning documents, Fields (2019) found that the plans "were virtually silent on housing affordability issues." While coalitions of advocates like the NewCity Partnership and HousingNOLA sought to include affordability issues in the broader recovery agenda, the recovery process broadly operated within a neoliberal sphere where the market was to decide who returned and who benefited from the emerging new resilience projects like the Lafitte Greenway (Gotham and Greenberg 2014). Instead of creating a clear equity strategy for the distribution and impact of resilience projects, the city often facilitated an ad hoc process where political and market demand determined where recovery resources were expended (Fields et al. 2017). As Brand and Baxter (2020, p. 222) argue, the "formerly declining city was reimagined as a city with a resilient future, but this future was promised by a market-based logic that guided public housing reform, public education, environmental resilience, racial integration, and gentrification." This is the template for market-oriented resilience discussed in Chapter 2 (Figure 2.2).

It is in this context that Brand and Baxter (2020, p. 229) critique the Lafitte Greenway project as creating a "compounding dilemma of market-based economic logic rooted in deeply racialized systems of spatial inequality." While this accurately reflects how new, amenity-centered green developments can increase unequal access, the larger narrative does not provide clear policy guidance on equitable inclusion of parks and green spaces in recovery planning.

Another alternative is to position affordable housing as a core component of resilience planning alongside climate adaptation and mitigation. For resilience planning to produce more equitable results in this political setting, planners need to consciously push to connect access to affordable housing into the political discussion to address the very increases in housing cost that the resilience projects are triggering (Rigolon and Németh 2018; Fields 2019; Brand and Baxter 2020; Morris and Diaz 2020). We call this the adaptation urbanism resilience process (Figure 2.3) and argue that it is central to addressing equity issues that can be generated from large green infrastructure projects. Without this step, resilience planning in a neoliberal context will not only not bounce forward, but could act to entrench preexisting equity problems and, in a larger context, generate climatological gentrification (Whitehead 2013) and enhance greenlining (Lamb 2020).

A key policy lesson is that housing affordability needs to be directly linked to resilience planning from the start to help address equity issues that arise from the enhanced amenity value of new park and greenway projects. While some resilience planners may feel, as Rigalon and Balan (2018, p. 76) report from Chicago, that they "are not in the business of housing," large green infrastructure and park projects add community amenities that will impact housing affordability. Resilience planners are in the business of affordable housing, whether they want to be or not.

While silos can prevent coordinated action (Jennings et al. 2019), numerous affordable housing policy tools can be used to address affordable housing issues and should be included directly in the planning for new, green resilience projects (Fields 2019).[9] Park and green space advocacy organizations in New Orleans have recognized this. The Friends of the Lafitte Greenway (2018) released a statement on affordable housing calling for focused attention to "public policies and financial tools that promote housing equity and affordability in the Greenway neighborhoods" to help address "development pressure in neighboring communities" (Friends of the Lafitte Greenway 2018). Providing broad access to the new, amenity-rich "safer spaces" like the Lafitte Greenway area needs to be recognized as a core task of resilience policy.

From green dots to integrated green infrastructure: Gentilly Resilience District

While the Lafitte Greenway helps to show the complex equity issues associated with resilience, it is just one of the post-Katrina projects that have moved forward. The largest resilience project to emerge after Katrina is the GRD. The GRD is the centerpiece of the city's resilience-planning effort, having emerged as a concept from the Urban Water Plan. The GRD, as we discussed above, was one of the national recipients of the US Department of HUD 2014 National Disaster Resilience Competition. The goal of the GRD is to reduce flood risk, slow land subsidence, and encourage neighborhood revitalization through an array of land and water management tools in the streets and public spaces of the Gentilly neighborhood.[10]

The GRD shows the evolution of thought in resilience policy in New Orleans. While initial resilience efforts after Katrina envisioned large-scale abandonment of existing low-lying neighborhoods in favor of added green space, the legacy of the green dot experience has resulted in a much more limited and narrowly targeted use of green infrastructure in newer resilience projects. The post-green dot wave of green infrastructure projects has focused on repurposing existing park, open space, and vacant lots rather than moving towards neighborhood-level resident relocation (Lamb 2020). In the same way that the Lafitte Greenway project was able to gain political purchase by repurposing existing open space, the GRD proposals have sought to reconsider the uses of existing park and open space as key locations for green infrastructure.

The GRD provides another interesting parallel to the green dot experience in that its project area encompasses one of the original proposed green dots in the Gentilly section of the city. Instead of abandonment as a risk reduction strategy, the city has moved towards integrating green infrastructure within existing neighborhoods as a flood control and risk reduction strategy. Lamb (2020) found a similar pattern in green infrastructure planning throughout the city. Lamb (2020, p. 86) quotes a senior city planner as arguing that "[m]any of the places where we are prioritizing these kinds of projects are in areas that were under the green dots. Without displacing people and without all of the negative connotations of the green dots." The GRD is the largest and most high-profile of this new generation of green infrastructure projects in the post-green dot era.

The GRD plan consists of 12 key projects focused on addressing water retention and improved quality of life for the neighborhood with an estimated budget of $141 million. The planned projects target a diverse range and scale of interventions, including corridor projects, scatter-site interventions on individual lots, and strategic insertions of green space in educational campuses and recreational facilities.

The flagship project is the Mirabeau Water Garden, a $20 million project on the 25-acre former site of the Sisters of St. Joseph Provincial House. The site, destroyed during Hurricane Katina, is being redesigned as a combination park and green infrastructure project designed to hold up to 9.5 million gallons of water (Phinney 2019). In terms of context, the Benthemplein Water Square in Rotterdam is designed to hold 450,000 gallons of water during a storm event. The Mirabeau Water Garden is transforming the multi-block open space into more of an urban wetland than a traditional water square. The process is ongoing with the initial phase set to open in the summer of 2021 (Toussaint 2020).

Most of the GRD projects are still in development. The projects are led by multiple teams of consultants and have included varying degrees of public involvement. At its core, the plans and vision underlying the GRD clearly recognize the placemaking potential of public spaces and the amenity value of streetscapes enriched with green infrastructure. What is less clear is how climate adaptation, mitigation, and equity goals will be tied together at the policy level. While the recently passed permeable pavement ordinance that mandates permeable surfaces for parking and sidewalks is a step in the right direction (Adelson 2020), there is no overarching policy vision and implementation template for advancing green infrastructure treatments into street projects more broadly.

Green streets: climate adaptation and mitigation

While parks, open spaces, and vacant properties have been the locus of green infrastructure planning in the post-green dot era, the precise role of street space in climate adaptation and mitigation is still emerging in New Orleans. The St. Anthony Green Streets project helps to show both the innovative nature of the GRD designs in terms of climate adaptation and the limited focus on climate mitigation.

The St. Anthony Green Streets project is a retrofit of ten blocks of residential streets linking three neighborhood parks and playgrounds. The central adaptation focus of the project has been on how to utilize the two parks as water management and recreational resources for the community. The City of New Orleans' submission to the National Disaster Resilience Competition (2015) points out that "[t]he main objectives [of the St. Anthony green streets] are to reduce localized street flooding, control subsidence through infiltration, improve water quality, and add aesthetic value to the neighborhood, thereby improving quality of life for residents" (p. 47). Planning outreach for the project has involved determining what types of recreational facilities to include in the designs and how to maintain the green infrastructure components over time.[11]

While the project is an important step forward in integrating green infrastructure in a neighborhood corridor, the actual design changes planned for the streets themselves are somewhat minimal. The street segment designs are mostly focused on replicating the existing modernist auto and drainage systems. There has not been any major effort to focus on Vision Zero principles in road design or efforts to integrate the planned bioswales to create an integrated traffic-calming system. The green streets in the GRD are currently being planned more as a network of green parks with limited focus on the broader active transportation dimensions of the project. The planning documents for the project only peripherally mention active transportation as a project goal (see Appendix A for deeper plan analysis).[12]

While the St. Anthony Green Street is a good example of a climate adaptation project, it is not planned as part of a larger effort to create an integrated active transportation network that could be used to address GHG emissions. This disconnect is common in projects like this that are seen more as climate adaptation efforts rather than integrated resilience projects that focus on climate mitigation and adaptation simultaneously. Projects like St. Anthony Green Streets could benefit from more integrated planning for green streets found in other examples in the book like Rotterdam (Chapter 5), Copenhagen (Chapter 6), and Vancouver, Amsterdam, Delft, and Utrecht (Chapter 10). These example projects weave both climate adaptation and mitigation goals together to create multi-functional green and blue landscapes that make it safer and easier to walk and bicycle to neighborhood destinations.

New Orleans itself has an emerging template for green streets on Cherokee Street in the Uptown area of the city that could also be a useful model. Cherokee Street was once known to local residents as Lake Cherokee because of its propensity to flood. The City of New Orleans worked with the Sewerage and Water Board to improve drainage and also worked to narrow the road width of the street, add curb bulb-outs at the corners with bioswales, and add a parking lane with pervious gravel over a plastic mesh liner to keep gravel in place. Preliminary results show that flooding has been reduced on the street and residents seem pleased with the new design. Additions of more integrated traffic- calming features like speed tables could create a Vision Zero/Safe Systems street model that would be very similar to the Dutch or Danish models and simultaneously improve water management issues. Instead of Lake Cherokee, the Black Pearl could be a green village of slow-speed, safe streets. This could be a residential template for streets of the future.

The Cherokee Street project could be a stepping stone to a larger effort at green and blue streets currently being planned as part of the GRD. The green and blue corridors GRD project is designed to "include multimodal transportation connections, canals for rainfall storage, green infrastructure, and public meeting spaces" (City of New Orleans 2018). Overall, these green and blue corridors promise "to introduce a comprehensive rethinking of streetscapes to incorporate rainfall management with symbiotic community benefits" (City of New Orleans 2018). The green and blue corridors are currently in the planning stage and are expected to be completed by August 2021. As these street projects emerge from the planning phase, it will be important to reevaluate them in light of both climate adaptation and mitigation goals.

As the equity discussions in this chapter have indicated, new green amenities will also likely generate affordable housing pressure in impacted communities. Analysis of the GRD plans shows that, while equity is mentioned consistently as a key theme, it is not specifically defined in relation to affordable housing impacts of new green infrastructure amenities. The experience of the Lafitte Greenway indicates that resilience initiatives will be successful at improving the amenity value of the neighborhood and simultaneously put pressure on affordable-housing stocks. If equity is to be a core element of resilience planning, affordable housing planning needs to be articulated as a specific equity dimension and integrated into climate district planning as a co-equal element.

Bouncing forward: resilience policy implications

New Orleans has bounced back (more for some residents than others) and is struggling to find consensus on what bouncing forward looks like in practice. The post-Katrina experience shows that large-scale greening efforts in existing neighborhoods faced significant backlash. For neighborhood residents who would have been displaced by the new projects, these resilience proposals were clearly not seen as a way to bounce forward. The reaction to the green dots proposal resulted in significant revaluation of green infrastructure policy with a current focus on repurposing existing park and open space into green and blue neighborhood systems. Rather than green dots, New Orleans has now focused on building resilience districts with networks of green infrastructure and water parks designed to increase flood safety and enhance livability. This is the new vision of bouncing forward to a more resilient New Orleans.

While New Orleans has crafted a more functional and politically acceptable resilience vision, the case highlights two key limitations with existing articulations of resilience policy. First, the case highlights the need to plan for community equity as a central resilience goal. While large-scale displacement for green space was ruled out, smaller-scale greenlining around new resilience projects remains a key issue.

Green and blue infrastructure, as we have discussed, is designed to both limit flooding impacts and to enhance local livability as the new green and blue areas act as new amenities for the area. Instead of the drained city turning away from water, the new, resilient water-sensitive city is envisioned to integrate "the normative values of environmental repair and protection, supply security, flood control, public health, amenity, livability and economic sustainability, amongst others" (Brown et al. 2009, p. 854). Most resilience planners focus on the provision of these broad community benefits as a normative good for the whole community, but, as we have seen, the unequal distribution of these new community benefits can have important equity impacts.

If resilience planning is to truly act to bounce a community forward, equal access to the new more livable, safer city must be ensured. Affordable housing policy, in this context, is a core resilience-planning concern on the same level as climate adaptation and mitigation. Resilience planners should partner with and engage affordable housing advocates and administrators to help ensure that the new resilient water-sensitive city is accessible to all residents.

While the equity story is central to understanding the resilience challenges of New Orleans, the use of streets as a key resilience resource is a potential missing link in the bouncing-forward agenda in post-Katrina New Orleans. While efforts to improve active transportation have moved forward in the recovery period, resilience district planning has not fundamentally reexamined the role of streets. Resilience projects have primarily focused on parks and open space as locations for enhanced green infrastructure. While the city has moved forward on a parallel track to improve active transportation and is currently planning to add 75 miles (121 km) of bikeways by 2022 (Sneath 2020), resilience planning has not been the primary driver of these changes. Roads are both the source of and repository for the bulk of routine flooding. These roadways are also a leading GHG emissions source. Creating resilient streets that manage water and GHG emissions simultaneously should be a key goal of resilience district planning. While the green streets approach is being piloted in New Orleans, more effort to rethink street space itself could be a valuable addition to the resilience toolbox of the city.

Notes

1 Laska (2012) distinguishes between a disaster which has more localized impacts and a catastrophe which deeply impacts a large area. In this context, the Katrina flooding was

a city and regional catastrophe. Different types of governmental response are required to address a catastrophe versus the more common disaster approaches. We utilize the term "disaster" to refer to the more common language of disaster response, but refer to the Katrina experience as a catastrophe to connote the immense scale of the event.

2 The period that Colton describes (1900–1930) straddles two broad eras of water management philosophy. Brown et al. (2009) define a "sewered city" era focused on extending sewer services to address public health concerns. This matches the turn-of-the-century efforts in New Orleans to address significant public health issues of malaria and typhoid through enhanced drainage and sewerage system coverage. The drained city emerges in New Orleans as the backswamps of the city are drained and development of the low-lying areas significantly expands from the 1920s forward.

3 Robert Moses was the great "power broker" (Caro and Caro 1974) who, as the head of numerous public commissions, helped to deconstruct neighborhoods and construct much of New York's modernist infrastructure in its place. His vision also carried forward throughout the United States in his consultancy work. Moses' plan was not the first major transportation plan for New Orleans. Harland Bartholomew and Associates produced a plan in 1927 that originally proposed burying the New Basin Canal "as a measure of progressive civic development" to expand the street system and encourage growth of the city (Fields 2005, p. 93, quoting Bartholomew and Associates). Moses' plan takes Bartholomew's street expansion concepts into the expressway age.

4 There were multiple streams of planning processes that occurred after Katrina. Some of these were official, city-led processes, some were led by foundations, and some were even led by neighborhood groups. They often overlapped and sometimes moved towards competing aims (Nelson et al. 2007; Olshansky et al. 2008). The specific planning processes at play in the initial green dot controversy included the Urban Land Institute's initial work that set the stage for specific proposals in the Bring New Orleans Back Commission's planning process.

5 For example, not all of the lowest-lying areas of the city were targeted for the green dots. The largely white, low-lying Lakeview area of the city experienced catastrophic flooding due to the flood wall failures but was not targeted for a green dot. The greenlining was seen as targeting largely African-American areas of the city that had equal flood risk.

6 The distinction between hazard mitigation and climate mitigation should be noted again. In disaster and recovery planning, hazard mitigation is broadly conceptualized as decreasing (mitigating) potential impacts to natural hazards through policy mechanisms such as land use zoning and development management techniques (Burby et al. 2000). In a strange linguistic quirk, these activities are often very similar to climate adaptation where communities seek to decrease risk to a changing climate. Climate mitigation, on the other hand, involves a focus on decreasing GHG emissions.

7 Possibly because it was designed as a visionary document to spur interest in a new conception of water policy rather than as a document tied specifically to the preexisting bureaucracy, the Water Plan also included limited discussion of broader resilience issues such as compact development and sustainable transportation options. While the plan does mention decreases in CO_2 from water pumping, the plan does not substantively address how connecting the city in a more compact, water-sensitive manner could reduce GHG emissions through active transportation or linkages to transit. The plan did, however, focus on equity issues as a key dimension of planning, but did not directly address the potential for the enhanced amenity value of green and blue infrastructure to act to accentuate affordable housing pressures (see Appendix A).

8 It should be noted that transit ridership has significantly declined during the post-Katrina period. Prior to Katrina, New Orleans had a robust system with the highest rates of transit use in the southern United States. After the storm, service became more limited with a focus on adding streetcar lines. These projects were focused more on the economic development potential of light rail and less on encouraging transit use and access to jobs (Ride New Orleans 2019; Brand and Baxter 2020). The lack of a strong transit system is a key equity issue as approximately 20% of New Orleans households lack access to an automobile for transportation and rely on transit for access to jobs and medical care. The recent growth of transit advocacy organization, Ride New Orleans, presents an opportunity to push for more equitable, improved transit service in the city.

9 Jennings et al. (2019, p. 71), for example, argue that intersectional approaches that link green space planning with "other planning elements such as transportation, housing, and water management" can be effectively designed to improve equity outcomes. Drawing from the experience of the Los Angeles Regional Open Space and Affordable Housing Collaborative, Jennings et al. (2019, p. 74) find that consciously linking affordable housing with urban green space planning can provide "a voice to historically marginalized people" by focusing on collaborative planning across multiple agencies. Efforts like this that seek to break down siloed agency goals and broaden the perceived goals of green space planning provide an important procedural avenue towards more equitable resilience planning.

10 In terms of management and funding, the City's Office of Resilience and Sustainability is leading the effort, along with partners New Orleans Redevelopment Authority and the Sewerage and Water Board of New Orleans. Although some early projects included under the GRD umbrella were constructed using FEMA Hazard Mitigation Grant Program funds, the GRD is funded primarily through a grant awarded by the federal HUD National Disaster Resilience Competition (NDRC).

11 The maintenance issue has been identified as a key challenge in accelerating the expansion of green infrastructure projects, at both the community level and for the city agencies and contractors tasked with keeping up public spaces (Sullivan 2019).

12 The planning documents also strangely do not mention resilience, adaptation, or mitigation at all. While the plan clearly attempts to address resilience, the lack of specificity and connection to overall conceptual framing for the goals seems missing.

References

Adelson, J. (2020). To Reduce Flooding, New Orleans City Council Mandates Permeable Materials for Parking, Sidewalks. *Times Picayune-New Orleans Advocate.* May 21. Last accessed 6/24/2020 from www.nola.com/news/politics/article_0f047728–9bbb-11ea-91ea-5f1f267d28bf.html.

Baumbach, R. O. & Borah, W. E. (1980). *The Second Battle of New Orleans: A History of the Vieux Carré Riverfront Expressway Controversy.* Tuscaloosa: University of Alabama Press.

Brand, A. L., & Baxter, V. (2020). Post-Disaster Development Dilemmas: Advancing Landscapes of Social Justice in a Neoliberal Post-Disaster Landscape. In Louisiana's Response to Extreme Weather (Laska, S. ed.*)*, 217–240. Cham, Switzerland: Springer.

Brown, R. R., Keath, N., & Wong, T. H. (2009). Urban Water Management in Cities: Historical, Current and Future Regimes. *Water Science and Technology, 59*(5), 847–855.

Burby, R., Deyle, R., Godschalk, D., & Olshansky, R. (2000). Creating Hazard Resilient Communities Through Land-Use Planning. *Natural Hazards Review, 1*(2), 99–106.

Campanella, R. (2010). *Delta Urbanism: New Orleans*. Chicago, IL: American Planning Association.

Caro, R. A., & Caro, R. A. (1974). *The Power Broker: Robert Moses and the Fall of New York*. New York: Alfred A Knopf.

City of New Orleans. (2015). Reshaping the Urban Delta Exhibit A—Executive Summary. Last accessed 3/6/2020 from www.nola.gov/resilience/resources/ndr-docs/ndrc_phase2_neworleans_narrative_graphics/.

City of New Orleans. (2018). Blue and Green Corridors Fact Sheet. Last accessed 4/6/2020 from https://nola.gov/resilience-sustainability/resources/fact-sheets/blue-green-fact-sheet9–14-18_updated/.

Colten, C. E. (2002). Basin Street Blues: Drainage and Environmental Equity in New Orleans, 1890–1930. *Journal of Historical Geography*, *28*(2), 237–257.

Colten, C. E. (2005). Unnatural Metropolis: Wresting New Orleans from Nature. Baton Rouge: LSU Press.

Crompton, John. (2001). The Impact of Parks on Property Values: A Review of the Empirical Evidence. *Journal of Leisure Research,* 33(1), 1–31.

Fields, Billy. (2005). Urban Landscape Change in New Orleans, LA: The Case of the Lost Neighborhood of Louis Armstrong. University of New Orleans Theses and Dissertations. 151. https://scholarworks.uno.edu/td/151.

Fields, B. (2009). From Green Dots to Greenways: Planning in the Age of Climate Change in Post-Katrina New Orleans. *Journal of Urban Design*, *14*(3), 325–344.

Fields, Billy. (2019). Post-Disaster Amenity Politics: Livability, Gentrification, and Recovery in Post-Katrina New Orleans. In *Community Livability: Issues and Approaches to Sustaining the Well-Being of People and Communities* (F. Wagner, & R. W. Caves, eds.). Routledge.

Fields, B., Wagner, J., & Frisch, M. (2015). Placemaking and Disaster Recovery: Targeting Place for Recovery in Post-Katrina New Orleans. *Journal of Urbanism: International Research on Placemaking and Urban Sustainability*, *8*(1), 38–56.

Fields, B., Thomas, J., & Wagner, J. A. (2017). Living with Water in the Era of Climate Change: Lessons from the Lafitte Greenway in Post-Katrina New Orleans. *Journal of Planning Education and Research*, *37*(3), 309–321.

Fields, B., Thomas, J., & Wagner, J. A. (2017). Living with Water in the Era of Climate Change: Lessons from the Lafitte Greenway in Post-Katrina New Orleans. *Journal of Planning Education and Research*, *37*(3), 309–321.

Frank, T. (2019). After a $14-Billion Upgrade, New Orleans' Levees Are Sinking. *Scientific American*. April 11. Last accessed 4/4/2020 from www.scientificamerican.com/article/after-a-14-billion-upgrade-new-orleans-levees-are-sinking/.

Friends of the Lafitte Greenway. (2018). Statement on Housing Affordability. November 26. Last accessed 4/4/2020 from https://www.lafittegreenway.org/housing_affordability.

Goody Clancy. (2010). *Plan for the 21st Century: New Orleans 2030*. New Orleans, LA: New Orleans City Planning Commission.

Gotham, K. F., & Greenberg, M. (2014). *Crisis Cities: Disaster and Redevelopment in New York and New Orleans*. Oxford, UK: Oxford University Press.

Green, B. (2019). *The Smart Enough City: Putting Technology in its Place to Reclaim our Urban Future*. Cambrodge, MA: MIT Press.

Harris, L. M., Chu, E. K., & Ziervogel, G. (2018). Negotiated Resilience. *Resilience, 6*(3), 196–214.

Heard, M. (1997). *French Quarter Manual: An Architectural Guide to New Orleans Vieux Carré*. Oxford, MS: University Press of Mississippi.

Immergluck, Dan, & Balan, Tharunya. (2018). Sustainable for Whom? Green Urban Development, Environmental Gentrification, and the Atlanta Beltline. *Urban Geography*, 39(4), 546–562.

Jennings, V., Browning, M. H., & Rigolon, A. (2019). *Urban Green Spaces: Public Health and Sustainability in the United States*. Cham: Springer.

Kang, Simi. (2018). "I Have a Right Not to be Resilient": New Orleanians of Color Remember Hurricane Katrina. *The Migrationist*. March 2. Last accessed 4/4/2020 from https://themigrationist.net/2018/03/02/i-have-a-right-not-to-be-resilient-new-orleanians-of-color-remember-hurricane-katrina/.

Lamb, Z. (2020). Connecting the Dots: The Origins, Evolutions, and Implications of the Map that Changed Post-Katrina Recovery Planning in New Orleans. In *Louisiana's Response to Extreme Weather* (S. Laska, ed.). Cham: Springer.

Laska, S. (2012). Dimensions of Resiliency: Essential Resiliency, Exceptional Recovery and Scale. *International Journal of Critical Infrastructures*, *8*(1), 47–62.

Lewis, Peirce. (2003). *New Orleans—The Making of an Urban Landscape* (second edition). Charlottesville, VA: University of Virginia Press.

Lopez, J. A. (2006). The Multiple Lines of Defense Strategy to Sustain Coastal Louisiana. Metairie, LA: Lake Pontchartrain Basin Foundation. Last accessed 1/5/2015 from www.SaveOurLake.org/.

Markwell, P., & Ratard, R. (2014). Deaths Directly Caused by Hurricane Katrina. Last accessed 2/6/2020 from http://ldh.la.gov/assets/oph/Center-PHCH/Center CH/stepi/specialstudies/2014PopwellRatard_KatrinaDeath_PostedOnline.pdf.

Meyer, H. (2009). Reinventing the Dutch Delta: Complexity and Conflicts. *Built Environment*, 28(4), 432–451.

Morris, A. M., & Diaz, L. (2020). Reimagining Housing: Affordability Crisis and Its Role in Disaster Resilience and Recovery. In *Louisiana's Response to Extreme Weathe*. (Laska, S. ed.), 241–259. Cham, Switzerland: Springer.

Nelson, M., Ehrenfeucht, R., & Laska, S. (2007). Planning, Plans, and People: Professional Expertise, Local Knowledge, and Governmental Action in Post-Hurricane Katrina New Orleans. Cityscape: A Journal of Policy Development and Research, 9(3), 23–54.

Olshansky, R. B., Johnson, L. A., Horne, J., & Nee, B. (2008). Longer View: Planning for the Rebuilding of New Orleans. *Journal of the American Planning Association*, 74(3), 273–287.

Phinney, P. Jr. (2019). Managing Our Holy Water. *Clarion Herald*. August 13. Last accessed 4/6/2020 from https://clarionherald.org/2019/08/13/managing-our-holy-water/?fbclid=IwAR2WG_3GZpeJ_2inFopgCsrO4IG75LtkIiXY97mmLW68YKus3a9mFdYCi20.

Piazza, T. (2005). *Why New Orleans Matters*. New York, NY: Harper Collins.

Regis, H. A. (1999). Second Lines, Minstrelsy, and the Contested Landscapes of New Orleans Afro-Creole Festivals. *Cultural Anthropology*, 14(4), 472–504.

Ride New Orleans. (2019). New Links and Next Steps: State of Transit 2019. Last accessed 4/6/2020 from https://rideneworleans.org/wp/wpcontent/uploads/2019/08/SOTS2019_FINAL_V2_Digital.pdf.

Rigolon, A., & Németh, J. (2018). "We're not in the Business of Housing:" Environmental Gentrification and the Nonprofitization of Green Infrastructure projects. *Cities*, *81*, 71–80.

Schleifstein, M. (2019). What it'll Take to Raise New Orleans-Area Levees: $3.2 Billion, 50-Year Plan, Corps Says. *Times Picayune*. December 9. Last accessed 4/4/2020 from www.nola.com/news/environment/article_a160ff42–1ace-11ea-bd3b-cbcf2a74b089.html.

Shaw, K. (2012). "Reframing" Resilience: Challenges for Planning Theory and Practice. *Planning Theory and Practice*, *13*(2), 308–312.

Smith, G., Duda, S., Lee, J. M., & Thompson, M. (2016). Measuring the Impact of the 606: Understanding How a Large Public Investment Impacted the Surrounding Housing Market. Chicago, IL: Institute for Housing Studies at DePaul University.

Sneath, Sara. (2020). New Orleans Starts Construction on New Stretches of Bike Lanes. Times-Picayune-New Orleans Advocate. May 21. Last accessed 6/9/2020 from www.nola.com/news/coronavirus/article_f4619f9c-993d-11ea-a5f8–4753c6e89f36.html.

Sullivan, Z. (2019). Could Water Management Be New Orleans' Next Big Export? *NextCity*. October 29. Last accessed 4/6/2020 from https://nextcity.org/daily/entry/could-water-management-be-new-orleans-next-big-export.

Toussaint, Kristin. (2020). How These New Orleans Nuns Helped Turn their Convent into a Beautiful, Flood-Preventing Urban Wetland. *Fast Company*. February 26. Last accessed 4/6/2020 from www.fastcompany.com/90458827/how-these-new-orleans-nuns-helped-turn-their-convent-into-a-beautiful-flood-preventing-urban-wetland.

Trancik, R. (1986). *Finding Lost Space: Theories of Urban Design*. Hoboken, NJ: John Wiley.

Waggonner & Ball Architects. (2013). Greater New Orleans Urban Water Plan. Last accessed 2/6/2020 from http://livingwithwater.com/urban_water_plan/Reports/.

Wagner, J. A. (2006). Creole Urbanism: Searching for an Urban Future in the Flooded Streets of New Orleans. *Space and Culture*, *9*(1), 103–106.

Wagner, Jacob, & Frisch, M. (2009). Introduction: New Orleans and the Design Moment. *Journal of Urban Design,* 14(3), 237–255.

Whitehead, M. (2013). Neoliberal Urban Environmentalism and the Adaptive City: Towards a Critical Urban Theory and Climate Change. *Urban Studies*, *50*(7), 1348–1367.

Zaccaro, H., & Atherton, E. (2017). Complete Streets for Health Equity: An Evaluation of New Orleans and Jefferson Parish. *National Complete Streets Coalition and Bike Easy*. Last accessed 4/4/2020 from http://bikeeasy.org/files/Complete_Streets_for_Health_Equity_Report_NO__JP.pdf.

9

SOUTH FLORIDA AND MIAMI

Rising seas and a fragmented response

Introduction

Miami sits in a precarious position surrounded by water with the Atlantic Ocean to the east and the massive Everglades wetland network to the west. This complex location presents the yearly challenge of hurricane season, but also offers emerald blue waters and trade routes to Latin America. These challenges and opportunities have drawn large numbers of residents since the city's founding in the late 1800s, making Miami and the surrounding South Florida region the seventh largest metropolitan area in the United States with over six million residents.

Miami was founded in 1896 as the terminus of Florida East Coast (FEC) railway that extended north to Jacksonville. The project was led by Henry Flagler who was John D. Rockefeller's partner in Standard Oil. Much of the surveying for the FEC took advantage of a natural limestone ridge, known as the Cutler Ridge, that runs along the mainland of the east coast of South Florida. Standiford (2002, p. 85) points out that, "At scarcely ten feet above sea level, the 'ridge' was more of a barely perceptible rise…But its elevation made enough of a difference."

The Miami region, including Broward, Miami-Dade, Monroe, and Palm Beach Counties, is built along this ridge between the ocean and the Everglades. The ridge provides a level of protection from storm surge but also, importantly, an avenue for the sea to push inland. The limestone ridge is porous and allows sea water to infiltrate inland at high tide (Butler et al. 2016; Portes and Armony 2018). As we described in Chapter 1, sea water is increasingly bubbling up through the limestone at high tides, temporarily flooding streets like those in Hollywood, FL, just north of Miami. As sea level rise (SLR) is added to the equation, the Miami region faces an existential challenge. Jeff Goodell (2017, p. 9) describes these conditions as making the greater Miami region "a modern-day Atlantis-in-the-making."

In the greater Miami region, some local governments have begun to adopt adaptation urbanism elements, which as outlined in Chapter 4 include compact development, sustainable transport, focus on equity, and inclusion of blue/green infrastructure. However, much of the current resilience policy and planning efforts is focused on hardening infrastructure to keep the invading seas away through sea walls, pumps, raising road elevations, and other adaptive measures. At present, synergistic transportation policies to connect climate adaptation and mitigation are not widely in use in the greater Miami region. Fragmented governance structures and lack of political will limit broader policy efforts to implement significant land use and transportation reforms in South Florida to reduce carbon emissions to promote safer, healthier, and more equitable communities. Urban transportation resilience planning in South Florida, while advancing rapidly, has been mostly focused on climate adaptation with limited pilot work to advance a more holistic adaptation urbanism framework.

While there are a number of promising developments highlighted in the chapter, the Miami case study provides a window into the gravity of the climate change problem. Miami is a heavily populated, low-lying area that is hemmed in by water on all sides. As the seas begin to rise, the complexity of the planning challenge is immense. Adaptation urbanism tools are designed to equitably assist as coastal communities adapt to a changing climate, decrease greenhouse gas (GHG) emissions, and improve quality of life. The speed of change and difficult environmental characteristics of the South Florida region stretch the limits of adaptation urbanism planning. At the same time, the decisions made now and in the near future to reduce carbon emissions and adapt our communities to become more resilient will play a role in how dire that future will become.

This chapter summarizes efforts to promote adaptation urbanism planning efforts to address SLR and other related climate change issues across the politically fragmented region. The chapter begins with a short overview of key resilience challenges in the transportation and water management sectors. This is followed by an overview of selected resilience plans in the Miami area. Finally, this chapter focuses on more detailed analysis of efforts in the City of Miami and the City of Miami Beach and discusses policy implications for resilience planning and policy.

From challenging to existential threat: South Florida resilience background

The greater Miami metropolitan area (South Florida) has grown dramatically since its founding just over a hundred years ago. In 1900, Miami-Dade County had just 5,000 residents, but population of the southeast part of Florida grew dramatically with population growth rates averaging 90% per decade from 1900 to 1980 (Smith 2005). While population growth in the Miami Metro area has slowed since 1980, population still grew at a rate of 26% in the 1980s, 24% in the 1990s, and 11% in the 2000s (Frey 2012). Miami has emerged as a global city (Portes and Armony 2018) with a diverse population and, unfortunately, a large income gap and threatened middle class. Metropolitan Miami's population now sits at approximately six million people and is incredibly diverse with 46% Latino/Hispanic, 20% black, and 29% white population (Frey 2020). While the image of Miami often centers on glitzy South Beach, large shares of the population live in high-poverty neighborhoods inland with limited access to higher-paying jobs. Kneebone and Reeves (2016) estimate that 20% of the metropolitan population is living in a household that is doubly disadvantaged with a combination of high family poverty, living in a concentrated poverty neighborhood, low educational attainment, family unemployment, or lack of health insurance. These numbers place Miami as one of the metropolitan areas with "the highest rates of multidimensional poverty" (Kneebone and Reeves 2016, np) in the United States.

It is within this difficult socio-demographic context that resilience-planning efforts are beginning to take shape. South Florida is precariously perched between water and swamps along a fairly narrow limestone ridge of higher ground. Rising seas are increasingly surging inland during the highest tides. A recent report by Savitch et al. (2020) points out that in just 20 years in 2040 sea levels are projected to rise by 10–17 inches (25–43 cm). Projections for the year 2070 are for a 21–54-inch (53–137-cm) SLR and 40–136 inches (101–345 cm) by 2110. Savitch et al. (2020, p. 10) note that every inch of SLR

> bring[s] greater exposure to people and their properties. Once the tide line rises, more assets are covered in its wake. At less than three feet above the high tide line, over 2,000 square miles in the flood zone along with an estimated $145 billion in vanished housing; at six feet above that tide line the amount of exposed land jumps to over 4,000 square miles and $544 billion in lost property value.
>
> *(Savitch et al. 2020, p. 10)*

To put these figures into context, current property in the Miami region is assessed at $833 billion (p. 9).

Climate change creates an intense spatial challenge for Miami region as there is limited higher ground land and a large population jockeying for access to these zones. Portes and Armony (2018) lay out the political and spatial components of Miami's growth as an emerging global city. They note that, "Within cities, the competition for space always triggers political confrontation" (2018, p. 3).

While traditional spatial politics in Miami has focused on access to the amenities of the coast, spatial politics is growing more complicated and intense with the rise in sea levels and limited higher ground land available for development/redevelopment. Portes and Armony (2018) link this spatial competition between transportation and climate change in their aptly titled chapter "Driving into the Flood: Traffic and Climate Change." The chapter lays out the lack of regional cooperation to address what the authors describe as "traffic gridlock" and the impacts of that lack of cooperation in addressing the even larger challenge of climate change. Portes and Armony (2018, p. 177) note that, while other areas of the world like the Netherlands have created large systems of coastal defenses that protect against SLR, South Florida is challenged because of the underlying limestone that allows sea water to bubble up at high tides. They note that, "Building a dike on limestone is like putting a wall on top of a tunnel; the water will simply go underground" (p. 177). Portes and Armony (2018) see four current strategies that simultaneously define planning for SLR: "denial, technology, infrastructure above the sea, and exodus" (p. 181). The challenges are immense, and the will is diffused within the fractured political interests.

While there are a fairly large number of climate denialists in the state government, local communities have watched the tide coming up into their yards and are increasingly taking action to address SLR. Butler et al. (2016, p. 321) argue that there are three typical forms of adaptation that planners use for SLR: protection, accommodation, and managed retreat. These components essentially lay out a continuum of actions that communities can take from protective measures like sea walls, pumps, and levees to living with water-adaptive measures to, finally, abandonment of the most impacted areas.

Within this context, Butler et al. (2016) argue that an ideal community response to SLR should focus on vulnerability assessments to determine risk, adaptation policies based on the risk assessments, and, finally, systematic land use planning employed based on risk management factors such as climate risk, local impacts, and effectiveness of SLR strategies. While this framework provides an important conceptual guide for adaptation to SLR and speaks to the intense complexities of land use and infrastructure policy, the hazard mitigation lens is too narrow to confront the full scope of the climate change challenge. While climate adaptation is a strong focus of Butler et al.'s (2016) ideal type, climate mitigation is not substantively addressed. The land use and transportation decisions that are impacted by hazard mitigation policy can significantly influence GHG emissions. Coastal resilience planners need to not just adapt to the changing climate, but also actively work to decrease GHG emissions through their planning decisions. In Florida overall and Miami in specific, the largest area of GHG emissions comes from the transportation sector, but resilience planners are not currently actively planning for GHG impacts of their projects. Current iterations of resilience planning in Florida focus almost exclusively on climate adaptation and are often planning for only half of the climate challenge.

Planning for half of the challenge is still, however, incredibly difficult and important. Butler et al. (2016, p. 324) examine plans from Florida coastal communities to address SLR and show how communities are currently planning for climate resilience. They find that 98% of communities have access to detailed SLR projections, 76% of communities have conducted vulnerability assessments, and 43% of communities have begun to plan for and implement land use and adaptation strategies to SLR. Butler et al. (2016, p. 323) find that the strategies laid out in these communities "mirror the traditional objectives of coastal hazard mitigation and coastal natural resource protection." That is, that they are focused on decreasing susceptibility to flooding and improving public safety and limiting

TABLE 9.1 Miami-Dade climate adaptation project funding by category 2011–2017

Climate adaptation project type	*Total project investment*	*Percentage*
Infrastructure hardening	$171 million	52.50%
Critical facility hardening	$91 million	27.90%
Drainage improvement	$7 million	2.10%
Emergency preparedness	$18 million	5.50%
Recovery operation	$39 million	12%
Total	$326 million	

Modified from Kim (2019, p. 10).

"public expenditures in and direct development away from hazardous coastal areas." Overall, Butler et al. (2016, p. 327) find that "[m]ost of the coastal communities in Florida we observed have demonstrated a predilection for cautious, low-regrets, incrementalism."

Miami-Dade County has also begun to invest in a series of adaptive measures over the last decade. From the second quarter of 2011 to the last quarter of 2017, Kim (2019) estimates that the county invested $326 million in climate adaptation in over 300 projects (Table 9.1). While these figures represent a large community investment, the types of projects continue the traditional approach of infrastructure and critical infrastructure hardening to create sea walls or elevate infrastructure like roadways and buildings. The protective measures are designed to keep water out and, when that becomes infeasible, accommodate water and protect infrastructure. These traditional hazard mitigation investments represent 80.4% of the climate adaptation investments in Miami-Dade County. At the same time, investments in green infrastructure are beginning to be included in project work, but currently represent a small percentage of the drainage improvement category that is itself only 2.1% of overall spending. Despite the small overall budgetary emphasis, these green infrastructure improvements have made a significant impact on housing prices with a 9.7% housing appreciation for properties close to these new, green amenities. While the increases in property value are important for landowners, they also speak to the potential problem of climate gentrification that often follows adaptation investments. These issues are examined later in the chapter.

While the Miami area has begun to address the complex water management challenges of the region, the transportation issues that have, as Portes and Armony (2018) note, gridlocked the region remain difficult challenges. The South Florida region is overall a fairly dispersed area of lower-density housing with higher densities along key nodes of the amenity-rich coast. The region has grown during the auto age and is filled with streets of the past that generate high car throughput and speeds. The result, predictably, is high fatality rates and high GHG emissions. Florida has consistently ranked as the most dangerous state for walking in Smart Growth America's *Dangerous by Design* overview of the most unsafe places to walk in the United States. The 2019 report notes that "eight of the top 10 most dangerous metropolitan areas [are] in the state of Florida" (Smart Growth America 2019 p. 14). While Miami falls outside the top ten, its ranking of 14th most dangerous pedestrian region in the United States is not comforting. Between 2008 and 2017, there were 1,548 pedestrian fatalities in the Miami Metropolitan area and many times more serious injuries.

While the Miami area is dominated by streets of the past, there are glimpses of streets of the future beginning to emerge. Traditional downtown cores of the smaller cities have increasingly been retrofitted to become more pedestrian and bicycle-friendly. West Palm Beach has created a number of traffic-calmed streets and the beginning elements of bicycle transportation system. This system links to both the TriRail commuter rail line along the Interstate-95 corridor and the new Brightline high-speed line closer to the coast that connects Miami with West Palm Beach and, in the future, to Orlando. This emerging system of rail access and the concerted efforts to improve walking and bicycling conditions in the region are beginning to create optimism for a more sustainable transport system, but mode share numbers for sustainable modes are overall still very low. In metro Miami, only 6.6% of trips are by walking, bicycling, or transit (see Appendix A). This is the lowest of the case study areas and places the region within the lowest category for sustainable transportation use.

The result of the car-centric transportation system is high transportation GHG levels. Transportation accounts for the highest share of any category of emissions at 48% of all GHG emissions in the region (Southeast Florida Regional Climate Change Compact (SFRCCC) 2017). The overall level of transportation emissions has fallen only slightly from 2005 to 2015 and essentially represents status quo trends.

While there is technological optimism for uptake in electric vehicles, transportation policy at present essentially represents extensions of current trends. As we have noted, this business-as-usual transportation model is a significant contributor to GHG emissions overall. Recent modeling of SLR by the Center for Urban and Environmental Solutions (CUES) at Florida Atlantic University shows what streets will look like as the ocean pours into communities. The three-dimensional models show the streetscape of Las Olas Boulevard in Fort Lauderdale under varying scenarios of SLR (Figure 9.1). The goal of the project is to use immersive visualizations to show residents what the sometimes abstract SLR projections will look like in their communities. The results are stark. The Atlantic Ocean will inundate Las Olas Boulevard by about 3 feet (91 cm) at high tides by 2100.

Resilience plan overview

While the challenges in South Florida are complicated and daunting, planners in the area have begun to engage in resilience planning to help address these challenges. The City of Miami and Miami-Dade County have engaged in an iterative process of planning for climate change and updating the City's Comprehensive Development Master Plan (CDMP) to reflect a strategic approach to mitigation and adaptation.

FIGURE 9.1 Las Olas sea level rise 2100.

This includes plan documents explicitly focused on resilience: the Miami-Dade County Climate Change Action Plan, Miami-Dade Green Print, Resilient 305 Strategy Report, and the recently released Miami Forever Climate Ready Strategy.[1] Overall, analysis of the recent plans, strategy documents, and recommended comprehensive plan amendments using the adaptation urbanism normative evaluation model reveals growing awareness of adaptation/mitigation concepts and project-level elements but shows limited synergistic planning across areas (see Appendix A, Table A.10).

Sustainable transportation is consistently highlighted, emphasizing public transit and related developments. Notably, as in many of the other case study cities, equity is not a key theme woven throughout the plans. Housing is considered in the plans, however. Historic development patterns that may increase risk are recognized, even if clear policy paths forward to address these are not always evident.

These tensions can be seen in the Resilient 305 Strategy Report developed in 2019. The plan was created through the 100 Resilient Cities program through a partnership of local and county governments. The plan links climate adaptation and mitigation criteria to evaluating new developments through checklists, guides, grant programs, and resilience-focused staff positions. Resilient 305 identifies growing traffic congestion, SLR and coastal erosion, aging infrastructure, decreasing housing quality and affordability, and income inequality as key areas that focus the strategy. The plan also connects these issues to social justice efforts, a large foreign-born population, and an overwhelmed criminal justice system that costs taxpayers $180 million per year. The goals of the strategy seek to enhance places, people, and pathways towards equity.

In addition to these larger elements, green infrastructure begins to take a more central role in climate response. Connections between transportation and green amenities that make sustainable transport options more appealing are drawn, and enhanced green infrastructure in park spaces is specifically called for. In addition, equity concerns are explicitly recognized and linked to policy interventions, including the inclusion of affordable housing in lower-vulnerability areas and promotion of "moderate- to high-density development along transit corridors in areas less susceptible to flooding, and strong protection of the natural systems that attenuate coastal hazards" (p. 58).

The overall plan review reveals ways in which Miami differs from other climate-focused cities due to the specific nature of the region's most immediate environmental threats: rising sea levels and related saltwater intrusion are the most significant priority issues. Policy responses to rainwater-driven flood events, droughts, and/or subsidence are not as prominently featured in the plans. As a result, green infrastructure does not seem to be as prominently addressed as observed elsewhere. While green infrastructure may not feature as prominently in plans, adaptation urbanism key themes where present in the plans frequently go beyond aspirational visions to directly address specific regulatory tools and policy actions needed to advance regional goals.

Sea level rise adaptation efforts

While analysis of these planning documents presents an ambitious vison for regional resilience, the area has moved forward with a number of adaptation projects (Kim 2019). Infrastructure investments have recently been completed or are under way to adapt local communities to SLR in Miami and other cities across the region. The situation is becoming urgent as some residents are experiencing saltwater intrusion flooding their driveways and pools and even bubbling into their homes through shower drains during King Tides (Loria 2018). As Portes and Armony (2018) note, the limestone ridge geology of the region leads to saltwater intrusion as seas rise.

City of Miami

Nevertheless, several local governments are making investments and plans to adapt their communities to the impacts of SLR. The City of Miami is beginning to attempt to look at this from a holistic viewpoint on how adaptation and mitigation efforts relate to the bigger picture, including transportation systems and affordable housing. Jane Gilbert, the Chief Resilience Officer for the City of Miami, has been focusing on planning efforts. Her focus is on addressing the combined issues of SLR, hurricane protection, housing affordability, and transportation through the lens of flood protection (Loria 2018). In addition, the City of Miami is attempting to address carbon reduction strategies as part of a holistic strategy. Miami Mayor Francis Suarez serves as a Commissioner on the Global Commission on Adaptation, a United Nations effort to encourage the development of measures to manage the effects of climate change through technology, planning, and investment. By 2030, the Commission is working on financing for climate-resilient cities, including initiatives focused on the urban poor (Global Commission on Adaptation 2020).

Suarez and Gilbert are guiding the City of Miami towards greater resilience through recent plans and policies that address climate adaptation, carbon mitigation, sustainability, and partnerships. In November 2019, the Mayor and Commission declared a climate emergency, mandating a comprehensive response to the vulnerabilities of climate change. The Miami Forever Climate Ready plan includes five goals: (1) ensure decisions are data-driven and human-centered; (2) inform, prepare, and engage residents and businesses; (3) protect and enhance the waterfront; (4) invest in resilient and smart infrastructure; and (5) promote adaptive neighborhoods and buildings.

Understanding the connections between elevation and investments in infrastructure to promote adaptation is emerging as a key equity concern in Miami. Little Haiti, a low-income neighborhood located north of Downtown, is one of the first neighborhoods to experience climate gentrification pressures. Little Haiti is located on the coastal ridge and elevated 7–14 feet (213–427 cm) above the sea. It is also located in the path of intense investment which extends north from Downtown along Biscayne Bay. The investments in luxury condos, museums, parks, infrastructure, and mixed-use projects total over $10 billion (Malura Luxury Real Estate 2013). Moreover, massive investments in Wynwood, Midtown, and the Design District have led to significant displacement of local residents as new luxury towers rise.

Little Haiti lies in the path of this wave of investment. A billion-dollar development proposal for a project known as Magic City received approvals from the City Council in June 2019. While the area is safer from SLR, local residents feel threatened by the tide of development dollars washing over their neighborhood that threatens to push them out. The City of Miami has set aside a $400 million bond program to invest in infrastructure and housing to address climate impacts. This includes funding to build 12,000 affordable units on higher ground, in neighborhoods like Little Haiti. Whether this investment from the city is enough given the tide of investment is an open question.

This creates a dilemma: the more the city invests in directing public and private investment into higher-ground "safer" locations, the more expensive those neighborhoods will become. This could result in a shift of affordable housing to more flood-prone areas. This is the market-oriented resilience dilemma. As we saw in New Orleans, without clear guidance for resilience planning to include affordable housing, climate gentrification will increase vulnerabilities among low-income residents. The adaptation urbanism resilience process includes affordable housing as a key resilience goal on par with climate adaptation and mitigation. Engaging local residents to build this vision and help guide transportation and housing resilience investments is vital to avoid the pitfalls of the market-oriented resilience dilemma. While the construction of some additional affordable housing on high ground is good news in Miami, the larger issue of how to address a wave of development in higher-elevation neighborhoods will require more serious discussion of how affordable housing can be included in resilience planning.

City of Miami Beach

Located across Biscayne Bay, the City of Miami Beach is also becoming a national leader for investing in infrastructure to combat climate change. Famous for its Art Deco Arts District and South Beach, the City of Miami Beach has been one of the first cities in the United States to invest millions in raising streets. Streets in some areas were elevated approximately 2 feet (61 cm). In many instances, the streets and sidewalks have been raised, but the homes adjacent to the sidewalks remain at the original elevation. As Miami Beach planned for more road elevation projects, local residents began to push back on the proposals because of warranted fear that higher streets would result in flooding private property adjacent to the streets.

The pushback has resulted in the development of a more holistic approach to addressing resilience in Miami Beach. The Rising Above Plan seeks to move past engineering-only solutions to incorporate blue–green solutions and an integrated design solution among engineers, urban designers, landscape architects, and other design and sustainability professionals. The plan seeks to invest $600 million to raise roads, improve pumping stations, elevate sea walls, and replace outdated infrastructure.[2] Sunset Harbor, located in eastern Miami Beach, became the first neighborhood to undergo the full treatment of climate investments. As a result, tidal flooding has been reduced and new public space along the streets allows for expanded landscaping, shade trees, and sidewalk cafés. The full suite of policies and actions implemented in Sunset Harbor is being touted as the first climate-adaptative neighborhood in South Florida.

While innovative and a step in the right direction, this type of plan does not address the role that streets play in generating GHG emissions. Raising streets to avoid flooding while not addressing the role that these streets are playing in the climate crisis does not match the high bar that resilience projects need to clear in the climate change era.[3] While Miami Beach is one of the largest tourist destinations in Florida and includes a number of streets that are pedestrian-friendly, investments in regional transit connectivity and bicycle infrastructure remain minimal compared to best-practice leaders.

In 2018, an Urban Land Institute (ULI) Advisory Services Panel brought global experts in stormwater management and climate adaptation to the city for three days to review the city's practices and plans. The city asked the panel to address if the city was on the right track in its stormwater approach, including elevating roads, harmonizing, placemaking, and aesthetics. They also asked the panel what other investments in public infrastructure should occur in ongoing projects. The panel made several recommendations, endorsing the city's approach in applying good practice in its initial stormwater pump rollout and elevating roads. The panel also recommended integrating flood management with a broader resilience strategy, to embrace a plan to live with water. They also recommended elevating public aesthetics to enhance the local culture of arts, heritage, and placemaking, as well as a recommendation to actively use green and open space to manage and infiltrate water through permeability and sponge features of landscaping (Urban Land Institute 2018).

While these are important and needed recommendations that will enhance community resilience, the ULI proposals and the current investments and planning in Miami Beach do not actively address transportation climate mitigation.[4] While the City of Miami Beach has been forthright in identifying the need to reduce carbon emissions by encouraging green buildings, they have not directly addressed one of the largest carbon generators—their streets. While the streets of the past are being retrofitted with some green trimming, they are still being designed to carry large flows of cars. As we have discussed, adaptation urbanism streets are designed to both be adapted to the changing climate and act as important tools in decreasing GHG emissions.

Miami Beach has some of the highest urban densities in the United States and the north–south orientation could work well for light-rail or even bus-rapid transit. At present, however, Miami Beach has poor transit connectivity to Downtown Miami. Bus stops fail to provide protection from the sun and rain. Street crossings are often unsafe for vulnerable populations. The City of Miami Beach should be commended for their progressive approach in combating SLR by investing over a half-billion in adaptation efforts. They should also be commended for asking the ULI what other investments in public infrastructure could be made in ongoing projects, but the limited acknowledgment of the climate mitigation potential of redesigning streets illustrates the problems of professional silos and the limits of narrow, adaptation-oriented view of resilience. Streets themselves are a public resource that can be redesigned to adapt to the changing climate and act as a key policy tool to decrease GHG emissions.

Miami 2100: Atlantis and Venice

The future of South Florida is challenged by the pace and potential scale of SLR. Harold Wanless, Professor and Chair of Geology at the University of Miami, argues that the speed and impact of SLR will present difficult challenges in the immediate future. He argues that the rate of SLR will be too fast for many neighborhoods to be habitable beyond 2050. He notes that much of the planning efforts in South Florida are based on a gradual SLR, but the potential for quick, catastrophic SLR is a distinct possibility based on historical analysis of previous rapid change events (Wanless 2014).

This stark vision outlines one potential pathway for South Florida: a suburban sprawl Atlantis of buried neighborhoods and protruding high-rise towers. An alternative future could still be written with significant changes in GHG emissions and urban development policies that adapt the landscape to climate change and encourage low-carbon neighborhoods. In this vision, Miami could rethink streets and work to live with water. This vision of South Florida as more of a Venice is being advanced by architect Jeff Huber. Huber, a professor at Florida Atlantic University and practicing architect with Brooks + Scarpa, outlines a vision that he calls salty urbanism. The concept recognizes that some buildings and neighborhoods may need to be abandoned but investments could be made to protect and adapt communities to promote a living-with-water approach (Brooks + Scarpa 2020). Designs for salty urbanism include built environment typologies such as surf and tidal neighborhoods, green streets to blueways, and a transit-oriented development ridge. A salt-tolerant landscape palette is presented along with identifying the need for potential strategic retreat from some neighborhoods. This vision is difficult as some neighborhoods will be surrendered to the ocean. This will require difficult decisions about how to ensure equitable relocation assistance for residents who are losing their homes and difficult equity challenges concerning access to affordable housing in the higher-ground protected zones.

In summary, the future for Miami and the South Florida region is challenging. Already-emitted GHG emissions will raise the seas. Decisions about how much more GHG is emitted will determine the magnitude of the challenge. The scale of change required to alter the future is significant, but significant change is sometimes possible. The COVID-19 crisis showed that travel behavior can be changed if for a terrible reason. A recent study found that temporary global carbon emission reductions for surface transportation, due to COVID-19, fell by approximately 20% in April 2020 (Le Quéré et al. 2020). While such restrictions are temporary, the magnitude of this reduction provides a lesson that rapid change in travel is possible, and in fact may be necessary due to external emergencies such as a pandemic or the impending climate crisis. As we have argued, just because something is necessary does not mean that it will happen. Significant push is needed to make changes of this order. In the other case study chapters, we lay out how changes to street and public space can add amenities to communities and decrease GHG emissions. Instead of a terrible tragedy pushing change, change could be pushed by a desire for a better, more livable community. While hopeful in this framing, there are few places in the world that have more at stake in finding sustainable and resilient solutions than Miami and South Florida. Building towards a salty version of adaptation urbanism may be a potential pathway.

Notes

1 In addition, the Seven50 Plan from 2014 and the Southeast Florida Regional Climate Action Plan in 2012 and 2017 are important regional documents, but are not covered in this chapter.

2 Miami Beach notes that, due to the subsurface limestone bedrock, rising roads and property above seas is the only long-term solution since pumping and sea walls will only result in temporary solutions. The city is working to promote a process called harmonization that over time will allow private property owners to adjust landscaping or redevelop their

property to adjust for higher streets. Moreover, new land use codes require that ground floors be located at least 1–5 feet (30–152 cm) above the Federal Emergency Management Agency base flood elevation. The new code also encourages native and salt-tolerant landscape vegetation and greater tree canopy.

3 It should be noted that there has been movement to reduce GHG emissions in other sectors such as revisions to the land use code that encourage more green buildings.

4 There were 20 mentions of mitigation in the ULI review document, but these references were to flood or hazard mitigation rather than climate mitigation. There was one graphic with climate mitigation included. While there were 189 mentions of resilience in the document, there were only three mentions of GHG emissions and none of these references were to transportation-related emissions. There were three references to walking and bicycling in relation to co-benefits of "alternative transportation" and no references to transit.

References

Brooks + Scarpa. (2020). Salty Urbanism Website. Last accessed 7/6/2020 from https://brooksscarpa.com/salty-urbanism.

Butler, W. H., Deyle, R. E., & Mutnansky, C. (2016). Low-Regrets Incrementalism: Land Use Planning Adaptation to Accelerating Sea Level Rise in Florida's Coastal Communities. *Journal of Planning Education and Research*, *36*(3), 319–332.

Frey, W. H. (2012). Population Growth in Metro America Since 1980. March. The Brookings Institution. Last accessed 7/8/2020 from www.brookings.edu/wp-content/uploads/2016/06/0320_population_frey.pdf.

Frey, W. H. (2020). The Nation is Diversifying Even Faster than Predicted, According to New Census Data. Brookings Institution. July 1. Last accessed 7/10/2020 from www.brookings.edu/research/new-census-data-shows-the-nation-is-diversifying-even-faster-than-predicted/.

Global Commission on Adaptation. (2020). Cities Action Track. Last accessed 7/6/2020 from https://gca.org/global-commission-on-adaptation/action-tracks/cities.

Goodell, Jeff. (2017). The Year is 2037. This is What Happens when the Hurricane Hits Miami. *Guardian*. 17 December. Last accessed 6/30/2020 from www.theguardian.com/us-news/2017/dec/17/miami-hurricane-2037-climate-change.

Kim, S. (2019). The Economic Effects of Climate Change Adaptation Measures: Evidence from Miami-Dade County and New York City. May 2019. Joint Center for Housing Studies of Harvard University. John R. Meyer Dissertation Fellowship Working Paper. Last accessed 7/8/2020 from www.jchs.harvard.edu/sites/default/files/harvard_jchs_kim_economic_effects_climate_change_adaptation_2019.pdf.

Kneebone, E., & Reeves, R.V. (2016). The Intersection of Race, Place, and Multidimensional Poverty. April 21. Brooking Institution. Last accessed 7/8/2020 from www.brookings.edu/research/the-intersection-of-race-place-and-multidimensional-poverty/.

Le Quéré, C., Jackson, R. B., Jones, M. W., et al. (2020). Temporary Reduction in Daily Global CO_2 Emissions During the COVID-19 Forced Confinement. *Nature Climate Change*, 10, 647–653. https://doi.org/10.1038/s41558–020-0797-x.

Loria, Kevin. (2018). Miami is Racing Against Time to Keep up with Sea-Level Rise. *Business Insider*. April 12. Last accessed 7/6/2020 from www.businessinsider.com/miami-floods-sea-level-rise-solutions-2018-4.

Malura Luxury Real Estate. (2013). Discover the $10 Billion Mile. Last accessed 7/6/2020 from www.youtube.com/watch?v=8D1Ae7PbNM4.

Portes, A., & Armony, A. C. (2018). *The Global Edge: Miami in the Twenty-First Century*. Berkeley, CA: University of California Press.

Savitch, Hank, Sawislak, Josh, & Renne, John. (2020). Protecting South Florida: A Discussion of Sea Level Rise, Property and Regional Planning. Center for Urban and Environmental Solutions, Florida Atlantic University. Last accessed 1/4/2021 from http://cues.fau.edu/.

Smart Growth America. (2019). *Dangerous by Design*. Washington, DC. Last accessed 7/8/2020 from https://smartgrowthamerica.org/app/uploads/2019/01/Dangerous-by-Design-2019-FINAL.pdf.

Smith, S. K. (2005). Florida Population Growth: Past, Present and Future. Gainesville, FL: Bureau of Economic and Business Research, University of Florida.

Southeast Florida Regional Climate Change Compact (SFRCCC). (2017). Sustainable Communities and Transportation. Last accessed 7/4/2020 from https://southeastfloridaclimatecompact.org/recommendation-category/st/.

Standiford, L. (2003). Last Train to Paradise: Henry Flagler and the Spectacular Rise and Fall of the Railroad That Crossed an Ocean. New York, NY: Broadway Books.

Urban Land Institute. (2018). Miami Beach Florida: Stormwater Management and Climate Adaptation Review. 16–19 April, 2019. Last accessed 7/6/2020 from https://ulidigitalmarketing.blob.core.windows.net/ulidcnc/2018/09/Miami-Beach_PanelReport-1.pdf.

Wanless, Harold. (2014). Rising Sea Levels will be Too Much, Too Fast for Florida. *The Conversation*. 28 May. Last accessed 7/6/2020 from https://theconversation.com/rising-sea-levels-will-be-too-much-too-fast-for-florida-27198.

10

ADAPTATION URBANISM

European and North American examples

Introduction

The case study chapters that we have just presented provide an in-depth analysis of resilience plans and projects and point to a widespread disconnect between project-level implementation of climate adaptation and mitigation goals. At the same time, the cases also highlight the potential to reconceive streets and public spaces as key physical places that can act to tie climate mitigation and adaptation together. While this suite of case study cities provides a reasonable overview of the beginning movements towards adaptation urbanism, multiple other cities are innovating new street and public space projects and these examples help to show the diversity and breadth of the burgeoning movement.

In this chapter, we examine a select set of these projects from Barcelona, Vancouver, and a collection of cities in the Netherlands (Amsterdam, Delft, and Utrecht). Instead of the more detailed analysis of the case study chapters, we seek to highlight specific projects or connected sets of projects to highlight key innovations. It should be noted that there are multiple other cities (like Paris, Seville, Malmo, Madrid, Singapore, Montreal, New York, Philadelphia, Portland, Seattle, and many others) innovating adaptation urbanism projects as well. In addition, cities around the world are rethinking street space more broadly in response to COVID-19. Our examination here is intended to provide creative examples of changing streetscapes rather than provide an exhaustive analysis of emerging projects.

Overall, what we found was a type of proof of concept where multiple cities are moving towards rethinking streets as key tools to improve neighborhoods and address complex global problems like climate change. The motivations for and the coalitions pushing these projects vary from city to city. Some cities see local air pollution and livability as driving imperatives for change, while others include public health and broader resilience concerns as key factors. There is, as yet, no clear movement that links all of these efforts. Seeing all of these projects as a whole, however, points to a dramatic repositioning of streets as tools to enhance local quality of life, address climate resilience goals, and improve public health and safety outcomes. Key connecting features of the projects examined below include an emphasis on slower-speed streets to improve safety, a focus on linking streets together into an active transportation system, increasing the use of green infrastructure both as a placemaking and a climate adaptation tool, and, overall, a focus on streets as public spaces of value. These cases show what is possible today when groups begin to push for change. The window of the possible is expanding.

Barcelona: *superillas*

One of the most prominent developments to emerge over the last few years has been the Barcelona *superillas* plan for traffic calming multiple block areas of the city center to lower traffic speeds and add public space to the core of the city. This effort is sometimes translated as the superblock plan, but this translation can make the changes seem like a type of high modernist scheme. A more apt translation of *superilla* from Catalan to English focuses on the term "*illa*." In Catalan, this broadly translates as island. The feeling of *superillas* is more akin to that of a village-like island in the city where traffic is slowed (but not stopped) and public space is valued over speed.

A recent multi-part series by David Roberts (2019) for *Vox* examines the origins and ambitions of the *superillas*. The *superillas* concept in Barcelona was first used in 1993 in the Born neighborhood to help limit through traffic in the area. The idea slowly developed and expanded with a second and third version of *superillas* implemented in 2003 in central Barcelona neighborhoods. The results showed increasing levels of walking and biking and, not surprisingly, decreasing levels of car use in these areas. By 2015, the small-scale vision had been dramatically increased with plans to build 503 *superillas* across the city. This would, as Roberts points out, transform the city and devote "almost 70 percent of city streets to mixed use" patterns of the *superillas* (Roberts 2019b).

The potential public health impacts of transforming Barcelona into a walkable, transit-oriented super village are impressive. Mueller et al. (2020) conducted a quantitative health impact assessment to project the impact of the potential decreased air pollution, heat island impacts, and increased physical activity that could be expected to be achieved if the full *superillas* plan was implemented. Mueller et al. (2020) project that 230,000 trips will be shifted from cars to walking, bicycling, and transit and result in an overall car mode share decline of 19.2%. The decline in auto mode share and the shift to active transport are projected to result in 667 averted premature deaths annually because of improved air quality, increased physical activity, and decreased heat island impacts in the city. The shift from car to active transport and transit opens up space for additional green space in the city with the Eixample neighborhood, for example, projected to show an increase in green space from 6.5% to 19.6% of all neighborhood area. These shifts are also projected to have an annual economic impact of Euro 1.7 billion ($2.08 billion). Overall, Mueller et al. (2020) note that the *superillas* plan is a "promising urban model as well as public health strategy to reclaim public space for people and help the city become cleaner, more physically active and climate change resilient through the reconfiguration of urban and transport structures" (p. 11). They also note that to avoid potential gentrification impacts of increased green space, "equitable implementation of the model across the entire city is recommended" (p. 11).

While the full *superillas* vision has many projected positive impacts, change is hard. The vision of reclaiming the city streets for local residents has created political tensions as many residents worry more about what they may lose than what they may gain. Roberts (2019a) outlines a particularly strong initial pushback from local residents in the Poblenou area and the broader political pushback from governmental factions seeking to tag the controversy on opposing political parties. The result, according to Roberts (2019a), was that the Poblenou *superilla* implementation was tenuously hanging on for political support during its initial phase. After more investment and outreach to the community the project gained a foothold and eventually grew into a popular neighborhood feature.

This political tension is matched in other cities attempting to push broad change in street use. In Paris, for example, the yellow vest movement pushed back strongly against a raising of the gas tax and efforts to minimize car use. In Madrid, efforts to close central areas of the city to car traffic were met with counter proposals from differing political parties to keep the car landscape the same. In both cases, political pressure, though intense, has been met with counter pressure to keep moving forward with reforms. In Paris, efforts are under way to link residents to the city's expanding metro system through a network of safe bicycle infrastructure (O'Sullivan 2019b). The changes in Paris are starting to impact the number of cars on the street with the city's car ownership rate dropping from 60% in 2001 to 35% in 2019 (Nossiter 2019). The coronavirus response has also added reasons to address air pollution in the city and increase space for active transportation (see Prologue). In Madrid, the city had pushed for efforts to limit cars in the center of the city and add extra space for walking and bicycling (Medina 2018), but efforts were scaled back after political changes to a right-wing, pro-car government (O'Sullivan 2019a; Rodriguez-Pena 2019).

While the politics of *superillas* and car-free centers more generally remain in flux, the existing projects speak to the simplicity of the technology needed to repurpose streets. In the Poblenou project in Barcelona, for example, sections of streets are blocked off to through car traffic with planters and the remaining street sections are "activated" as public places with benches and stenciled games on the pavement itself. In one section, there is a 50-meter (55-yard) running track painted down the middle of the street to encourage kids to run and have fun. There are also other sections where more elaborate makeovers have taken place with full playgrounds taking over street space.

Overall, what stands out is both the low-cost, simplicity of the designs and the impact on city life that these small changes accomplish. Currently, large potted

FIGURE 10.1 Poblenou *superilla*.

plants have been added to the streets as a type of placeholder for green infrastructure. Paint and bollards are used to guide cars through narrow sections of the streets (Figure 10.1). The result is slow-speed access to cars in the area and a return of citizens to the neighborhood streets. Older residents sit on the benches reading in the Catalan sun. Kids with parents play in the neighborhood streets. At the same time, pedestrians, cyclists, and cars move slowly through the streets.

The difference between the repurposed Poblenou streets and the adjacent streets that have not received these treatments is stark. In the nearby streets, there are no benches and no older residents enjoying the Catalan sun. There are no playgrounds in the streets and no parents and children playing. There are, however, cars parked in every possible portion of the streets. The street corners have even been shaved to add extra parking at just the space needed for pedestrians to cross. The result is higher-speed traffic with pedestrians and bicyclists jockeying for space in a fairly hostile streetscape.

While the Poblenou *superilla* is noteworthy compared to the adjacent neighborhoods, it is not, as Roberts (2019b) points out, "a perfect urbanism postcard. It is, for lack of a better term, somewhat ragged." The efforts in Barcelona, though noteworthy, are really only small-scale efforts to transform individual neighborhood areas through strategic traffic calming and minimal public space enhancement. We have already discussed efforts in Rotterdam (Chapter 5) and Copenhagen (Chapter 6) that effectively create neighborhood traffic-calmed streets at a large scale across these cities. The *superillas* in Barcelona might better be seen as an important neighborhood-based pilot project for change. Scaling up these pilot projects across the city could provide a tangible mechanism for moving towards the more advanced Dutch or Danish models quickly. As these *superilla* efforts begin to scale, adding permanent green infrastructure and working with the neighborhoods to further activate the spaces could make these initial attempts to reclaim city streets even more successful and truly transform these areas into a series of linked urban islands. As Mueller et al. (2020) note, these changes are projected to have important impacts on the public health and livability of the city.

The coronavirus response has further pushed these issues to the front of the policy agenda. Pollution levels in Barcelona dropped 62% in the immediate months of the crisis and many residents did not want to return to the previous status quo of clogged streets and dirty air (United Nations 2020). At the same time, the need for more space for safe movement in the city became a pressing issue (Carey 2020). Barcelona responded with plans to add 12 km (7.4 miles) of additional space for pedestrians, increased use of 30-km (18.6-mile) zones, and created an additional 21 km (13 miles) of bicycle infrastructure (Guerrero 2020). As Barcelona emerges from the crisis, the difficult push and pull of street space politics will continue to be negotiated.

Vancouver: green islands linked by transit and an all ages and abilities (AAA) bicycling network

While the *superillas* of Barcelona have received a great deal of well-deserved attention, a number of other similar approaches to neighborhood traffic calming and city placemaking are developing in other areas around the world. Vancouver's push to remake neighborhood streets to enhance walking and biking and simultaneously address water management issues is a powerful model of change within a North American context. The Vancouver example shows how it is possible to change car-oriented streets into neighborhood amenities and, importantly, highlights how these changes can begin to be scaled up to help address transportation greenhouse gas (GHG) emissions (mitigation) and form a more holistic water management system through insertion of well-designed green infrastructure (adaptation).

While Vancouver is becoming a model for remaking its streets, it is really a city in transition with the streets of the past still dominating most of the landscape. Most streets in Vancouver resemble those of other North American cities with large multi-lane, one-way roadways dominating downtown. Over the last 20 years, however, the city has significantly expanded its rail rapid transit system, begun a program to reclaim streets as public spaces through traffic calming, and expanded its protected bicycle facility network. Brent Toderian (2013), the former Director of City Planning for Vancouver, notes that these changes are based on privileging "active, healthy and green" modes of transportation first and then adding in the car "as the last priority." He notes that, while this hasn't happened in all projects, "the decision to prioritize rather than balance" provides an important policymaking framework for creating the "multi-modal city." This suite of changes has resulted in a 21% increase in walking, biking, and transit from 2006 to 2016 with the city's walk, bike, transit mode share now standing at 50% for all trips (City of Vancouver 2018). At the same time that the city began to move towards building the multimodal city, Vancouver began expanding green infrastructure components into the street system both as water management and traffic-calming tools. While many of the city streets are still car-dominated, the emerging system offers a glimpse at what is possible within a North American context and speaks to an emerging city resilience framework, the seeds of an adaptation urbanism system.

Vancouver urban resilience: transit

Vancouver's transit system has greatly expanded over the last 20 years and now provides fairly broad coverage in central Vancouver. The light-rail system, for example, is a fully automated system with 50 miles (80 km) of track and service as often as every 100 seconds at peak hours. This system has been integrated with land use planning to help encourage development around the light-rail stops with 146 new development projects planned in station areas (Gutman 2018). When combined with the regular bus and bus rapid transit routes, the Vancouver system provides a robust transportation alternative in the city core. It is also notable that Vancouver is the only North American city without an urban expressway system. Increasing transit and limiting auto infrastructure can go hand in hand to build more livable cities.

Vancouver urban resilience: green islands

During this same time period, Vancouver began to add on-street bike lanes and connect a set of residential bike boulevards that often include integrated green infrastructure. The traffic-calming system began as a way to limit and slow down car travel in residential areas through the use of small, green traffic circles. In some areas, full street closures have been added for a block or two that act as mini-parks for the neighborhood and as traffic-calming tools. Bikes and pedestrians are led through the street closures into the green blocks. The neighborhood traffic management systems have also grown to include more explicit green infrastructure treatments like curb bulb-outs with bioswales that act as both traffic calming and as "mini-sponges" for water management. As Paul Krueger from the Vancouver Department of Transportation points out, "Traffic diverters are opportunities for green infrastructure or public space or both" (author interview August 2019).

A good example of these types of changes can be seen in the network of streets in the West End area of the city. Streets in this area lead from downtown through the neighborhood and out to the Stanley Park peninsula. Multiple generations of traffic calming are woven through the neighborhood with first-generation small traffic circles and street diversions sharing space with more recent parklets and traffic-calming systems. The effect of this suite of traffic-calming systems is dramatic

FIGURE 10.2 Bute/Robson Plaza.

as traffic speeds are slow, public use of the mini-parks is high, and a shared sense of being in a place rather than on a road permeates the neighborhood.

Probably the most interesting project of this type can be seen at the Bute/Robson Plaza (Figure 10.2). The street area was closed to through car traffic, but bikes and pedestrians filter through the new public space. Benches and chairs extend into the street from the local bakery. New green planters have been added and even a piano has been placed in the street to encourage public life. The day we visited an older gentleman was playing the piano in the summer sun with neighborhood residents and café guests sitting in the new public park in the space that had once been a street. When it rains, the employees of the café come out and put a cover over the piano. Streets can be more than movement corridors: streets as public space, public space as streets.

This full model of green street closures is being pursued in other areas of the city as well and forms a type of North American version of the *superilla*. Taking inspiration from the Barcelona naming scheme, perhaps these could be called green islands. The feeling of transformation in these places is powerful.

Vancouver urban resilience: all ages and abilities bicycle network

In downtown, the city has begun to build out a network of protected cycle tracks to link the neighborhood systems. To the south, new protected bicycle lanes have been added to the Burrard Street Bridge connecting out to the Arbutus Greenway and to the east similar treatments have been added to the Georgia Viaduct that connect to the Union/Adanac Corridor. The Union/Adanac Corridor, one of the busiest bicycle corridors in Vancouver, provides a glimpse into a broad set of adaptation urbanism street components. Green street elements like bioswales and mini-park modal filters are combined with placemaking features like street ping pong and skateboard elements (City of Vancouver n.d.). This corridor feels like a fully fleshed-out version of the green street concept with traffic calming, water management, and placemaking combined together. Compared to the initial green streets designs like the still lovely but eminently upgradeable Ankeny Street design in Portland (or the initial version of the Adananc Corridor, for that matter), the new design feels like a leap forward. The Vancouver approach to continuous improvement shows how traffic calming local streets with green infrastructure and strategic placemaking can be connected with a downtown network of cycle tracks to create a protected system. The process of building this system took political push through an intense multi-year process, but the end results are the backbone of arguably the best active transportation system in North America.

All of this is designed to begin to create a full All Ages and Abilities (AAA) network that makes cycling safe and easy for kids, older residents, and all ages in between. The system is based on two simple but powerful principles of street design. The City of Vancouver's (2017) *Transportation Design Guidelines: All Ages and Abilities Cycling Routes* defines these two elements as: "Ensuring low motor vehicle speeds and volumes on local streets, or [p]roviding physical separation on busy streets." These direct guidelines also match closely with the Dutch and Danish approach to bicycle design and create a clear pathway to Vision Zero street design (Toderian 2019). Instead of fighting street by street to include active transportation, the street design guidelines place appropriate and safe active transport provision into all designs with either traffic calming on slower streets or physical separation on higher-speed, higher-volume streets. The policy innovation here is the movement from ad hoc active transportation decisions to systematic use of proven Vision Zero guidelines that create a new expectation for how city streets should be designed.

Designing an AAA system is not technically hard, but rather politically challenging. Strong design guidelines that include traffic-calmed neighborhoods and protected bike and pedestrian facilities on higher-speed streets and then tenacious adherence to these components are the foundation of the AAA system. Failure to integrate these elements creates a far less safe system. It is a policy choice between a safer, low-carbon system and a less safe, carbon-intensive system.

Following these design precepts, Vancouver has strategically been remaking its streets into far safer and more attractive places that encourage cycling by citizens of all ages with 25% of the system now rated AAA (City of Vancouver 2018). The suite of changes to Vancouver's streets has begun to show how North American cities can truly be transformed. In 1994, for example, Vancouver's mode share for cycling was very similar to many other North American cities at about 1%. The city slowly began to add bike lanes and connect to neighborhood greenways throughout the late 1990s and early 2000s. The AAA movement has developed over the last 10 or so years and has begun to move the needle on the share of trips taken by bicycles. In 2018, Vancouver reported that 7% of all trips in the city were taken by bike utilizing the over 200-mile (325-km) network of bike facilities as the base for these trips (City of Vancouver 2019a). By measuring the extent of AAA infrastructure and committing to increasing this total and linking the network together, Vancouver has begun to create an important template for systematically changing streets over time.

Streets, public spaces, and green infrastructure

In addition to remaking streets to be safer and more encouraging for active transportation and transit, Vancouver has begun to layer green infrastructure into street and public space projects. Beginning with pilot projects and objects of opportunity like the Olympic Village, Vancouver has tested green infrastructure inclusions in its street projects over the last 10–15 years and is now ready to begin to move towards more systematic inclusion of green infrastructure into new street projects in a more systematic fashion.

Vancouver's Rainwater Management Plan and Green Infrastructure Strategy (City of Vancouver 2016) links current outcome data with benchmarks to help push the city departments towards this more systematic integration of green infrastructure. The plan notes that about 30% of city space is currently filled with impermeable roads (p. 5). These roads and adjacent public space are increasingly seen, however, as opportunity spaces for collecting and managing the plentiful rainwater of the Pacific Northwest. The plan sets the goal of capturing and infiltrating 90% of annual rainfall before it reaches the marine environment by treating rainfall as a resource, greening land use and streets, and returning rainfall to natural pathways. To accomplish these goals, Vancouver has created a green infrastructure toolkit (Table 10.1) designed to link policy actions with water management benefits. While the toolkit represents a detailed set of green infrastructure landscape tools, the use of larger water squares and water boulevards is currently not included in the list as distinct policy tools. Given the success of water boulevards in the Netherlands and water squares in Copenhagen and Rotterdam, including these elements as additional toolkit items may make sense in the future, particularly in light of Vancouver's placemaking initiatives.

Finally, the Plan notes that a key part of achieving the policy goals is creating multi-departmental teams aimed at coordinating city actions across differing landscape categories. The Plan points out that, "To achieve the long-term goal and target of the Rainwater Management Plan, the Green Infrastructure Strategy will need to be planned through a focused and dedicated multi-departmental effort" (City of Vancouver 2016, p. 6). The planned approach focuses on the creation of

TABLE 10.1 Vancouver green infrastructure toolkit

Tools
Absorbent landscapes
Infiltration swales
Raingardens and infiltration bulges
Pervious paving
Green roofs
Tree well structures
Rainwater harvesting
Infiltration trenches
Water quality structures
Detention tanks
Daylighted streams and channel improvements
Constructed wetlands

a green infrastructure team with representatives of engineering, planning, finance, and the park board of the city. The green infrastructure team then will jointly build work plans, identify resources and needs, and develop key metrics for policy implementation. Overall, this plan represents an important framework for building green infrastructure into business-as-usual practices of city departments. As City of Vancouver landscape designer Paul Lightfoot argues, the goal is to make green infrastructure inclusion "just another component of how to rebuild a street" (author interview August 2019).

Climate emergency: streets as places for urban resilience

As these efforts have moved forward, the urgency of climate as a policy issue has increased. Vancouver is attempting to wrap multiple efforts together through its Climate Emergency policy designation (City of Vancouver 2019b). In the transportation sector, the goal is to increase the walking, biking, transit share of trips to two-thirds of all trips by 2030 (Toderian 2019). For the remaining trips that are taken by cars and trucks, the goal is to make 50% of these trips taken by zero-emission vehicles by 2030. This is a good example of how active transport and transit can be prioritized while including targeted electric vehicle goals.

Vancouver shows what happens when policy, funding, and resolve come together to reshape transportation priorities. This is a powerful template for the North American resilient city that emphasizes both zero-emission vehicles and a changing street design to push emission reductions. When taken together with the work to enhance green infrastructure in neighborhoods to address water management and slow traffic, Vancouver can be seen as an emerging model of adaptation urbanism transformation where climate adaptation and mitigation are being woven together into projects designed to enhance neighborhood livability.

The Netherlands deep urban resilience: Amsterdam, Delft, and Utrecht

While Vancouver shows the potential to rethink and reclaim streets for urban life, cities in the Netherlands have both piloted and institutionalized dramatic street makeovers, collectively taking the ideas of adaptation urbanism and putting them into practice across the country. While we have already discussed Rotterdam and several other examples in depth, the transformation of Dutch streets to encourage safe active transportation and the deep relationship with living with water warrant more discussion.

Across the country, 70% of Dutch city streets have been transformed into 30-km (18.6-mile) zones (19 mph or less) and most larger streets have protected cycle tracks (SWOV 2018). While any individual Dutch city will have streets that could be improved, the majority of streets in the entire country have essentially been transformed to address these two basic principles of safe streets: traffic-calmed neighborhood streets and protected bicycle infrastructure on higher-speed streets. These safe active street connections provide access to a well-integrated bus, tram, and train system that, taken together, makes low-carbon transportation the easy choice for most residents. The whole country seems to be a functioning example of well-designed transit-oriented development with easy active transportation access (Jonkeren et al. 2019).

At the same time, the base of long-standing water management integration into the urban environment shows how green and blue infrastructure can be used to create highly livable systems. The ubiquitous canals of the Netherlands linked with water boulevards connect across the country. They are increasingly being linked with extended rural bicycle trails that create a functioning bicycle highway system. The base of Dutch resilience is this interconnected system of water management and active transportation connectivity.

We highlight a suite of three Dutch cities that are pushing forward with significant street and water conversions that build on this base: Amsterdam, Delft, and Utrecht. These cities show how Dutch resilience builds on a base of centuries of water management governance, a new spirit of living with water, and, importantly, the underlying components of a safe systems transportation system.

Amsterdam: the street of the future emerges from the push of the past

Amsterdam has often been seen as a city of bicycles, but the decline of bicycling in the 1960s and its resurrection in the 1980s and 1990s is less known (Feddes and de Lange 2019). Amsterdam in the 1960s was essentially following the US model of transportation planning that focused on extending high-speed streets into the cores of cities. Amsterdam had a series of expressways inserted, streets widened, and canals covered over before significant political pushback in the 1970s reversed the policy direction. The hard-political battles of this era and the subsequent policy shifts towards a safe systems street-planning system helped to usher in the resurgent Amsterdam of bicycles that captures the public imagination.

Amsterdam has begun to innovate again and the developments over the last few years offer guidance about the potential of streets to be used as key physical locations for innovative climate adaptation and mitigation projects. While the entire city seems to offer valuable lessons on integrating active transportation and water management, two recent projects stand out. The first, as we discussed in Chapter 1 of the book (Figure 1.2), focuses on the use of street closures for cars and repurposing of street space for transit, walking, and bicycling through a park-like setting. The street design example of Plantage Middenlaan privileges active transportation and transit as key tools for climate mitigation, integrates a permeable green median and adjacent canals to address climate adaptation, and, simultaneously, creates a new *place* in the center of the city. This modest street segment in the heart of Amsterdam offers a glimpse at what a resilient street can look like and may offer a vision of an emerging climate street network.

It is worth revisiting this example again in light of the previous discussions in this chapter of *superillas* and green islands. Plantage Middenlaan and adjacent water boulevards feel more like a fully realized version of the green island concept. Instead of the unfinished feel of the *superillas* in Barcelona or the more minimal green islands in the midst of larger street networks in Vancouver, Plantage Middenlaan acts as a green island amidst the blue connections of canals and the cycle tracks on adjacent larger streets. It acts as a new layer on the resilient base of water and bicycle infrastructure that was already in place. Amsterdam is still a big city with people moving at pace through the area, but the movement is more like a dance than a competition. The green island here acts like a place to take a break, to enjoy the quiet, or, as need or mood dictates, continue moving through the corridor connecting into the streets and water boulevards of the city. While quantifying the impacts of these existing features is difficult and seems like a public health intervention worthy of a health impact assessment (Mueller et al. 2020), the full suite of features creates the base of a truly resilient street system with climate mitigation, adaptation, and placemaking embedded as core elements.

Standing here, or in many other places in Amsterdam, you can see a distinctly different future of transportation beginning to take shape where streets have both movement and place functions. Some people move along the tram tracks or cycle tracks, while others sit and watch the world go by in the park-like setting. The movement and place functions are not in conflict here, but rather function together. When the place, movement, and climate mitigation and adaptation components of the street are taken together, the outlines of a well-planned resilient street system begin to come into focus. Scaled up, a system like this works for local needs and simultaneously has a global function of limiting GHG emissions and managing water.

Imagining the scaling potential of this short road segment gives a sense of a different future for cities and streets. Creating this street of the future does not happen in one moment but is instead built through a series of projects (safe neighborhood bicycle infrastructure, light-rail investment, compact urban development, use of canals, and then the specific green median project). Resilience planning needs to begin to better understand the funding, bureaucratic structures, and political coalitions necessary to build these layers over time to help uncover the potential of adaptation urbanism to create and sustain places like this.

Another place in Amsterdam that offers a glimpse of the future and simultaneously shows how political push is vital to change is the De Pijp neighborhood. The neighborhood offers a window into the history of the last 50 years of street planning in the Netherlands all within several square blocks. The area was one of the neighborhoods that was supposed to be sacrificed for the creation of a 1960s expressway system. The expressway was planned to move through the heart of the neighborhood and then slice across the entire city paving over the Singel Canal to create a ring road for the city (Not Just Bikes 2019).

The plan, Geef de Stad Een Kans, translated from Dutch, means Give the City a Chance. This plan fits within the broad set of modernist plans from the 1950s and 1960s from around the world that argued that cities must be remade for the car to make them relevant. As Le Corbusier argued,

> Statistics show us that business is conducted in the centre. This means that wide avenues must be driven through the centres of our towns. *Therefore the existing centres must come down.* To save itself, every great city must rebuild its centre.
>
> *(Hall 2014)*

As proof of the need to destroy the city to save it, these plans often pointed to the increasing number and projected increases in cars as forecast in the frictionless models of future demand. Feddes and de Lange (2019) capture this sentiment well when they argue that planners of this era believed that "the future was a linear continuation of prevailing trends. Essentially, there were no alternative scenarios" (p. 30). The modern future was to be as solid as the trend lines that always extended upward. Arguing against these trends was arguing against the future.

The residents of De Pijp and other impacted neighborhoods, however, envisioned an alternative scenario where their own neighborhoods would not be sacrificed on the altar of the modern expressway. They envisioned a city where their homes and families were included in the future of the city rather than erased because of trend lines that did not include them in their equations.[1]

In De Pijp and other neighborhoods, the fight for the appropriate future was joined with a protest movement focused first on stopping the expressway and then more broadly on rethinking the role of cars in the city. After the initial success at stopping the expressway, De Pijp was one of the first locations for the Stop the Child Murder protests from the early 1970s that, in a direct Dutch way, pointed out the growing number of children who were being killed in car crashes. In 1972, the highest recorded year for fatality crashes, 457 children aged 14 and under were killed in transportation crashes in the Netherlands (SWOV 2020).

The Stop the Child Murder movement helped to spark a wider effort for safe streets across the Netherlands. Feddes and de Lange (2019) provide a detailed history of this movement and how Amsterdam streets were gradually taken back from the car in the 1980s and 1990s. The analysis shows how political push in Amsterdam and other cities led to a succession of small changes that resulted in shifts in organizational practices that finally scaled to the institutionalization of improved safe systems standards across the country. The result is that transportation fatalities for children aged 14 and under across the Netherlands decreased from 457 in 1972 to 15 in 2017. While the country as a whole grew by almost four million residents from 1972 to 2017, the transportation fatality numbers for children 14 and under declined by 97% during this same period (SWOV 2020).

The overall transportation fatality numbers from the Netherlands dropped from 3,264 to 535, an 84% decline. While US transportation fatalities have also declined significantly (41% decline from 1972 to 2011), the United States did not match the safety improvement rate of the Netherlands. Evans (2014) calculates that if the United States had matched the overall transportation fatality decline achieved in the Netherlands, 22,075 fewer deaths would have occurred in the United States from 1972 to 2011 (Evans 2014). For context, this is 566 additional fatalities per year because of the failure to institute safe street policies. This is the equivalent of about three Boeing 737 Max aircraft crashing per year for 39 years. If 117 planes crashed because available safety procedures were ignored, this would be a large political issue.

Resilient streets need to be safe streets. We have the technology to significantly improve street safety today, but only if we *push* for it. The lessons from the Netherlands show what is possible when street safety is taken seriously. Changing streets is hard political work that doesn't come all at once, but, in the case of Amsterdam and the Netherlands more broadly, in a succession of waves that opens new potential as they move forward.

The process of reinvention is still ongoing. Amsterdam is now seeking to remove 10,000 parking spaces from the streets over the next few years to open more neighborhood green space and improve livability. The first pilot project is in De Pijp. Some of the on-street parking in De Pijp is being moved to underground garages, but some of it is being removed from the streets for the benefit of city residents who don't own a car. Currently, green planters, children's play areas, and bike parking are being added as car parking is being removed. Over the next few years, these temporary tactical urbanism measures will be made permanent through a process of working with the neighbors to identify key items that would make the neighborhood a better place. New mini-green spaces, mini-parks, and slower, safer streets are being planned (Eckerson 2019a). The new space in the city will help to infiltrate water and, probably more importantly for area residents, add spaces for kids to play, residents to garden and sit in the new green places, and overall add a village-like quiet charm back into the heart of the city.

The changes in De Pijp show how long-term political push can change the course of what is possible. From a neighborhood that was seen as expendable to a place for children to play in the slow streets, negotiating and pushing on each present moment open up new potential for the future. The alternative city may always be just out of reach, but it can be shaped by public discourse to better meet the needs of citizens.

Delft: from Woonerfs to climate streets

Another example of this type of citizen-led planning can be seen in the Dutch university town of Delft. The story of the transformation of Delft mirrors the changes in Amsterdam in many ways. The city's beautiful town square, framed by the 1554 Nieuwe Kerk cathedral, was being used as a car-parking lot in the 1970s. As Peter Newman notes in the Foreword the small streets of the city were overrun with cars and the city planners of the day, using the latest linear projection models, argued that the city needed a highway through the center of the city.

As in Amsterdam, the citizens began to push back. One of the earliest efforts to push back on the inevitability of these trend lines was the citizen effort to slow traffic on the narrow streets near the city's train station. Residents pulled couches out of their houses, placed plants in the streets, and created an early version of traffic calming on Westerstraat. This became one of the first examples of a *woonerf* or living street.

Mobycon Consulting, headquartered in Delft, leads tours down this tiny unassuming street and highlights the small design changes that create a safe, livable street. While each living street will incorporate slightly different, contextual elements, the key elements on Westerstraat in Delft are identified in Table 10.2. Before the *superillas* or green islands, the humble *woonerf* on Westerstraat in Delft began to show planners how to rethink streets. The simple design elements show how streets can be remade with inexpensive elements into safe neighborhood streets that are the backbone of an adaptation urbanism system.

Angela van der Kloof of Mobycon points out that visitors to the Westerstraat are drawn to "the simplicity of it. It looks so doable." For van der Kloof, the design helps to build safety and sociability, especially for kids. She says,

> One of the things I like about the woonerf is that it is easier for kids to play outside and in some woonerfs, it is not just in a street but in a little playground...There is this sense that it is inviting for kids to play.

TABLE 10.2 Delft *woonerf*/living street elements

Woonerf signage	Street trees
Transition zone across cycle track/sidewalk	Bike and car parking
Change in brick color	Speed tables
Change in elevation between street segments	Mini-park
Brick pavement	Murals
Chicanes	Benches
Green curb bulb-outs	Green island public space

This freedom of kids to play and move about on their own is a hallmark of contemporary Dutch streets. Younger kids are free to move in their neighborhoods and older kids are free to move about the city on their own. Waves of kids will pass you on bicycles laughing and talking. The safe city is the social city.

The elements of the Delft *woonerf* and Dutch neighborhood street design in general are simple and effective in creating slow-speed streets that are safe and inviting. These designs filter out high-speed, non-local traffic. These straightforward street designs are the foundation of healthy neighborhoods in multiple contexts and deserve serious consideration for outright "copying" in other areas. Robert Weetman (2018) notes that

> The Netherlands residential street design can be copied **here and now**. And in many ways relatively little actual engineering is required to get started. Designs needn't be perfect—the Netherlands ones aren't. They just need to be definite in controlling motor vehicle permeability.

While the "historic" *woonerf* in Delft shows the first generation of Dutch street redesigns from the 1970s and early 1980s, Delft's city center is filled with multiple projects that showcase other adaptation urbanism approaches. The city experimented with creating a full network system of connected bicycle infrastructure during the 1980s as part of the Dutch bicycle pilot program (Wagenbuur 2019). The program, according to Van Goeverden and Godefrooij (2011, p. 1), was part of a larger "paradigm shift in thinking about traffic." This shift in thinking about the role of the car in the city has continued since the pilot program with a new model for climate streets (*klimaatstraats*) with permeable pavement and green infrastructure on Hof van Delftlaan, the replacement of a central roadway at Delft University of Technology (TU Delft) with a cycle track that connects to the city center, the addition of a new tram system from the train station into the heart of the university campus, and removal of car parking from the Nieuwe Kerk and Beestenmarkt, creating beautiful well-used city squares. Meanwhile multiple streets and traffic circles have been redesigned into templates of safe systems road design.

The largest example of these types of city redevelopment projects is the massive redesign of the Delft train station and adjacent area. Delft Centraal had been separated from the city by elevated tracks that created an unattractive seam across the city. The redesign of the station buried the train tracks, redesigned the streets to add protected bicycle access, opened up the front of the station for tram access, daylighted canals, and created new land for development in the center of the city. The space has been transformed into an attractive, multi-purpose place with a new City Hall, cafés, and student housing that now sit on the edge of a network of daylighted waterways. The station has a massive underground bicycle-parking facility that allows for easy, direct access into the station. The train routes connect to Rotterdam and The Hague about every 15 minutes. Overall, these elements create a connected urban environment and frequent train service, key characteristics of strong rail station planning (Loukaitou-Sideris et al. 2017, p. 14).

The integrated elements also create a powerful example of a connected low-carbon transportation system. All of this is accomplished because of the synergy of station access from active transportation and local buses that link directly to the station. There is no car parking at the station and the station area is filled with city life. If the Delft redevelopment was in the United States, it would be a model that planners would visit with a sense of wonder and awe. In the Netherlands, it is just another project, a step in pushing the city forward.

Utrecht: the modern city as a resilient city

While the Delft station redevelopment is a model for smaller cities, the transformation of Utrecht is a prototype for larger cities planned to be connected with high-speed rail lines (Loukaitou-Sideris et al. 2017). Utrecht, the fourth largest city in the Netherlands, is in the process of uncovering its medieval canals that were buried in the car experiment of the 1960s. The project is creating a dramatic transformation of its city center from the high-rise modernism of Le Corbusier to a livable, water city focused on active transportation and transit/train access.

In the 1950s, however, the template of the modern city was considerably different. Many cities in the Netherlands, like those in the United States and many others around the world, were attempting to find space to expand their roadway networks. The reductive, "efficient" location for many of these new roads was often seen in burying canals and using the new city space for roadways. As we discussed in the case studies of Rotterdam and New Orleans, this process resulted in the "drained city" (Brown et al. 2009) where water was buried, and automobile space expanded.

This process took place in Utrecht where the 12th-century medieval canal that surrounded the old city was slated for burial with a new ring road added to connect the city to the modern world. Mark Wagenbuur's (2016) practical history of the area highlights the political struggles that saved some parts of the canal, but eventually resulted in burying the north and west parts of the canal for a new, 1960s roadway.

In the United States, this is usually where the story ends with a before image and then the after shot of a radically changed space replacing the historic landscape. There is even a series of books, the Then and Now series, that highlights the changing city (see, for example, Campanella and Campanella 1999 or the city series by Pavillion Books). The "now" image is almost always a shot of a forlorn space that evokes a sense of sadness compared to the history that was lost.

In Utrecht, however, the story doesn't end with the historic demolition. As Schuetze (2017) notes, Utrecht is now pioneering a "concept of progress [that] looks quite different." The city is in the process of daylighting the 700-year-old canal on Catharijnesingel and resurrecting the new waterscape as a vital feature of a more appropriate version of the modern city (Figure 10.3). This development creates a new city archetype of change, the "Before–After–Resilient" series where the history of the city is destroyed and then brought back to life again like a disaster movie in reverse. This moves Utrecht towards a water-sensitive city approach, outlined by Brown et al. (2009), where water is managed to become an amenity for

FIGURE 10.3 From ring road to living with water (Catharijnesingel).

the resilient city. In Utrecht's case, they have resurrected the traditional Dutch water boulevard concept of traffic-calmed streets with a center canal as the embodiment of the living-with-water ethos.

Utrecht takes this approach further by linking the newly uncovered water resource to a broader reconsideration of the transportation system overall that improves livability and decreases GHG emissions. Utrecht currently has 51% of commuters traveling to the city center via a combination of trains and bikes, the highest percentage in the Netherlands (Bruntlett and Bruntlett 2018, p. 136). Utrecht has become one of the world's leading cycling cities, currently ranked number 3 in the world in the Copenhagenize ranking of top bicycling cities (Copenhagen and Amsterdam are numbers one and two). The path to improving the bicycle system is not rocket science, but instead involves improving the connections to safe bicycle infrastructure in a structured, methodical fashion. Utrecht spends about $55 million annually on improving bicycle infrastructure, but saves $300 million in improved health and air quality impacts (Schuetze 2017). As Saskia Kluit, CEO of Fiesterbond, argues in an excellent compilation of Utrecht cycling changes in Clarence Eckerson's Utrecht *Streetfilms* (2019b), "things have changed radically in the last years so you can see what happens if you choose the radical choice; get the car out and the bikes and people in."

Eckerson's full *Streetfilms* piece on Utrecht presents a template for city transformation. The film interviews key planners and advocates and explains how a series of changes have transformed the city. Key projects include the Croeselaan street redesign in front of Centraal Station that transformed a four-lane road into a traffic-calmed street interwoven with cycle tracks and green infrastructure, the Mariaplaats street redesign, where 75 car-parking places were removed at the request of local

FIGURE 10.4 Utrecht transformed.

businesses, the Dafne Schippersbrug cycle track/bridge project that moves seamlessly over a school, the world's largest bike-parking station at Utrecht Centraal with 12,500 bicycle-parking spaces, the introduction of bicycle streets that create a special type of 30-km (18.6-mile) street where cars are guests, and finally the canal/road/canal transformation. This is a single sentence of projects with years of effort and a fully transformed central city as a result (Figure 10.4). Mark Waggonbuur, interviewed in the film, sums up the changes as the canal returns to the city center. He says, "Soon that motorway will only be a footnote in history" (Eckerson 2019b). The future of the city can be different if we want it.

Conclusion

The modern future is not preordained. It is contested. The present in Utrecht, Delft, or Amsterdam was a vision a few short years ago. The emerging changes in Barcelona and Vancouver show how pilot projects can gradually be scaled up, beginning to create broader systems of safe, climate-adapted streets and public spaces. The key transportation components of this transformation are traffic-calmed neighborhood streets and protected bicycle facilities on higher-speed roads. When these components are combined with green and blue infrastructure like the bioswales in Vancouver or the canals in the Netherlands, streets and public spaces can act as fundamental resilience components in climate mitigation and adaptation systems. At the same time, the street spaces begin to act as livable places for the community. Resilient streets weave climate mitigation in the form of safe, inviting active transport/transit together with climate adaptation in the form of green and blue infrastructure to create places of long-term value. This is the vision of adaptation urbanism.

This future won't come in one large step, but rather needs to be guided through a succession of local processes of reinvention to steer the city forward. Within this complicated process of local engagement, we need to begin to figure out how to accelerate these processes, to deliberately layer on the key components of safe streets and green and blue infrastructure to create a network of truly resilient streets. While the street of the future on Plantage Middenlaan in Amsterdam resulted from decades of purposeful changes to the streets and neighboring public spaces, the pressing climate crisis requires that we begin to figure out how to scale up adaptation urbanism solutions with much greater speed. In essence, we need to identify how to make the resilient street the default street design if cities are serious about addressing climate change.

Note

1 Marshal Berman's discussion of modernism comes to mind here. The modern city should be "a dialogue among the past, the present and the future" (Berman 1982, p. 6) where the positive characteristics of the existing place are accentuated to build livable, safe neighborhoods for all residents. In this modern city, "the streets, our streets, are where modernism belongs. The open way leads to the public square" (Berman 1982, p. 12). The challenge is finding the appropriate modernism for the time that helps to build the type of city, the type of streets, that help that vision grow.

References

Berman, M. (1982). *All That is Solid Melts Into Air: The Experience of Modernity*. New York: Penguin.

Brown, R. R., Keath, N., & Wong, T. H. (2009). Urban Water Management in Cities: Historical, Current and Future Regimes. *Water Science and Technology*, *59*(5), 847–855.

Bruntlett, M., & Bruntlett, C. (2018). *Building the Cycling City: The Dutch Blueprint for Urban Vitality*. Washington, D.C.: Island Press.

Campanella, R., & Campanella, M. (1999). *New Orleans Then and Now*. Gretna, LA: Pelican Publishing.

Carey, Christopher. (2020). Barcelona Traffic Down 80 Percent Since Coronavirus Lockdown. *Cities Today*. April 27. Last accessed 6/15/2020 from https://cities-today.com/barcelona-traffic-down-80-percent-since-coronavirus-lockdown/.

City of Vancouver. (n.d.). Adanac Vernon Plaza. Last accessed 3/29/2020 from https://vancouver.ca/streets-transportation/adanac-vernon-plaza.aspx.

City of Vancouver. (2016). Rainwater Management Plan and Green Infrastructure Strategy. Last accessed 3/29/2020 from https://council.vancouver.ca/20160419/documents/rr2.pdf.

City of Vancouver. (2017). Transportation Design Guidelines: All Ages and Abilities Cycling Routes. Last accessed 3/29/2020 from https://vancouver.ca/files/cov/design-guidelines-for-all-ages-and-abilities-cycling-routes.pdf.

City of Vancouver. (2018). Walking and Cycling in Vancouver 2017 Report Card. Last accessed 3/29/2020 from https://vancouver.ca/files/cov/cycling-report-card-2017.pdf.

City of Vancouver. (2019a). Catalogue of Protected Bike Lanes. Last accessed 3/29/2020 from https://vancouver.ca/files/cov/protected-bike-lane-catalogue-part-1-one-way-bike-lanes.pdf.

City of Vancouver. (2019b). Climate Emergency Response. Last accessed 3/29/2020 from https://council.vancouver.ca/20190424/documents/cfsc1.pdf.

Eckerson, Clarence Jr. (2019a). Amsterdam's Removing 10K Parking Spaces: See What That Can Look Like! *Streetfilms.* June 2. Last accessed 3/30/2020 from www.streetfilms.org/amsterdams-removing-10k-parking-spaces-see-what-that-can-look-like/.

Eckerson, Clarence Jr. (2019b). Utrecht: Planning for People & Bikes, Not for Cars. *Streetfilms.* June 27. Last accessed 3/30/2020 from www.streetfilms.org/utrecht-planning-for-people-not-for-cars/.

Evans, L. (2014). Traffic Fatality Reductions: United States Compared with 25 Other Countries. *American Journal of Public Health, 104*(8), 1501–1507.

Feddes, F., & de Lange, M. (2019). *Bike City Amsterdam: How Amsterdam Became the Cycling Capital of the World.* Amsterdam: Nieuw Amsterdam.

Guerrero, D. Barcelona convertirá espacios destinados al coche en aceras ampliadas y carriles bici. *La Vanguardia.* April 25. Last accessed 6/15/2020 from www.lavanguardia.com/local/barcelona/20200425/48704357907/barcelona-espacio-coches-aceras-carriles-bici-desconfinamiento-coronavirus.html.

Gutman. (2018). Is this the Future of Seattle Transit? A Look at Vancouver, B.C.—a City that Figured it Out Years Ago. *Seattle Times.* April 19. Last accessed 3/30/2020 from www.seattletimes.com/seattle-news/transportation/seattle-struggles-with-growth-and-transit-while-vancouver-b-c-figured-it-out-years-ago/.

Hall, P. (2014). *Cities of Tomorrow: An Intellectual History of Urban Planning and Design Since 1880.* Hoboken, NJ: John Wiley.

Jonkeren, O., Kager, R., Harms, L., & te Brömmelstroet, M. (2019). The Bicycle–Train Travellers in the Netherlands: Personal Profiles and Travel Choices. *Transportation*, 1–22. Published online October 26.

Loukaitou-Sideris, A., Peters, D., Colton, P., & Eidlin, E. (2017). A Comparative Analysis of High-Speed Rail Station Development into Destination and Multi-Use Facilities: The Case of San Jose Diridon. Mietta Transportation Institute. MTI Report 12–75. Last accessed 3/30/2020 from https://transweb.sjsu.edu/sites/default/files/1502-high-speed-rail-station-development-san-jose-diridon_0.pdf.

Medina, Miguel Angel. (2018). Madrid Takes Historic Step to Becoming a Car-Free City Center. *El País.* November 30. Last accessed 3/30/2020 from https://elpais.com/elpais/2018/11/30/inenglish/1543565577_207058.html.

Mueller, Natalie, Rojas-Rueda, David, Khreis, Haneen, Cirach, Marta, Andrés, David, Ballester, Joan, & Bartoll, Xavier. (2020). Changing the Urban Design of Cities for Health: The Superblock model. *Environment International, 134*, 105132.

Nossiter, Adam. (2019). The Greening of Paris Makes Its Mayor More Than a Few Enemies. *New York Times.* October 5. Last accessed 3/30/2020 from www.nytimes.com/2019/10/05/world/europe/paris-anne-hildago-green-city-climate-change.html.

Not Just Bikes. (2019). The Highway Plan that Almost Destroyed Amsterdam—Plan Jokinen. October 21. Last accessed 3/30/2020 from www.youtube.com/watch?v=vI5pbDFDZyI.

O'Sullivan, Feargus. (2019a). Is This the End of the Road for Madrid's Car Ban? *CityLab.* June 20. Last accessed 3/20/2020 from www.citylab.com/environment/2019/06/madrid-election-car-ban-traffic-congestion-emissions-spain/591961/.

O'Sullivan, Feargus. (2019b). In Paris's Suburbs, a Bike Trail Plan Carries a Big Promise. *CityLab.* August 15. Last accessed 3/20/2020 from www.citylab.com/transportation/2019/08/paris-bike-lanes-rer-v-cycle-track-petite-couronne/596089/.

Roberts, David. (2019a). Barcelona's Radical Plan to Take Back Streets from Cars. *Vox.com.* Last accessed 3/30/2019 from www.vox.com/energy-and environment/2019/4/9/18300797/barcelona-spain-superblocks-urban-plan.

Roberts, David. (2019b). Barcelona Wants to Build 500 Superblocks. Here's What it Learned from the First Ones. *Vox.com*. Last accessed 3/30/2019 from www.vox.com/energy-and-environment/2019/4/9/18273894/barcelona-urban-planning-superblocks-poblenou.

Rodriguez-Pena, Gloria. (2019). Madrid to Ease Low-Emissions Zone Restrictions: More Cars, Lower Parking Fees. *El País*. September 30. Last accessed 3/30/2020 from https://elpais.com/elpais/2019/09/30/inenglish/1569845738_731257.html.

Schuetze, Christopher F. (2017). If You Build It, The Dutch Will Pedal. *New York Times*. September 6. Last accessed 3/30/2020 from www.nytimes.com/2017/09/06/world/europe/bicycling-utrecht-dutch-love-bikes-worlds-largest-bike-parking-garages.html.

SWOV. (2018). *30 km/h Zones*. SWOV Fact Sheet. May. The Hague: SWOV.

SWOV. (2020). Road Safety in Numbers: Crashes. Last accessed 3/30/2020 from www.swov.nl/en/factsandfigures/road-safety-numbers-crashes.

Toderian, Brent. (2013). The Most Important Urban Design Decision Vancouver Ever Made. *Planetizen*. February 25. Last accessed 3/30/2020 from www.planetizen.com/node/60918.

Toderian, Brent. (2019). If Only Experienced Cyclists Feel Safe in a Bike Lane, Then is it a Bike Lane at All? *Fast Company*. June 10. Last accessed 3/30/2020 from www.fastcompany.com/90361034/if-only-experienced-cyclists-feel-safe-in-a-bike-lane-then-is-it-a-bike-lane-at-all.

United Nations. (2020). UN Eyes Bicycles as Driver of Post-COVID-19 'Green Recovery'. Department of Global Communications. May 22. Last accessed 6/15/2020 from www.un.org/en/coronavirus/un-eyes-bicycles-driver-post-covid-19-%E2%80%98green-recovery%E2%80%99.

Van Goeverden, C. D., & Godefrooij, T. (2011). The Dutch Reference Study: Cases of Interventions in Bicycle Infrastructure Reviewed in the Framework of Bikeability. TU Delft Department of Transport and Planning. Last accessed 3/30/2020 from www.cycling-embassy.org.uk/sites/cycling-embassy.org.uk/files/documents/Report%20Dutch%20cases.pdf.

Wagenbuur, Mark. (2016). Motorway Removed to Bring Back the Original Water. *Bicycle Dutch*. January 5. Last accessed 3/30/2020 from https://bicycledutch.wordpress.com/2016/01/05/motorway-removed-to-bring-back-original-water/.

Wagenbuur, Mark. (2019). The 1979 Delft Cycle Plan. *Bicycle Dutch*. February 27. Last accessed 3/30/2020 from https://bicycledutch.wordpress.com/2019/02/27/the-1979-delft-cycle-plan/.

Weetman, Robert. (2018). Amsterdam vs. Copenhagen Part 3. *Nicer Cities Livable Places*. February 15. Last accessed 3/30/2020 from https://robertweetman.wordpress.com/2018/02/15/amsterdam-vs-copenhagen-part-3/.

11

ADAPTATION URBANISM

Policy implications

Introduction

Our survey of international best practices highlights the growing trend of reimagining streets and public spaces as key tools to help manage greenhouse gas (GHG) emissions, improve safety, and, increasingly, manage water. At present, the projects we have highlighted in the case study and international survey chapters show more of an ad hoc use of adaptation urbanism tools in individual street projects rather than a full-fledged, citywide plan to implement a more holistic resilience agenda focused on both climate mitigation and adaptation.

While we found no city that had integrated adaptation urbanism into daily planning activities as a whole, we found multiple projects and even some smaller districts that were being planned based on adaptation urbanism principles (Table 1.2). In essence, we found that the street of the future exists today, but the resilient street is only beginning to take shape. We found variations of adaptation urbanism streets developing in multiple countries around the world. Some of these, like Plantage Middenlaan in Amsterdam or Sankt Kjelds Plads in Copenhagen, are fully formed examples of the best existing practices in incorporating active transportation and green and blue infrastructure. Others, like Cherokee St. in New Orleans, Ackney St. in Portland, and Union/Adanac in Vancouver, show the beginning movements towards a new vision for adaptation urbanism streets.

Overall, the most fully formed representation of adaptation urbanism projects was in Copenhagen where the suite of resilience plans and strong active transportation planning culture has resulted in a wide number of projects moving forward. While no individual plan or specific policy measure analyzed in Copenhagen integrated all of the adaptation urbanism elements in a strong fashion, the full suite of resilience plans and projects taken as a whole provides examples of highly advanced policy guidance for adaptation urbanism planning. In the Netherlands, a slightly different model of street and public space designs has relied on the deep resilience of legacy water and active transportation projects to act as a powerful adaptation urbanism base. This adaptation urbanism base is arguably stronger in Dutch cities than in Copenhagen.[1] New projects around the Netherlands are increasingly adding to this base with targeted efforts to enhance resilient street and public space systems. In London, we found that the Healthy Streets Approach offered a promising new policy tool to begin to move towards adaptation urbanism design, but there were still significant administrative hurdles to overcome to begin to push the new streets into wide adoption. On the flip side, we found that North American cities like Miami and New Orleans were only beginning to move in this direction. In Miami, we found promising projects, but there was no evidence of a broader movement towards more holistic street and public space resilience planning focused on adaptation urbanism indicators. New Orleans was a little more advanced with the Gentilly Resilience District, but wide adoption of these resilient street templates was still contested.

In this chapter, we synthesize the key policy lessons that are beginning to emerge as this new wave of street resilience projects is put into practice. We first focus on discovering key barriers to adaptation urbanism planning identified from case study and best-practice cities. While there are multiple, overlapping barriers that limit adaptation urbanism, three key barriers emerged through the research. These are bureaucratic silos and inertia that limit innovation, targeted public resistance movements that act to entrench the status quo, and overarching conceptual tensions about resilience and urbanism.

Next, we identify policy and governance reforms that can help to address these barriers. Specifically, we address the need to:

- Conceptually, reenvision streets as a central resilience platform for creating the safe/climate/equitable/space-efficient city
- Substantively, link funding to core outcomes of policy concern in the climate change era
- Politically, build towards a linked agenda between Vision Zero, equity, climate, smart growth, and public health interests in planning and programming for resilience.

Finally, we set forth a brief speculative agenda to push adaptation urbanism practice forward. There is no singular path forward, but instead a number of promising developments that could form the foundation of a strong movement towards more livable, safe, equitable, and climate-resilient communities. At the core of these reform initiatives is the imperative to begin to act now to build a new positive vision for cities as a key platform to address climate change. Inaction is clearly a potential policy choice that is currently acceptable to a large portion of the public and institutions. Urban resilience can be a powerful unifying movement to find avenues to overcome these barriers and build places that act to adapt and mitigate against the climate crisis. Adaptation urbanism is a pathway to place streets and public spaces as central tools in building livable, climate-resilient cities.

Obstacles to change

Bureaucratic inertia and siloing at the street level

One of the key impediments to rethinking the multi-functional capacity of streets is the firm set of auto-centric constraints constructed by the transportation bureaucratic state. This network of government organizations, state and national/federal rule-making bodies, and economic beneficiaries of the status quo has helped to create a set of strict auto-centric rules, funding mechanisms, and political constituencies that act to push narrow auto efficiency policy solutions to nearly all transportation problems (Aldred et al. 2019).

These overlapping institutions, rulemaking bodies, and Congressional committees that generate the funding for the system form a type of transportation iron triangle that acts to limit potential policy options and steer resources towards a narrow set of preexisting options. If the transportation policy problem is conceived to be strictly related to auto congestion and funding is tied to addressing congestion through increasing capacity of cars, then the only item on the policy agenda that can be funded is widening the arteries of the system with more lanes and larger intersection capacity for cars. This set of locked logic walls acts to limit discussions of the implications of induced demand, GHG emissions, and potential alternatives as they are outside the limits of the status quo policy domain (Green 2019). As we discussed in Chapter 3, this narrow, reductionist approach continues to ignore the last 75 years of empirical results of these policies and is carried forward through the bureaucratic inertia of rules that limit asking different policy questions, much less facilitating funding of different policy choices. In our interviews and case study research, we found that the underlying structures of the transportation bureaucratic state were a pervasive policy limitation on local decision makers in the United States (Green 2019) and the United Kingdom (Aldred et al. 2019). Evidence from Denmark and the Netherlands, however, points to increasingly successful efforts to challenge auto-focused hegemony.

In addition to the limited set of policy options open to local policymakers to enhance multi-modal street design, we found that integrating more green and blue infrastructure into water projects faced similar bureaucratic hurdles. Modernist water management practices have also been codified with hardened bureaucratic silos of funding that perpetuate status quo practices and limit inclusion of co-benefits in cost–benefit calculations (O'Donnell et al. 2017). Green and blue infrastructure projects in street design are not broadly seen as proven methods to manage water and face funding and statutory hurdles in planning and implementation.

We argue that strategically deconstructing the transportation and water bureaucratic states through new outcome metrics is necessary to begin to address pressing climate, safety, and public health concerns. The status quo is not neutral and privileges high speed, high levels of runoff, high carbon emissions, and low safety outcomes as standard operating procedure. Changing funding and performance metrics is necessary to break through the bureaucratic inertia of the present system (Fields and Hull 2013).

Local political resistance to change

In addition to bureaucratic inertia and strict siloing of outcome metrics, adaptation urbanism approaches also often face targeted public resistance to changing street designs. These efforts are often effective at limiting innovation and act to privilege status quo systems. Our interviews and case examples match the broader academic and policy discourse that finds that car drivers often form a vocal and sometimes powerful political force that actively pushes back on adaptation urbanism street proposals (Filion 2018). The status quo has power and locks in the past decisions that perpetuate the climate crisis, particularly in terms of street width and parking reduction discussions.

The power of this pushback, however, varies across our study cities. In the Netherlands and Copenhagen, bicycle planning has moved through the initial stages of outright opposition to a new normal where planning for active transportation is now seen as a legitimate part of the transportation dialogue. There is still tension about the design solutions that are proposed, but active transportation is not perceived to be an existential threat to the economic health and well-being of the city. In other cities like Vancouver or London, for example, active transportation planning has begun to find a tenuous foothold in the broader transportation-planning dialogue. In Vancouver, intense initial pushback to bicycles as a legitimate transportation mode has given way to a type of limited acceptance of the All Ages and Abilities network. In London, a similar process of public protest around the Mini-Hollands project (Aldred et al. 2019) has been subsumed by the sheer numbers of new cyclists using the projects and the broader expanded system advanced through the Healthy Streets Approach. In both cities, bicycle mode shares are still fairly low compared to the Netherlands or Copenhagen, but significant growth has been visible and broadly accepted. On the other end of the spectrum, broad public support is still lacking in many US cities with hopeful change at the margins in New Orleans and limited structural reform to auto-oriented transportation systems in Miami.

While changing the spatial configuration of roads to decrease parking and add active transportation space has often been contentious, we found through our interviews that adding green and blue infrastructure was often welcomed by the community, particularly on residential streets. We found no evidence of growing political movements in case study cities to oppose green and blue infrastructure solutions for small-scale projects. In New Orleans, however, we did find that large-scale greening efforts proposed after Hurricane Katrina that would have displaced residents created significant backlash. In addition, we found that housing affordability and gentrification issues along the Lafitte Greenway project created concern about the impact of new green amenities. In Miami, we also found evidence of increasing property values associated with green infrastructure (Kim 2019) and the potential growth of climate gentrification in certain neighborhoods. To address these issues, housing affordability needs to be included as a central issue when adding substantial green and blue infrastructure in neighborhoods (Fields 2019). Policy efforts to ensure equitable access to the new green city need to have the same priority for resilience planners as climate adaptation and mitigation concerns. With that caveat, adding green components to street plans and building broader green networks were predominantly seen as positive developments.

Missing the street for the trees

While there is a continuum of public political opposition and support for changing street systems to meet adaptation urbanism goals, there is limited awareness across case study communities about the potential of streets to be used as key planks in resilience policy. While some cities have begun to institutionalize safe active transportation street designs, no city examined has broadly moved towards incorporating green and blue infrastructure systematically in street systems. Copenhagen and Vancouver show promise in terms of prototyping adaptation urbanism street designs, but most study communities have not moved towards creating connected green street systems.

While bureaucratic and public opposition form important political barriers (Aldred et al. 2019), a more conceptual barrier seems to hover over policy discussions of adaptation urbanism street change. This conceptual barrier is the lack of integration of streets into the broader environmental and resilience policy dialogue. While managing transport GHG emissions through technological innovation of automobiles is seen as a mainstream environmental policy issue, street design itself is not broadly seen as a key environmental and resilience issue.

Environmental discussions of transportation emissions are popularly framed as technological issues to be solved through the expansion of electric (EV) and autonomous vehicles (AV). As we discussed in Chapter 3, the environmental and spatial demands of cars are often swept aside in waves of technological optimism where EVs and AVs are perceived as silver bullets that will slay the urban transportation problem once and for all. A broader historical lens, however, shows that waves of misplaced techno-optimism about new automotive technologies have been at play for a century and ignore the key political dimensions of street space regulation. Green (2019, p. 30) describes this as the "smart city trap of embracing technology without considering how to create more livable urban environments." He goes on to argue that, "For although an automobile-dominated city with AVs is likely preferable to an automobile-dominated city without AVs, both pale in comparison to a livable city where public transit, walkability, and public transit can thrive" (Green 2019, p. 30).

The technological optimism is also sometimes tinged with an anti-urban environmental ethic, discussed in Chapter 3, that questions the need and the potential to remake cities into more compact places linked by a restructured street network. Developing more compactly to accentuate accessibility and decrease travel distances is sometimes seen as unnecessary with the perceived potential of EVs and AVs negating any pressure to change urban form. Pointing out the successes of Copenhagen and Amsterdam or even Vancouver can seem like identifying a success story on another planet well beyond the scope of what is possible in sprawling Phoenix or Houston or Miami, the very types of car-centric cities that are literally driving the transportation side of the climate crisis. Flipping the fuel source of cars to renewable energy (and maintaining the sprawling pattern) is seen by some as the realistic environmental position given the scale of the challenge.

As we have shown throughout the book, however, "Copenhagen wasn't always Copenhagen" (Colville-Andersen 2018, p. 64). Amsterdam wasn't always Amsterdam (@fietsprofessor 2019; Norton 2019). In fact, the Vancouver of today isn't the Vancouver of 25 years ago. Vancouver's mode share 25 years ago looked like many other North American cities. Focused investment helped move bicycle mode share in Vancouver from 1.7% in 1996 to 7% in 2017 (Pucher et al. 2011; City of Vancouver 2018). Vancouver's share of walking, bicycling, and transit in the core of the city is now just over 50% (City of Vancouver 2019). At the same time, kilometers driven by Vancouver residents declined by 27% (Robinson 2016). Policy change of supporting new investments in transit and active transportation, coupled with efforts to encourage more infill development, are effective policy tools in remaking cities into low-emission communities with a high quality of life.

Even in the United States, 50% of all trips are under 3 miles (4.8 km), well within the range of bicycles or micro-mobility options like scooters or e-bikes. Planning for making these trips safe and convenient is not only possible, but effective at significantly decreasing carbon emissions and remaking cities into the type of amenity-rich places that have long-term value. Overcoming the conceptual pessimism to remaking streets is vital to addressing transportation-driven GHG emissions. Moving towards EVs fueled by renewable sources *and* rethinking the role and form of streets are interlinked dimensions of a 21st-century environmentalism in the climate change era. The both/and approach is vital to transitioning cities towards a carbon-free transportation system (Winkleman et al. 2019). This approach needs to, however, be centered on key principles that place safety, low emissions, spatial efficiency, and equity as the guiding values of the emerging new transportation system.

Adaptation urbanism street design, as we have pointed out in the book, can be used to not only help manage GHG emissions through privileging active transportation and transit, but also as a key tool to add green space into the heart of the street system itself through green infrastructure. Instead of a conceptual divide between the city and nature, streets and public spaces can be reclaimed to help address water demands and build linked green corridors for active transportation and transit. This could be accomplished through micro-level insertions of bioswales to calm traffic or through more extensive redesigns of linked greenway systems like the Green Route in Copenhagen, the Arbutus Greenway in Vancouver, or the

Lafitte Greenway in New Orleans. If environmental and resilience planning is seen as bouncing back to the present system of car dominance, this opportunity to bounce forward towards a green city will be missed. Resilience planning for streets is not just about building our streets higher to withstand flooding or switching to a new fuel source for cars, but instead about bouncing forward toward designs that enhance climate mitigation and adaptation, livable communities, and a greener city. As we discussed in the New Orleans and Miami chapters, bouncing forward must be also be premised on creating equitable access to the new green city.

Building momentum for resilience

The safe/climate/equitable/space-efficient city

The obstacles to change are entrenched and significant, but the analysis of our city cases shows emerging, successful avenues for addressing these hurdles. As we have argued throughout the book, systematic, targeted reform of the transportation and water bureaucratic states is beginning to change the arc of the possible. While this movement is still early, three interlinked policy and political shifts appear to be promising. Again, these are:

- Conceptually, reenvisioning streets as a central resilience platform for creating the safe/climate/equitable/space-efficient city
- Substantively, linking funding to core outcomes of policy concern in the climate change era
- Politically, building towards a linked agenda between Vision Zero, equity, climate, smart growth, and public health interests in planning and programming for resilience.

As we discussed in the previous section, the resilience movement has the potential to create a platform for important discussions about how our city streets can be used to help bounce forward towards a new, green urban fabric. Resilience planning in the transportation sector has, however, frequently focused more on the bouncing-back ethos of maintaining the status quo auto-orientation of streets in context to disaster planning and recovery. This approach focuses on rebuilding roads to the same specifications as they were before a disaster (Chapter 8) or raising road heights to prevent flooding (Chapter 9). Both approaches essentially bounce back to or even accentuate the safety, equity, spatial efficiency, and climate weaknesses of the present system. We call this approach market-oriented resilience (Figure 2.2) where the focus is almost exclusively on climate adaptation with limited emphasis on interrelated issues of climate mitigation, safety, and equity. Transportation resilience needs to be redefined in an urban context if it is to be effective at addressing the mitigation demands of the climate crisis. The adaptation urbanism resilience process (Figure 2.3) lays out the conceptual framework of this more holistic approach centering resilience as an ongoing community dialogue on climate adaptation, mitigation, safety, and equity.

At the neighborhood level, redefining the role and meaning of the street is a crucial component of urbanizing resilience. In Chapter 1, we discussed Whyte's conception of the street as the "primary place" of the city (Whyte 1988, p. 7) and how this place component has been buried beneath a purely movement-focused approach to street planning. Over the last 75 years, the movement function of streets has been elevated as the central bureaucratic goal of transportation planning through the engineering values of speed and auto flow, ignoring the place functions of streets. As we discussed, great streets, however, have both a movement function and a place function. They are places to travel through and linger, places of residence and commerce, of beauty and movement. In New Orleans, as we discussed, there is even a rhythmic function to great streets embedded in the parading culture of the city. The multi-purpose nature of great streets has, however, been ignored, forgotten in the hegemony of Le Corbusier's vision of movement and burning through wilderness and resources. In the climate change era, using this vision of the streets of the past as the template for climate adaptation locks in high emissions and the sundry of negative externalities of the status quo transportation system.

The movement and place functions of great streets need to be explicitly defined for the climate change era within a context of climate mitigation and adaptation. The movement function needs to be defined in a way that minimizes GHG emissions and privileges low-carbon modes. By privileging low-carbon modes through slow-speed corridors, safety is enhanced and, importantly, the place functions of streets are not overwhelmed by the noise, speed, and pollution of the high-speed street. The place function of great streets in the climate change era must also include water management functions to enhance adaptation through the use of green and blue infrastructure to manage pulses of water and add to the amenity value of neighborhoods. As we have argued throughout, bouncing forward towards the great street of the climate change era needs to be one of the central goals of urban resilience.

This type of great street is developing in our study cities. The streets of De Pijp in Amsterdam, in the Resilience Districts of Copenhagen and Rotterdam, the West End of Vancouver, and the bubbling set of other examples emerging in our case study cities show what an urbanized resilience looks like and how redefining resilience to focus on integrated climate adaptation and mitigation can produce great streets. This is what bouncing forward towards urban resilience looks like.

Building momentum for change

Fund urban street projects by measuring what matters

In addition to articulating how streets can be central features of an urbanized resilience, we find that policy changes in our case cities are showing how to institutionalize these types of great streets. Efforts to change measurement metrics are beginning to be institutionalized, providing an important leverage point for transportation and water management innovation. In Chapter 3, we identified core outcomes of transportation in the climate change era as decreasing emissions/vehicle miles traveled (VMT), improving safety, targeting active transportation mode share goals, and improving spatial efficiency. Altering transportation metrics is part of a wider trend beginning to emerge arguing for even greater structural changes in funding and goal setting for transportation (Bellis et al. 2019; Lewis et al. 2019). Throughout the case study chapters, we have identified best-practice examples that show how these policy shifts operate in practice at the local level.

Copenhagen, again, shows how targeting active transportation mode share and prioritizing funding for key outcomes can generate success. Copenhagen is pushing towards the goal of 50% of all metropolitan trips by walking, biking, and transit by 2025 (Henderson and Gulsrod 2019, p. 23). These goals form the core of the transportation side of its climate change target of being climate-neutral by 2025. These goals are tied to a suite of 300 projects, like Tåsinge Plads, Sankt Kjelds Plads, and Hans Tavsens Gade, that remake the city's streets into a climate-adapted and mitigated system able to withstand pulses of water and better manage GHG emissions.

Utrecht provides an important example of how street space can be remade based around spatial efficiency standards and, with the removal of cars from many roads in the center of the city, improved open space for enhanced livability and water management. Utrecht provides direct and easy access to high-speed rail and its city center by privileging transit, walking, and cycling because these are the most spatially efficient modes of transportation. They take up less space, decrease GHG emissions, and make the city center more livable. Spatial efficiency as a planning principle needs to be expanded to enhance urbanized resilience.

Another example that stands out is, as we discussed earlier in this chapter, Vancouver's efforts to target decreased VMT and emissions while increasing funding for transit and active transportation. Vancouver has transformed its streets by adding a robust all ages and abilities (AAA) network of bicycle facilities, traffic calming neighborhood streets with green infrastructure, and with strategic additions to its transit system. The city is pushing forward even further with the Climate Emergency policy and aims to make walking and bicycling a safe and convenient choice for 90% of the city's residents. Taken together, the suite of policies provides an inspiring vision of what street transformation policies can accomplish in a short time. This is a strong North American version of a resilient city that links street transformation with emission reductions (climate mitigation) and green infrastructure to address water management (climate adaptation).

The London Healthy Streets Approach is another promising example where key indicators of great streets are beginning to be tied directly to funding. Moving from the auto-oriented systems of the past is hard, but the Healthy Streets Approach shows great promise in creating a holistic system of indicators that places health, safety, green infrastructure, and community livability as key goals of transportation policy.

Most of the other case examples, however, have not systematically linked outcomes to transportation funding explicitly. There are numerous examples covered in the book that show how systems are being rethought at the project or district level, but they have not been linked to broader structural policy change in terms of funding and prioritizing investments. Siloed administration of transportation and water projects and funding often limits adaptation urbanism thinking beyond pilot projects. Working to advance new outcome metrics and linked funding systems is vital to pushing adaptation urbanism street and public space systems forward. More research on the technical systems barriers to this type of planning is necessary to move from the pilot stage to wider adoption.

Adaptation urbanism as platform for transformation

While there is increasing awareness about the need to change our streets to meet urban resilience goals, the political will to push these changes forward is often lacking. Whether this is because of well-placed opposition groups or because of the overarching bureaucratic inertia of the status quo systems (or both), it is often difficult to move towards more holistic urban resilience solutions that create safe, climate and space-efficient streets.

At present, there are multiple groups pushing on various aspects of street, land, and public space reform. As we have argued throughout, successful streets are spaces of movement and places of community. They are the central connecting places of our communities and should be safe and welcoming to all residents and, in an era of climate change, help to limit GHG emissions and manage water as a community amenity. Multiple coalitions are currently advocating for parts of this agenda. Vision Zero advocates are pushing for systematic reforms of the transportation system to address the deep safety problems of the current system. The public health community is focused on addressing the overlapping issues of transportation safety, air pollution, and active living solutions to the obesity epidemic. Responses to the coronavirus pandemic have also begun to address the need for safe spaces within cities to walk and bike. Climate advocates are pushing for strict limits to GHG emissions. Smart growth advocates are pushing to limit energy-intensive sprawling developments and offer more options for walkable urbanism (Leinberger 2007). Equity advocates are concerned about environmental racism, climatological gentrification, housing displacement, police violence, and access to high-quality education and jobs. These groups share a broad vision of cities that are safer, more equitable, and less polluting, but clearly have differences in core goals that have limited coalition-building opportunities.

The urban resilience community is potentially positioned as a key connection point between these movements advocating for an urbanized vision of climate adaptation and mitigation that encompasses many of the goals of the broad array of urban actors. While we certainly do not see urban resilience broadly and adaptation urbanism specifically as papering over these important differences, we see the potential for a network of urban reformers to come together in the fight to remake our streets into safer, less polluting places accessible to all residents. It is clear that a new urban movement that builds across multiple sectors is necessary to help push against targeted opposition and the power of the transportation and water bureaucratic states. While adaptation urbanism does not offer clear answers on how to build this movement, we identified what could be the beginning stirrings of a broader movement to use urban resilience as a key platform for change. A couple of examples help to show the overlapping nature of these movements and the potential opportunities of building a shared agenda focused on urban resilience broadly and adaptation urbanism more specifically.

In London, we found that the Mini-Holland program provided a base of practical knowledge about street transformation but was seen conceptually as being too narrow a frame to use for a city-wide program. Many of the concepts learned in the Mini-Holland approach have been wrapped into the broader initiative of the Healthy Streets Approach with a wider coalition of advocates who could generate more power for change (TransportationXtra 2019). This approach brings together public health concerns of air pollution and transport safety into a focused approach designed to shift trips towards active transportation and transit. The program ties the public health goal of increasing active travel to the mode share goal of having 80% of all trips in London taken by walking, bicycling, and transit by 2041 (Transport for London 2017). This is an important partnership model that, when coupled with the Livable Neighborhoods program of targeted grants for walking and cycling infrastructure and green space, deserves more study as it moves forward. In addition, from the water sector in the UK, the Learning and Action Alliance (LAA) approach of pulling together multi-sectoral stakeholders to co-produce green infrastructure designs (O'Donnell et al. 2017) appears promising and could be potentially expanded to address broader concerns of adaptation urbanism street design.

Other examples in the book speak to this type of coalition-building potential as well. In New Orleans, we examined the Gentilly Resilience District and Lafitte Greenway planning efforts and the broader efforts to bring groups together to discuss disaster recovery, economic development, affordable housing, and how greenways could help connect neighborhoods. In Rotterdam, we saw citizens working with the city to redesign their streets to add green space, improve water management, and address transportation safety. We also delved into the redevelopment of Tåsinge Plads in Copenhagen with the instant *hygge* approach to public space engagement. These examples, and others throughout the book, speak to the potential of engaging a broad array of urban coalitions in redefining resilience planning from a technical exercise to an approach that builds on local concerns and needs. As we have argued throughout, this is the "negotiated resilience" (Harris et al. 2018, p. 2) that builds from community needs to a project-level agenda.

For this negotiated resilience to take root, equitable access to the new, safer, greener places needs to be a central resilience goal. As Rigolon and Nemeth (2018) note, cross-sectoral partnerships between green infrastructure planners and affordable housing coalitions are vital to help address the potential of green gentrification. These types of approaches help to show how urban resilience could begin to tackle pressing problems of equity and livability within a broader frame of climate adaptation and mitigation planning. They are not fully formed examples that tie all of the adaptation urbanism components together, but instead are examples that provide a foundation to link local concerns together with the larger planning goals of urban resilience. While more research is needed to understand how to help create meaningful coalitions that link local concerns with the larger climate issues of urban resilience, these promising examples help to trace a path forward.

Scoping an agenda for urban resilience

Adaptation urbanism

Throughout *Adaptation Urbanism*, we have articulated an urban resilience agenda based around a redefinition of the role of streets and public spaces to address climate change, water management, safety, equity, and livability issues. If adaptation urbanism streets and public spaces were a new technology that could be deployed (and sold) to cities to address these issues, there would be a mass of tech entrepreneurs working to create the hive-like buzz of inevitability that seems to give technological developments policy purchase. Instead, the base of adaptation urbanism streets and public spaces is already owned by the public and can be redesigned based on current technology. They are ours to use to solve our collective problems and needs. They can't (or shouldn't) be bought and sold for the profit of entrepreneurs. This creates a problem for a world that seems to rely on technology solutions to guide social and economic change and, at the same time, a potential opportunity to redefine what public solutions can look like.

Resilient public management of our streets and public spaces requires new goals, engagement processes, metrics, and funding systems. Bouncing forward is hard work. As we have outlined, however, the new systems needed to build these types of places are already being used in communities around the globe. Translating these systems into new structural circumstances is a technical and cultural challenge requiring deep commitment from multiple levels of government, leadership from above, and the political push from citizens to give license to local agencies as they innovate. The first articulations of the scholarly examination of these processes is beginning to take shape (Glaser et al. 2019) through analysis of projects like the EU's Civitas Handshake program of best-practice knowledge transfer, the accumulated knowledge of the Global Designing Cities Initiative and National Association of City Transportation Officials (NACTO 2016) and the Global Compact of Mayors (a partnership of C40 Cities, ICLEI, and United Cities and Local Governments). While much more work is necessary to understand the knowledge-sharing systems, the new work shows that knowledge transfer from best-practice leaders provides both inspiration and technical information needed to overcome policy challenges. As Tim Beatley (2012, p. 220) argues, studying best-practice cities can help us overcome "a failure of imagination" of what is possible.

From our case study analysis, the most promising platform for change seems to be the incubation of new ideas through the resilience district framework. We found that resilience districts appear to provide a focusing mechanism for local bureaucracies that helps to provide a mechanism for, paraphrasing Rene Lindsay in Copenhagen, telling a new story about the city. This storytelling component offers important leeway for city agencies to see problems in new ways and begin to build new relationships, both technical and budgetary, needed to articulate adaptation urbanism approaches. When coupled with deep local engagement, new opportunities for innovation emerge that generate shared goals acceptable to both local citizens and the governmental institutions themselves. Building new approaches to managing streets and public spaces requires building these new institutional and engagement pathways. Pilot projects at the district scale offer an opportunity to begin to build these new relationships.

The resilience districts provide a platform for learning, but the systematic change necessary to scale projects up from neighborhood to neighborhood across the city and region will require deeper structural change and needs to be linked to measuring (and funding) what matters (Piatkowski and Marshall 2018). We point out that four key metric alterations could help to provide the foundation for systematic change. Again, these are managing for decreased emissions/VMT, targeting transportation safety goals along the lines of Vision Zero, aiming towards active transportation mode share goals, and, finally, prioritizing the most spatially efficient urban modes. Current examples of these types of urban policies currently exist and are helping to transform case cities. More research and practical investigation on how to best implement this suite of policies with other complementary policies such as land use zoning reform, affordable housing improvements, district heating, impervious cover modifications, and other related systems will also be necessary.

Again, just because it is necessary does not mean that it is easy or even likely given the current political climate. Political push needs to be deep and sustained to affect the scale of change that will be needed to transform the auto age into the era of adaptation urbanism. We see the seeds of a potential new urban movement in the connections between resilience, Vision Zero, public health, equity, design, smart growth, and climate advocacy. While there are multiple points of disagreement, there are potentially greater connections that could help create a powerful voice for changing streets and public spaces into something resembling the outlines of adaptation urbanism.

This process is likely to be non-linear and uneven. Some cities will move forward more quickly and begin to build places that are better adapted to a changing climate and altered to decrease GHG emissions. These places will increasingly be more livable as well. Other cities will lack resources, political will, or both and remain stuck with congested, polluting streets and deepening cycles of disaster response. The unequal world of climate change era and its impact on cities is just beginning. Creating programs to help translate best practices into culturally appropriate local variants across cities, both North and South, is both necessary and complex. Efforts will require sustained engagement to help avoid the potential for deepening inequities.

Note

1 The Dutch have probably the most advanced and long-standing planning system for urban water management in the world. Over the last two decades, this water management system has moved towards a living-with-water ethos that seeks to integrate water into the landscape to both decrease flood risk and enhance livability. The Dutch have also, as discussed in Chapter 5 on Rotterdam, developed a safe systems approach to building roadways that ensures that safe systems designs are part of the DNA of the Dutch road network. These two systems developed outside of the resilience policy sphere but are the key base of adaptation urbanism in the Netherlands. New resilience projects are emerging, but they often do not explicitly call out this base in the resilience plans. It is rather almost presupposed in the Netherlands that strong active transportation and urban water management components will be included in project planning. In Copenhagen, on the other hand, the water management systems do not appear to be as fully integrated into administrative systems. Active transportation in Copenhagen is, as in the Netherlands, an expected component of street projects. Resilience planning in Copenhagen appears to be a key tool to help more fully integrate water management into street and public space projects. More research on how resilience projects develop in specific locations and how they can be integrated with other policy spheres is needed.

References

@fietsprofessor (Marco te Brömmelstroet). (2019). 'But our city isn't Amsterdam!' Well, so wasn't Amsterdam ... Policies only changed after serious bottom-up protests in which people fought to take the streets back from #Motordom in the 1970s. Quite literally! Twitter. June 30. https://twitter.com/fietsprofessor?lang=en.

Aldred, R., Watson, T., Lovelace, R., & Woodcock, J. (2019). Barriers to Investing in Cycling: Stakeholder Views from England. *Transportation Research Part A: Policy and Practice*, *128*, 149–159.

Beatley, T. (2012). Conclusion: Green Cities of Europe as Compelling Models. In *Green Cities of Europe* (T. Beatley, ed.). Washington, DC: Island Press.

Bellis, R., Osborne, B., & Davis, S. L. (2019). Repair Priorities 2019. Transport for America and Tax Payers for Common Sense. Last accessed 4/1/2020 from http://t4america.org/wp-content/uploads/2019/05/Repair-Priorities-2019.pdf.

Colville-Andersen, M. (2018). *Copenhagenize: The Definitive Guide to Global Bicycle Urbanism*. Washington, DC: Island Press.

City of Vancouver. (2018). Walking and Cycling in Vancouver 2017 Report Card. Last accessed 3/29/2020 from https://vancouver.ca/files/cov/cycling-report-card-2017.pdf.

City of Vancouver. (2019). Walking and Cycling in Vancouver 2018 Report Card. Last accessed 3/31/2020 from https://vancouver.ca/files/cov/walking-and-cycling-in-vancouver-2018-report-card.pdf.

Fields, B. (2019). Post-Disaster Amenity Politics: Livability, Gentrification, and Recovery in Post-Katrina New Orleans. In *Community Livability* (F. Wagner, & R.W. Caves, eds.): 123–136. New York, NY: Routledge.

Fields, B., & Hull, T. (2013). Policy Implications of the Nonmotorized Transportation Pilot Program. In *Transport Beyond Oil* (J. Renne, & B. Fields, eds.). Washington, DC: Island Press.

Filion, P. (2018). Enduring Features of the North American Suburb: Built Form, Automobile Orientation, Suburban Culture and Political Mobilization. *Urban Planning*, *3*(4), 4–14.

Glaser, M., Te Brömmelstroet, M., & Bertolini, L. (2019). Learning to Build Strategic Capacity for Transportation Policy Change: An Interdisciplinary Exploration. *Transportation Research Interdisciplinary Perspectives,* 1 (June).

Global Designing Cities Initiative and National Association of City Transportation Officials. (2016). *Global Street Design Guide.* Washington, DC, Island Press.

Green, B. (2019). *The Smart Enough City: Putting Technology in its Place to Reclaim Our Urban Future.* Cambridge, MA: MIT Press.

Harris, L. M., Chu, E. K., & Ziervogel, G. (2018). Negotiated Resilience. *Resilience, 6*(3), 196–214.

Henderson, J., & Gulsrud, N. M. (2019). *Street Fights in Copenhagen: Bicycle and Car Politics in a Green Mobility City.* London: Routledge.

Kim, S. (2019). The Economic Effects of Climate Change Adaptation Measures: Evidence from Miami-Dade County and New York City. May 2019. Joint Center for Housing Studies of Harvard University. John R. Meyer Dissertation Fellowship Working Paper. Last accessed 7/8/2020 from www.jchs.harvard.edu/sites/default/files/harvard_jchs_kim_economic_effects_climate_change_adaptation_2019.pdf.

Leinberger, C. B. (2007). *The Option of Urbanism: Investing in a New American Dream.* Washington, DC: Island Press.

Lewis, P., Davis, J., & Grossman, A. (2019). Refreshing the Status Quo: Federal Highway Programs and Funding Distribution. Eno Center for Transportation. October 1. Last accessed 4/1/2020 from www.enotrans.org/eno-resources/refreshing-the-status-quo-federal-highway-programs-and-funding-distribution/.

Norton, Peter. (2019). The Hidden History of American Anti-Car Protests. *Citylab.* October 8. Last accessed 3/31/2020 from www.citylab.com/perspective/2019/10/street-safety-american-history-dutch-cities-traffic-protests/599566/.

O'Donnell, E. C., Lamond, J. E., & Thorne, C. R. (2017). Recognising Barriers to Implementation of Blue–Green Infrastructure: A Newcastle Case Study. *Urban Water Journal, 14*(9), 964–971.

Piatkowski, D., & Marshall, W. (2018). We Count What We Care About: Advancing a Framework for Valuing Investments in Active Modes. *Research in Transportation Business & Management, 29,* 63–70.

Pucher, J., Buehler, R., & Seinen, M. (2011). Bicycling Renaissance in North America? An Update and Re-Appraisal of Cycling Trends and Policies. *Transportation Research Part A: Policy and Practice, 45*(6), 451–475.

Rigolon, A., & Németh, J. (2018). "We're Not in the Business of Housing:" Environmental Gentrification and the Nonprofitization of Green Infrastructure Projects. *Cities, 81,* 71–80.

Robinson, Matt. (2016). Vancouver Leads the Pack for Bike Commutes. *Vancouver Sun.* May 5. Last accessed 4/1/2020 from https://vancouversun.com/news/local-news/vancouver-leads-the-pack-for-bike-commutes.

Transport for London. (2017). Healthy Streets for London. Last accessed 03/28/2020 from http://content.tfl.gov.uk/healthy-streets-for-london.pdf.

TransportationXtra. (2019). Mini-Holland is Making Streets People-Friendly, Says Clyde Loakes. Last accessed 03/28/2020 from www.transportxtra.com/publications/local-transport-today/news/61522/mini-holland-is-making-streets-people-friendly-says-clyde-loakes/.

Whyte, W. H. (1988). City: Rediscovering the Center. Ann Arbor, MI: The University of Michigan.

Winkleman, S., Deweese, J., & El-Geneidy, A. (2019). Car-Oriented Sprawl Increases Driving and GHGs in Greater Montreal. Green Resilience Strategies. Last accessed 4/1/2020 from www.greenresilience.com/montreal-sprawl.

12

CONCLUSION

The emerging era of resilient streets

Introduction

Throughout *Adaptation Urbanism*, we have focused on examples of cities transformed. As we have argued, the Amsterdam of today with its low-speed, safe green streets is vastly different than the Amsterdam of the 1970s with high fatality rates and traffic-clogged streets. The same is true for Copenhagen and Vancouver and increasingly for a number of other cities around the world. In many ways, you get the city you dream, but, at a more foundational level, you get the city you push for.

Adaptation Urbanism is about creating a new vision of the resilient city. The resilient city is a compact city of neighborhoods linked with slow, safe streets and green and blue corridors that connect the city together. The resilient city helps to decrease greenhouse gas (GHG) emissions by creating safe active transportation and transit options and helps to manage water with the green and blue infrastructure. While it is climate-mitigated and adapted, it is, probably more importantly for residents, highly livable with ribbons of green connecting the city. These new public investments will also increase housing cost without a serious commitment to affordable housing. The new resilient city must engage affordable housing with the same intensity dedicated to climate mitigation and adaptation. The hard work of resilience requires engaging in a long-term push to create an equitable, adapted, low-carbon city.

For urban resilience to be a transformative movement, it needs to be animated with a deep sense of the *good* city (Wagner and Frisch 2009; Hall 2014), the city that is worth struggling for. *Adaptation Urbanism* begins to point towards what the good city can look like in the climate change era, but to get there will require both a new vision and tremendous political momentum. In this final chapter, we lay out a distilled vision of the resilient city and political struggles necessary to push this vision forward. We finish by emphasizing again that, through the existing technology of safe, green streets, the more resilient city is feasible today. Adaptation urbanism requires the vision and push to make it happen.

Adaptation urbanism

The safe/climate/spatially efficient/compact/affordable city

We have argued throughout that streets are a hidden public resource that can be repurposed to address the intense challenges of the climate change era. Streets and the space dedicated to car parking occupy between 30 and 50% of city space (UN Habitat 2013; Ellen MacArthur Foundation and McKinsey Center for Business and Environment 2015). Currently most of this space is dedicated to making the climate crisis worse by preferencing cars and SUVs that drive up GHG emissions on impervious surfaces that increasingly pulse water into flooding rivers. This system is highly inefficient as cars occupy vast swathes of the urban area and race forward to become clogged in choke points that no amount of new roadway space can fix (Bellis et al. 2020). The system also generates high rates of air pollution and fatalities and stress. At its core, this system also produces social stratification and inequality on the metropolitan level. As we've noted throughout, the modern city is the vision of Le Corbusier where we burn through wilderness and resources so that we can sit under separate pine trees 30 miles (48 km) from the city center pondering how we got here.

This vision of the future from the 1930s has been codified into administrative rules and design guidelines that now govern the minutiae of how we build roads. It's important to remember, however, that we created these rules and we can change them. A profoundly different future with a new design vocabulary is developing. The streets of the future are emerging in slow-speed corridors embedded with green infrastructure linked to higher-speed transit for longer trips. They are designed as part of a Vision Zero system where cars move slowly in cities and active transportation and transit are prioritized as the most efficient mobility options. These new streets enhance community livability, open the city with safe access for kids and older residents, and, when it rains, soak up the pulses of water. As part of a larger system, they can help to adapt the city to climate change all the while mitigating GHG emissions and, at the same time, make the city significantly safer. As we noted in Chapter 6, for example, if the United States were to match transportation safety trends seen in Denmark, the United States would see 20,000 fewer transportation fatalities and almost a million prevented injuries per year (Evans 2014, p. 1506). As we have seen throughout the pages of this book, these types of streets exist today and need no new technologies, but rather require a new vision and the political push to bring them into existence.

The experience with these emerging places also indicates that they will be successful to the point that they can impact property markets putting pressure on affordable housing (Rigolon and Nemeth 2018). Adaptation urbanism works, but it needs to work for the whole city and not just a select subset of wealthy residents. Successful adaptation urbanism requires integrating the new green and blue infrastructure with affordable housing. The new resilient streets of the future need to link the community together rather than drive it apart.

The status quo has power

Political and administrative inertia

While this vision is emerging in select cities today, most cities continue to build the streets of the past pushing us further away from solving the climate crisis and, just as importantly, from each other. We argue that status quo administrative systems in the transportation and water sectors help to perpetuate the high-speed mobility system where fatalities are high and water is buried away. The result is a sprawling city with consequent high GHG emissions, fatality rates, and, increasingly, flooding.

The status quo has power through the myriad of rules and regulations that guide funding and design standards. The assumption is often that the status quo system is the proven model and any changes to it need to reach a high bar to dislodge these proven systems. As we have shown throughout, the climate crisis is in many ways being driven by the transportation sector and outmoded visions of streets designed for speed and division. In the United States, the status quo system results in nearly 40,000 fatalities a year, congested streets that divide and pollute communities, and the largest share of GHG emissions of any sector. This is not a resilient system.

To put this in stark terms, defending the status quo means defending those nearly 40,000 fatalities per year in the United States and the largest share of GHG emissions by sector. The burden of proof needs to be placed squarely on the status quo system. The administrative rules and standards that produced these outcomes need to be re-vetted for the emerging climate change era.

In Chapter 3 and then again in the previous chapter, we outline a series of emerging metrics that challenge the underpinnings of the transportation bureaucratic system. We propose moving towards outcome measurements that create truly resilient communities that are safe and strong, climate-adapted and mitigated, and equitable places with a high quality of life for residents. We point towards a set of connected metrics to help move the transportation system towards more resilient outcomes:

- Emphasize Vision Zero goals as the foundation of street design
- Decrease vehicle miles traveled as a policy goal
- Increase active transportation and transit as a metric of success
- Prioritize spatial efficiency to improve accessibility, climate adaptation, and livability.

Advancing these policy metrics can help to move the system towards measuring what matters and open up the potential to create a system of streets of the future.

Currently, however, each of the proposed policy metrics is effectively blocked through comprehensive status quo rules and funding mechanisms. If we are to take the climate crisis seriously, these rules and funding structures need to be overhauled. This is the hard work of change, the boring minutiae of a system that continues to generate high levels of GHG emissions and fatalities.

Piloting towards adaptation urbanism

Engage, implement, learn, repeat

While sweeping changes to bureaucratic systems are needed, these systems are complex and difficult to dislodge. At present, working to create pilot projects that model the street of the future could be powerful steps in showing a type of proof of concept for adaptation urbanism. Pilot projects in the form of resilient districts or green streets projects can offer communities a way to begin to work through the necessary changes to bureaucratic structure within agencies and, just as importantly, show residents what change can look like in their communities.

While this is politically and administratively difficult, it is not technically complicated. The template for safe streets is based on traffic calming slow-speed streets with green infrastructure combined with separating vulnerable road users on higher-speed streets. Essentially, if cities begin to build safe, green neighborhood streets, add cycle tracks with bioswales on higher-speed streets, privilege space for transit, and integrate water squares into public spaces, they could begin to create the foundational elements of an adaptation urbanism system. The basic formula is direct:

> *Stop building streets of the past and start building and retrofitting safe, green streets linked to cycle tracks with green infrastructure, add water squares in key public spaces, and then repeat.*

Cities could begin with pilot projects in resilience districts, much like those found in Copenhagen, that create a green, low-carbon street network linked with new public spaces. By engaging residents in the difficult, but vital process of "negotiated resilience" (Harris et al. 2018, p. 2), the city can learn local needs and tailor resources for the communities.

As the experience from our case study cities suggests, these projects, if the engagement process is well done, will likely be successful and make streets safer, greener, and more amenity-rich. This is where the green gentrification challenge emerges as new amenities can put pressure on housing costs. Cities need to be proactive from the start and tie community-led planning for resilience districts and green infrastructure together with affordable housing planning (Rigolon and Nemeth 2018). This is a key process that links green infrastructure and affordable housing development and helps ensure that the resilient city becomes a more equitable city.

While this is technically not complicated to envision, piloting change is hard, administratively and politically. Scaling up and including transit for longer trips and addressing affordable housing needs add significantly to the complexity of integrating new streets into a truly resilient city. This will be a long-term process of change, but, as our case examples show, these changes can gradually transform the city street by street. Each new street can become an example of what is possible. Residents can begin to see the resilient city and experience how green and blue amenities create safe, slow-speed streets that increase the quality of life in their neighborhoods. Success in one neighborhood or city can generate calls for expansion into other areas. The question can then begin to change from whether to build these pilot projects to how to scale these projects up to levels where the impacts can begin to make a dent in the larger climate crisis. Streets and public spaces can change if there is demand and political will. Piloting resilience districts can be an important step in propelling this new vision of streets forward. More research and practical guidance on how these change processes can be successfully navigated and projects scaled up at a speed necessary to meet the climate challenge are needed.

Finally, sometimes all of this can seem too technical and complicated. Mobycon Consulting in the Netherlands sent out a simple tweet that cuts through the complexity of mode share, climate change, and street design and gets to the heart of what good transportation projects should be designed to accomplish. Mobycon (2019) asked community members:

> How would you prioritize space on your street to make it more welcoming?

This is such a simple, foundational question. Working with residents to create these welcoming places is the base of resilient communities. Resilient streets can welcome residents to slow-speed neighborhoods with green and blue places that create neighborhoods that we love, that are welcoming places to call home. Your turn: how would you prioritize space on your street to make it more welcoming?

Conclusion

While we are profoundly troubled by the dimensions of COVID-19 and climate crises, we are inspired by the people we have met who have shared their time, energy, and passion for improving their cities. The vision of this book has been collectively shaped by the stories of local victories and failures, of struggle and places transformed. Traveling and talking with local advocates, citizens, city employees, and researchers have offered a perspective on transformation that is at once daunting and inspirational. The changes in our case cities that have happened over the last 20–30 years have been paid for with equal parts hard work, practical push, and motivation for what could be. We have had the honor to look through the eyes of the people who have helped to transform their cities into places that are better adapted to a changing climate with urban systems that limit GHG emissions and that, most importantly for local residents, are places that they can be proud to call home. We look forward to talking with the countless other people who are pushing forward to remake cities that are safer, more equitable and resilient, and better places to call home.

References

Bellis, Rayla, Davis, Stephen Lee, McCahill, Chris, Sundquist, Eric, Mangan, Emily, & Osborne, Beth. (2020). *The Congestion Con: How More Lanes and More Money Equals More Traffic*. Washington, DC: Transportation for America. Last accessed 3/21/2020 from http://t4america.org/maps-tools/congestion-con/.

Ellen MacArthur Foundation, & McKinsey Center for Business and Environment. (2015). *Growth Within: A Circular Economy Vision for a Competitive Europe*. Cowes, UK: Ellen MacArthur Foundation.

Evans, L. (2014). Traffic Fatality Reductions: United States Compared with 25 Other Countries. *American Journal of Public Health, 104*(8), 1501–1507.

Hall, P. (2014). *Cities of Tomorrow: An Intellectual History of Urban Planning and Design Since 1880*. Hoboken, NJ: John Wiley.

Harris, L. M., Chu, E. K., & Ziervogel, G. (2018). Negotiated Resilience. *Resilience, 6*(3), 196–214.

@mobycon (Mobycon). (2019). A great collaboration of our colleagues for #Mobyday looking at creative solutions for people-focused street design. How would you prioritize space on your street to make it more welcoming? #livingstreets #livablecities #peoplefriendlystreets. Twitter. April 5. https://twitter.com/mobycon/status/1117756429803372544?fbclid=IwAR3sXQsqYH8X937tt0dbIjZFr8Ty97QiKh16I6MjhiZesxED_lMj4cqnfwM.

Rigolon, A., & Németh, J. (2018). "We're Not in the Business of Housing": Environmental Gentrification and the Nonprofitization of Green Infrastructure Projects. *Cities, 81*, 71–80.

UN Habitat. (2013). Streets as Public Spaces and Drivers of Urban Prosperity. Nairobi, Kenya: UN Habitat. https://unhabitat.org/streets-as-public-spaces-and-drivers-of-urban-prosperity.

Wagner, Jacob, and Frisch, Michael. (2009). Introduction: New Orleans and the Design Moment. *Journal of Urban Design,* 14(3), 237–255.

APPENDIX A

CASE STUDY RESILIENCE PLAN ANALYSIS

Co-written by Tara Tolford

This appendix provides a detailed analysis of resilience plans in Copenhagen, London, New Orleans, South Florida, and Rotterdam. The resilience plan analysis is augmented with place-based analysis of emerging resilience districts in these cities as well. The methodology for the plan analysis was laid out in Chapter 4. Again, the basic approach focuses on analyzing resilience plans to better understand how cities are planning for transportation climate mitigation and adaptation simultaneously. We use a structured summative content analysis framework (Hsieh and Shannon 2005; Appler and Rumbach 2016) to determine whether resilience plans actively utilize adaptation urbanism planning concepts and then examine the extent to which those concepts are linked to policy implementation. The approach identifies key words associated with adaptation urbanism within plans to uncover patterns of use and meaning. The focus is on understanding how adaptation urbanism concepts are or are not used in a policy context. These terms encompass both key project-level manifestations of adaptation urbanism categories such as green and blue infrastructure, sustainable transportation, compact development, and equity (Table A.1) and the overarching themes of resilience, adaptation, and mitigation. To help provide a more in-depth analysis of the meaning of the planning terms, we also evaluated the text more broadly in the context to adjacent plan language. We reviewed the quotes within each plan to search for broad patterns of meaning.

The plans for each city represent both a targeted selection of specific resilience plans and connected area plans. Because resilience is an emerging discipline, most of the case study cities did not have a wealth of resilience-specific planning documents to analyze. We added a series of related plans to examine the reach of resilience into key city-planning areas like transportation and land use plans.

The analysis is summarized for each city in tables that outline the degree to which each adaptation urbanism concept is reflected in the planning documents. Strong focus areas combined direct and significant focus on policy. Limited policy

TABLE A.1 Adaptation urbanism project-level categories and key terms

Blue infrastructure	*Green infrastructure*	*Sustainable transportation*	*Compact development*	*Equity*
• Blue infrastructure • Canal/creek • Water square • Water quality • Ponds • Stormwater	• Green infrastructure • Greenways • Parks • Bioswale • Green street • Cloudburst street • Open space • Water storage • Median/ neutral ground • Permeable/pervious pavement • Trees	• Walking • Pedestrian • Sidewalk • Bike • Bicycle • Cycle track • Trail • Bicycle superhighway • Transit	• Density • Dense • Development • Zoning • Mixed-use • Land use	• Equity • Equitable • Fair • Housing cost • Affordable housing • Social cohesion • Disadvantaged

focus areas had several mentions throughout the plan, but minimal policy focus. If the key word term was not mentioned at all or in a clear policy context, the category was labeled as "not addressed." This is a fairly course evaluation of term usage and is designed to provide a broad metric of plan emphasis in each area. As research in the resilience-planning sphere begins to emerge, more detailed analysis of plan quality should be included (Berke and Godschalk 2009). Despite these limits, patterns of use of the terms emerge that highlight gaps in transportation resilience planning.

Finally, each case study city overview includes summary statistics of key transportation-related resilience indicators for the metropolitan area and an analysis of transportation and open space characteristics in emerging resilience districts. The spatial analysis is intended to be a snapshot of the public realm characteristics and does not include analysis of private properties. The analysis also does not capture the qualitative characteristics of streets and public spaces that are vital to capturing both the movement and place functions of streets. Appendix B provides a more detailed tool to capture these interrelationships through an evaluation of Rotterdam with the Adaptation Urbanism Checklist.

Rotterdam resilience plan analysis

The plan overview in Chapter 5 provides a description of the changing focus of water and resilience planning in Rotterdam from the more structural orientation of early plans to more recent focus on a broader livability-focused resilience agenda. The broad outlines of resilience policy begin to be embedded in plans starting with the Rotterdam Climate Programme in 2008. Resilience became a key theme in the succession of planning documents that emerged in the 20-teens. While there has been significant progress in promoting and implementing resilience pilot projects focused on water and public space, there has been limited focus on policy mechanisms designed to move these projects from the pilot phase towards more comprehensive implementation. There has also been limited focus on integrating these public space/water concepts into street environments. This can be seen in the newer generation of Rotterdam plans (2008–2016).

Overall, each plan showed a strong resilience orientation focused on adaptation. For example, the Rotterdam Climate Adaptation Plan used the term *adaptation* a total of 379 times. This is not surprising as the plan's title focuses on adaptation, but it shows the extensive penetration of the concept within the plan. In the suite of plans analyzed, green and blue infrastructure projects were also addressed often and, in some plans, like the aforementioned Rotterdam Climate Adaptation Plan, were mentioned up to 50 times.

Mitigation and mitigation-related concepts were, however, given much less emphasis in the plans. In the Rotterdam Climate Adaptation Plan, for example, climate mitigation was mentioned only twice. Sustainable transportation, a key climate mitigation feature related to the built environment, was nearly absent from any of the plans. Compact development was also not emphasized to a large extent in any of the plans. In terms of equity, most of the plans did not strongly address this concept. The exception to this was the Rotterdam Resilience Strategy in 2016 which emphasized connections between resilience and social cohesion throughout the plan.

This analysis provides a surface-level sweep of the plans to identify varying levels of emphasis of adaptation urbanism terms. To provide a more in-depth analysis of the meaning of the planning terms, we evaluated the text more broadly in the context to adjacent plan language. We reviewed the quotes within each plan to search for broad patterns of meaning. Overall, as in the previous terms analysis, we found that adaptation was strongly identified as a key planning concept. Mitigation was, again, emphasized to a lesser degree. Despite this, we did find a more nuanced connection between concepts.

In the Climate Proof Plan, for example, planners argued that Rotterdam needed to focus on "the entire climate issue; the causes of climate change (mitigation) as well as the consequences (adaptation)" (Rotterdam Climate Initiative 2013, p. 3). This broad acknowledgment of the interconnection between adaptation and mitigation was, however, only mentioned in one other plan (Climate Adaptation Strategy). The Water Sensitive Rotterdam (WSR) and Rotterdam Resilience Strategy did not directly address the adaptation/mitigation relationship.

Despite this, the WSR and the Rotterdam Resilience Strategy better articulated equity-related concepts and the potential of pilot projects to help build political and technical momentum for change. The WSR (Urban Green-Blue Grids n.d.), for example, pointed to the need for equity/social cohesion and quality of life to be integrated into resilience planning. Planners state that "the objective of Water Sensitive Rotterdam is to make the city a better place to live and to promote social cohesion in addition to climate adaptation" (Urban Green-Blue Grids n.d.). As an example of this type of thinking, planners pointed to the ZoHo climate-resilient district that has "undergone a gradual urban regeneration" where the "unique multifunctional Benthemplein water square acted as a catalyst for the further development " (p. 3). While this type of project requires collaboration across sectors, WSR planners pointed out that the "central question" for planning moving forward "is therefore how the various municipal services can be motivated so that in every urban plan and project, water management and climate adaptation is taken into account" (Urban Green-Blue Grids n.d.).

The Rotterdam Resilience Strategy (City of Rotterdam 2016) echoes these concerns about equity and long-term change. From an equity perspective, planners pointed out that "Rotterdam must become resilient not just by fortifying its defences to a changing climate and rising seas, but also by building a more cohesive and inclusive society" (p. 8). Planners argued that resilience thinking had "penetrated into mainstream of city operations and water has added value for the city" (p. 8) and now it was time to help share positive experience from projects like that in ZoHo and "help to disseminate resilience thinking, encourage participation and support learning" (p. 82).

The findings are synthesized in Table A.2. Our findings suggest that there is a strong linkage between Rotterdam resilience plans and targeted adaptation policies, but very limited connection to mitigation policies in transportation and

TABLE A.2 Rotterdam adaptation urbanism plan analysis summary

Adaptation urbanism elements	*Rotterdam Climate Proof Progamme (2008)*	*Rotterdam Adaptation Strategy (2013)*	*Water Sensitive Rotterdam (2015)*	*Rotterdam Resilience Strategy (2016)*
Conceptual				
Resilience				
Adaptation				
Mitigation				
Project level				
Green infrastructure				
Blue infrastructure				
Sustainable transportation				
Compact development				
Equity				
Level of emphasis	**Not addressed**	**Limited policy focus**	**Strong focus**	

TABLE A.3 Sustainable transportation spatial analysis summary statistics, ZoHo resilience district, Rotterdam

Sub-area name	*ZoHo district*
Estimated % area paved streets and on-street parking	35.1%
Estimated % area surface parking lots	2.5%
Estimated % area public green space and water	8.2%
Active transportation mode share (metropolitan area)	*Rotterdam–The Hague Metropolitan Area*
Bike	23%
Walk	21%
Transit	10%
Total	**54%**

Mode share data source: Deloitte Insights (2019).

connected public space policy sphere. The area that is most striking in the analysis is the overall lack of integration of sustainable transportation into the resilience plans in a targeted manner.

Table A.3 presents the findings from a spatial analysis of the emerging ZoHo resilience district and overall sustainable transportation mode shares for the Rotterdam/The Hague Metropolitan Area. The intent of these small-area evaluations, conducted using publicly available spatial datasets and manual review of aerial photography, is to quantify the amount of space within a given area that is dedicated to the public right of way, and specifically, the amount of space that is paved for the primary or exclusive use of automobiles. In addition, we assessed the share of each district which is publicly accessible green space (parks, large vacant lots, landscaped medians, and in the case of Rotterdam, canal rights of way). The Rotterdam ZoHo district, discussed in Chapter 5, represents an area with a dense local street network, with approximately 37% of the area paved streets and parking (excluding dedicated rail right of way) and 8% unpaved green space. Finally, these figures are contextualized with overall mode share statistics for the metropolitan area, to begin to explore relationships between resilient streets and active transportation outcomes. In the Rotterdam/The Hague Metropolitan Area, over half of trips are completed by walking, bicycling, or transit.

Copenhagen resilience plan analysis

As the Copenhagen chapter suggests, Copenhagen has aggressively acted to expand a strong active transportation network as a key tool in meeting climate goals and is increasingly focusing on adding climate adaptation features into its street and public space system. This approach of building on the base of active transportation and adding climate adaptation features is embedded in the Copenhagen resilience plans.

This section examines key plans from 2011's Adaptation Plan to the 2016 Copenhagen Climate Resilient Neighborhood Policy Document. Overall, the Copenhagen plans themselves do not utilize the resilience concept to the same extent as Rotterdam, but the Copenhagen plans are much more targeted at integrating climate adaptation and mitigation plan elements in the transportation sector. Copenhagen was not as early an adopter of the resilience concept as Rotterdam. Four of the six plans analyzed do not in fact use the term *resilience* in a meaningful way. This is particularly interesting as most of the plans had a strong climate focus that integrated both adaptation and mitigation components. For example, the strongest plan in terms of integrating climate adaptation and mitigation, the Copenhagen Municipal Plan of 2015, does not integrate resilience language into the plan, but includes strong climate mitigation and project-level components of climate adaptation like the emphasis on green and blue infrastructure.

In terms of contextual language, the two plans that utilize the resilience term in the plan language, the Cloudburst Management Plan of 2012 and the Climate Resilient Neighborhood policy document of 2016, provide only broad language to help define the scope of the resilience concept. The plans tend to use the term in a very broad manner and do not clearly define the goals. They mostly focus on reducing susceptibility to flooding as a resilience goal.

While the plan language does not clearly define the scope of resilience, the actual policies articulated in the plans provide a strong adaptation urbanism-centered foundation for deep resilience. The later three planning documents in the analysis (Action Plan for Green Mobility, the Municipal Plan, and First Climate Resilient Neighborhood policy document) all include significant emphasis on the integration of sustainable transportation and green infrastructure. The most developed of these documents, the Municipal Plan, integrates all of the key policy elements of an adaptation urbanism framework. While it does not specifically utilize resilience language as a framing device, the underlying vision of a compact, adapted city linked with walking, bicycling, and transit options is well established and linked with municipal priorities. Key issues related to equity are also integrated into the planning language.

Table A.4 summarizes the results of plan evaluation and the degree to which adaptation urbanism concepts are linked to policy action. Our findings suggest that, while Copenhagen was slower than some other cities in adopting resilience language, it appears to be more advanced in integrating climate adaptation and mitigation in policies that advance the project-level components of an adaptation urbanism approach.

Table A.5 presents the findings from a spatial analysis of the St. Kjeld neighborhood within the Østerbro Resilience District and overall sustainable transportation mode shares for Metropolitan Copenhagen. Approximately 31% of the study area is comprised of paved streets and parking, while about 6% of land area is dedicated to parks and other public green space. It is important to note that this figure does not include the private green spaces found in many courtyards in the area. Meanwhile,

TABLE A.4 Copenhagen adaptation urbanism plan analysis summary

Adaptation urbanism elements	*Copenhagen Adaptation Plan (2011)*	*Copenhagen 2025 Climate Plan (2012)*	*Copenhagen Cloudburst Management Plan (2012)*	*Copenhagen Action Plan for Green Mobility (2013)*	*Copenhagen Municipal Plan (2015) (English Version)*	*Copenhagen Climate Resilient Neighborhood Policy Document (2016)*
Conceptual						
Resilience						
Climate adaptation						
Climate mitigation						
Project-level						
Green infrastructure						
Blue infrastructure						
Sustainable transportation						
Compact development						
Equity						
Level of emphasis	**Not addressed**	**Limited policy focus**	**Strong focus**			

TABLE A.5 Sustainable transportation spatial analysis summary, St. Kjeld, Østerbro, Copenhagen

Sub-area name	*Østerbro Resilience District–St Kjeld's Neighborhood*
Estimated % area paved streets and on-street parking	29.8%
Estimated % area surface parking lots	1.9%
Estimated % area public green space and water	6.0%
Active transportation mode share (metropolitan area)	*Copenhagen*
Bike	41%
Walk	6%
Transit	27%
Total	**74%**

Mode share data source: Deloitte Insights (2019).

Copenhagen has the highest overall sustainable transportation mode share of case study cities at 74%.

London resilience plan analysis

In London, a series of climate and resilience-focused plans were developed over the last decade, emphasizing adaptation to both increased flood and drought risk, correlated temperature increases, and energy efficiency.

Although the seven plan documents reviewed provide a range of strategies and actions oriented toward responding to climate threats, the conceptual themes as well as project-level elements of an adaptation urbanism approach are generally unlinked: plan documents tend to focus on either adaptation or mitigation, but not both (and in some cases, neither). The concept of resilience itself is only meaningfully connected to policy in two strategy documents (the Mayor's Climate Change Adaptation Strategy and London Resilience Partnership Strategy), while green and blue infrastructure are not discussed in the Delivering London's Energy Future, London Resilience Partnership Strategy, Zero Emissions City, or London Cycling Action Plan. Meanwhile, plans focused on adaptation do not substantively connect the mitigation potential of transport and compact development choices in a synergistic way. Conversely, the London Cycling Action Plan does not demonstrate any conceptual interest in resilience or climate, nor does it identify opportunities to connect proposed actions to green infrastructure. Most critically, despite being one of the highest-cost cities in Europe, equity is minimally discussed or absent from all seven of the reviewed plans.

In a few instances, clear, discernable connections about the interrelatedness of adaptation urbanism concepts are made. The 2010 Climate Change Adaptation

Strategy, the oldest of the suite of relevant plan documents, explicitly connects mitigation and adaptation right away: "There is no choice between mitigation and adaptation—we have to pursue complementary actions on both" (City of London Corporation 2010, p. 1), but this is not supported by potential synergistic policy actions. This strategy does focus on specific flood and drought adaptation infrastructure projects and discusses "sustainable drainage systems (SuDS)" and non-street open spaces, but excludes any discussion of transportation or land use concerns.

The 2011 Mayor's Climate Change Adaptation Strategy provides perhaps the most holistic view of how concepts and programs interrelate, and recognizes that goals evolve: "there is no state of being 'adapted' (because the climate, and hence the risk, will keep changing), therefore adaptation should be seen as a 'journey' rather than a 'destination'" (Greater London Authority 2011, p. 30). The Strategy references parallel climate mitigation and energy strategies, reinforcing those linkages without duplication, and focus in on green infrastructure, highlighting "pilot projects demonstrating how permeability can be retrofitted back into existing high-density urban areas, using sustainable drainage systems" (p. 52). The document does not mention equity in any context.

London's Resilience Partnership Strategy reiterates aspirational statements about achieving resilience, but does not support these with substantive policy discussion about any of the key concepts and/or project-level elements that would advance these goals. The subsequent Strategic Flood Risk Assessment (City of London Corporation 2017), narrow in focus, however, does balance adaptation and mitigation as key components of addressing climate resilience through a focus on blue and green infrastructure to manage water and notably, to improve water quality, defining "water compatible development" (p. 6) and "multifunctionality" (p.12) as goals of open space planning, with an emphasis on conserving existing green spaces and building/site-level interventions, although it does not discuss right of way as an asset other than to note the possibility of utilizing permeable pavements in some instances. The dense urban character of London is presented as a challenge, rather than an opportunity, impacting implementation of strategy ideas.

Finally, the two most recent plan documents focus (directly or implicitly) on mitigation: Zero Emissions City reiterates previously published energy ideas, with a strong focus on mitigation. Although it does not focus primarily on sustainable transportation, numerous policy options for incentivizing active modes are discussed. Conversely, the London Cycling Action Plan, light on conceptual vision, hones in on project-level elements to support active transportation, as well as links to development planning "around active and sustainable travel [that] will ensure that London's growth is good growth" (Transport for London 2018, p. 2). Equity and housing connections are also referenced, but not linked directly through policy to transportation infrastructure strategies.

Table A.6 summarizes plans evaluated and the extent of usage of concepts and elements therein, illustrating persistent gaps in the diffusion of these interrelated ideas across policy sectors and authorities.

TABLE A.6 London adaptation urbanism plan analysis summary

Adaptation urbanism elements	*London Climate Change Adaptation Strategy (2010)*	*Delivering London's Energy Future (2011)*	*Mayor's Climate Change Adaptation Strategy (2011)*	*London Resilience Partnership Strategy (2016)*	*Strategic Flood Risk Assessment (2017)*	*Zero Emissions City (2018)*	*London Cycling Action Plan (2018)*
Conceptual							
Resilience focus							
Adaptation focus							
Mitigation focus							
Project-level							
Green infrastructure							
Blue infrastructure							
Sustainable transportation							
Compact development							
Equity							
Level of emphasis:	**Not addressed**	**Limited policy focus**	**Strong focus**				

TABLE A.7 Sustainable transportation spatial analysis summary, Waltham Forest, London

Subarea name	*Waltham Forest*
Estimated % area paved streets and on-street parking	21.6%
Estimated % area surface parking lots	0.9%
Estimated % area public green space and water	7.5%
Active transportation mode share (metropolitan area)	*London*
Bike	3%
Walk	29%
Transit	29%
Total	**61%**

Mode share data source: Deloitte Insights (2019).

Table A.7 presents the findings from a spatial analysis of the Waltham Forest area, discussed in Chapter 7, and overall sustainable transportation mode shares for London. Less than a quarter (23%) of the study sub-area is comprised of paved streets and parking, with about 8% of the land area dedicated to green space. Overall sustainable transportation mode shares in Metropolitan London are estimated at 61%, though bicycles make up only a small share of this total.

New Orleans resilience plan analysis

New Orleans' policy efforts on resilience, as discussed in Chapter 8, were born from emergency, driven by a myriad of recovery efforts and processes, and characterized by critical tensions that have to some degree constrained implementation. This section focuses on the second wave of post-Katrina plans (2010 and later) that have centered on water and resilience. These plans have increasingly embraced adaptation urbanism concepts and linked these ideas to policy strategies (Table A.8). Overall, adaptation urbanism concepts and key project-level terms were utilized extensively throughout the planning documents. None of the plans, however, utilized all of the adaptation urbanism elements within each plan.

The city's comprehensive plan, *Plan for the 21st Century: New Orleans 2030* (Goody Clancy 2010), captured the language of resilience overall, but minimally mentions ideas of adaptation and mitigation. Of the five plans evaluated, this document (linked directly to the city's Comprehensive Zoning Ordinance) is the only one to focus on compact development, with significant attention dedicated to mixed land uses, with connections to transportation clearly delineated. Surprisingly given its origins in recovery from a disastrous flood, it dedicates little attention to issues pertaining to water.

This limitation is addressed in 2013's Urban Water Plan (Waggonner & Ball Architects 2013), which extensively outlines a multitude of policies, programs, and projects related to water management. The focus of the plan is on water with

TABLE A.8 New Orleans adaptation urbanism plan analysis summary

Adaptation urbanism elements	*New Orleans Comprehensive Plan (2010)*	*Urban Water Plan (2013)*	*Gentilly Resilience District Plan (2015)*	*Resilient New Orleans Strategy (2015)*	*Climate Action Plan (2017)*
Conceptual					
Resilience focus					
Adaptation focus					
Mitigation focus					
Project-level					
Green infrastructure					
Blue infrastructure					
Sustainable transportation					
Compact Development					
Equity					
Level of emphasis	**Not addressed**	**Limited policy focus**	**Strong focus**		

limited focus on land use and transportation issues or any explicit climate mitigation strategies. The Gentilly Resilience District Plan, which was drawn from concepts developed in the Urban Water Plan (Waggoner & Ball Architects 2013), is largely project-oriented. It broadly eschews discussion of conceptual underpinnings of resilience, as well as broader discussion of how the proposed projects relate to existing transportation networks. The later Resilience Strategy and Climate Action Plan continued to advance ideas around resilience. The Resilience Strategy brings a concentration on equity to the fore. The Climate Action Plan (City of New Orleans 2017) clearly links green infrastructure and active transportation to climate mitigation adaptation, but, for the most part, does not address equity and land use connections. Equity is, however, addressed through a subsequent interdepartmental effort resulting in the recently released "Taking Steps Together on Equity & Climate Change: A Report for and by New Orleanians" document. This document seeks to ensure that proposed resilience actions are equitably distributed throughout the community.

Overall, the plans create a strong conceptual foundation for adaptation urbanism, but the role of active transportation in climate mitigation and the mechanics of translating model projects into standard operating procedures often remain unclear. Equity, in terms of who is receiving resources and where place-based investments are being made, has become a clear goal in the more recent plans. The Urban Water Plan, for example, recognizes that "achieving socially just outcomes…presents a great opportunity in a city and region where the most disadvantaged often live in the areas most prone to flooding" (Waggonner & Ball Architects 2013, p. 32). The Climate Action Plan (City of New Orleans 2017) also directly connects equity, transportation, mitigation, and climate change, identifying climate action as an "opportunity to alleviate poverty and unemployment while improving neighborhoods and community connections" (p. 17). While this broader commitment has been expressed in plan language, there has been limited direct connection between the amenity-enhancing nature of green infrastructure projects and affordable housing. More clear connections can help to translate the aspirational language into reality.

Table A.98 presents the spatial analysis of the St. Anthony Green Streets project area, discussed in Chapter 8. This area is a relatively low-density, suburban neighborhood of primarily single-family homes. The right of way makes up approximately 26% of the surface area, including paved streets and on-street parking (14%), green medians (4%), and sidewalks/easement areas (8%). A total of 13% of the study area is green space, including medians, the two parks slated for improvements, and a segment of canal and adjacent green ROW. This indicates that, beyond the parameters of the current project, there is significantly more opportunity for comprehensive adaptive design to manage water throughout the transportation network than currently reflected within the St. Anthony Green Streets pilot. Meanwhile, approximately 17% of work trips in the City of New Orleans overall are made via sustainable modes, with one of the highest proportions of bike commuters among major US cities, at 3.7%. Metropolitan numbers are far lower.

TABLE A.9 Sustainable transportation spatial analysis summary, St. Anthony Green Streets, New Orleans

Sub-area name	*St. Anthony Green Streets*
Estimated % area paved streets and on-street parking	14.0%
Estimated % area surface parking lots	0.9%
Estimated % area public green space and water	12.8%
Active transportation mode share (metropolitan area)	*New Orleans-Metairie Metro*
Bike	1.3%
Walk	2.6%
Transit	2.7%
Total	**6.6%**

Mode share data source: U.S. Census, American Community Survey 2018 1-year estimates, Table B08301.

Miami resilience plan analysis

The 2010 Miami-Dade Climate Action Plan largely focuses on storm response. The plan points to the Miami region's extensive experience with hurricane adaptation and recovery, while also addressing general sea level rise. This document explicitly connects adaptation with mitigation, noting that "any responsible community must realize that it is equally important to maintain and even increase efforts to mitigate, or reduce GHGs [greenhouse gases] while moving forward with adaptation planning" (p. 5). It also recognizes the need to address multiple goals simultaneously, challenging the region to "pursue win–win strategies that accomplish multiple goals through coordinated cost-effective actions" (p.5). Although there is limited discussion of green or blue infrastructure, the potential co-benefits of open space strategies on water quality and transportation are noted. Connections between sustainable transportation and "healthy communities" initiatives are also addressed. Importantly, the plan observes that "compact development strategies are not typically highlighted in climate change mitigation because they are considered indirect measures" and seeks to address this topic within climate change planning (Table A.10).

The Miami-Dade Green Print document, updated in 2015, broadly addresses adaptation urbanism topics at the project-level. Sustainable transportation, transit-oriented development, and the interconnectivity of transportation with parks, food systems, health, and land use are highlighted. Despite a project-level orientation, there is little discussion of green or blue infrastructure as potential adaptation measures, nor is there any substantive discussion of equity considerations.

Adaptation-focused recommendations include the implementation of development impact tools and criteria to quantify climate impacts and integrate these in the development review process to ensure rigorous and consistent application. Mitigation strategies emphasize creating transit-supportive land use policy

TABLE A.10 Miami adaptation urbanism plan analysis summary

Adaptation urbanism elements	*Miami-Dade Climate Action Plan (2010)*	*Miami Dade Green Print (2015)*	*CDMP IRA 7 EAR (2019)*	*Resilient 305 Strategy Report (2019)*
Conceptual				
Resilience focus				
Adaptation focus				
Mitigation focus				
Project-level				
Green infrastructure				
Blue infrastructure				
Sustainable transportation				
Compact development				
Equity				
Level of emphasis	**Not addressed**	**Limited policy focus**		

TABLE A.11 Sustainable transportation spatial analysis summary, South Florida sub-areas

Sub-area name	*Las Olas Blvd*	*Grandview Market - West Palm Beach*
Estimated % area paved streets and on-street parking	11.7%	11.3%
Estimated % area surface parking lots	12.0%	28.2%
Estimated % area public green space and water	16.5%	13.1%
Active transportation mode share (citywide)	*Miami-Fort Lauderdale-West Palm Beach Metro*	
Bike	0.8%	
Walk	1.5%	
Transit	3.3%	
Total	**5.6%**	

Mode share data source: U.S. Census, American Community Survey 2018 1-year estimates, Table B08301.

and addressing how historic low-density development patterns exacerbate vulnerabilities and climate-related stressors. Finally, the Resilient 305 Strategy Report is covered in more detail in Chapter 9.

Evaluation of the Las Olas Boulevard sub-area reveals that approximately 24% of the total area is dedicated for automobile use, over half of which is off-street surface parking, and although the surrounding waterways account for over 16% of the area evaluated, less than 0.25%% of the space is pervious, public green space (Table A.11). In the Grandview Market peninsula sub-area in West Palm Beach, meanwhile, nearly 40% of the total area is composed of paved streets and parking, including 28% of the land area allocated to surface parking lots. Approximately 13% of the study area is comprised of publicly accessible green space or canals. Active transportation mode share in the Miami metro area is lower than any of the other case study cities at only 6%, suggesting that, despite the consistent emphasis on expanding sustainable transportation options and use, there remains considerable work to be done in this area.

References

Appler, Douglas, & Rumbach, Andrew. (2016). Building Community Resilience Through Historic Preservation. *Journal of the American Planning Association*, 82(2), 92–103.

Berke, P., & Godschalk, D. (2009). Searching for the Good Plan: A Meta-Analysis of Plan Quality Studies. *CPL Bibliography*, *23*(3), 227–240.

City of London Corporation. (2010). Rising to the Challenge—The City of London Climate Change Adaptation Strategy. London: City of London Corporation.

City of London Corporation. (2017). Strategic Flood Risk Assessment. London: City of London Corporation.

City of New Orleans. (2017). Climate Action for a Resilient New Orleans. New Orleans: City of New Orleans. Last accessed 1/14/2021 from https://nola.gov/nola/media/Climate-Action/Climate-Action-for-a-Resilient-New-Orleans.pdf.

City of Rotterdam. (2016). Rotterdam Resilience Strategy. Ready for the 21st Century. Rotterdam, The Netherlands: City of Rotterdam.

Deloitte Insights. (2019). Deloitte City Mobility Index. Last accessed 5/8/2020 from www2.deloitte.com/global/en/insights/focus/future-of-mobility/deloitte-urban-mobility-index-for-cities.html.

Greater London Auhtority. (2011). Managing Risks and Increasing Resilience: The Mayor's Climate Change Adaptation Strategy. London: Greater London Authority.

Hsieh, H. F., & Shannon, S. E. (2005). Three Approaches to Qualitative Content Analysis. *Qualitative Health Research*, *15*(9), 1277–1288.

Rotterdam Climate Initiative. (2013). Rotterdam Climate Proof Adaptation Programme: Connecting Water with Opportunities. Rotterdam: City of Rotterdam.

Transport for London. (2018). Cycling Action Plan: Making London the World;s Best Big City for Cycling. London: Transport for London.

Urban Green-Blue Grids. (n.d.). Water Sensitive Rotterdam. Last accessed 1/12/2021 from www.urbangreenbluegrids.com/projects/water-sensitive-rotterdam/.

Waggonner & Ball Architects. (2013). Greater New Orleans Urban Water Plan. Last accessed 2/6/2020 from http://livingwithwater.com/urban_water_plan/Reports/.

APPENDIX B

ADAPTATION URBANISM STREET ANALYSIS ROTTERDAM

As we discussed in Chapter 4, we are interested in creating a practical method for assessing the extent that key adaptation urbanism street and public space components are present in our study areas. The adaptation urbanism audit (Table B.1) provides a simplified way to analyze projects and outline the presence of green and blue infrastructure and core Vision Zero/Safe System components of streets. This helps uncover how green and blue infrastructure are (or are not) being integrated into streets. While much of the analysis in our case study chapters is more technical, the adaptation urbanism audit is intentionally designed to be a simplified way to synthesize adaptation urbanism concepts down to street level. As we argued in Chapter 4, we were inspired to create this straightforward tool by reading the National Association of City Transportation Officials (NACTO) *Urban Street Stormwater Guide*'s (2017) articulation of complete streets as green streets. In the age of climate change, green street elements are central to creating a truly complete street. The adaptation urbanism audit provides an easy-to-use tool to begin to gauge how close (or how far) streets in your community are from meeting the climate challenge.

Adaptation urbanism audit in practice

Rotterdam

To help show how the adaptation urbanism audit works, we examined the Centraal Station area of Rotterdam (Figure B.1). While not every component of an adaptation urbanism street is present, the suite of components currently in use helps to create a slow-speed street that enhances community livability and helps to address water management issues. As you look at these elements consider that each design feature used on the street had to be negotiated and layered together to create this

TABLE B.1 Adaptation urbanism audit

Green/blue street corridor elements	*Yes/no*	*Vision Zero/Safe Systems street elements*	*Yes/no*
Green medians		Brick pavement	
Street trees		Traffic calming (speed table, chicanes, etc.)	
Parks		Sidewalk	
Planters/bioswales		Continental cross-walk	
Pavement cuts into green space		Mid-block crossing treatment	
Permeable pavement		Cycle track	
Canals		Bike lane	
Rivers		Advisory bike lane	
Ponds		Protected intersection	
Water square		Roundabout	
Blue medians		Curb bulb-out	
Water boulevards		Trail/greenway	
Other:______________		Other:______________	

FIGURE B.1 Rotterdam adaptation urbanism street analysis.

type of place. Underlying the simple audit of adaptation urbanism features is a set of bureaucratic relationships and funding decisions that encourage or often limit community resilience.

The adaptation urbanism street analysis is designed to show the end design features that should prompt questions about the strengths and limitations of the street-planning process. While the Rotterdam analysis shows what happens when local placemaking, multi-modal transportation, safety, and amenity-driven water management are valued, it is easy to imagine another scenario where these design features are replaced to encourage high-speed mobility. The sidewalks, traffic-calming, permeable pavement, curb bulb-outs, green medians, trees, and planters, and canal might seem like quaint features that could be repurposed to something more important for regional mobility. Imagine that planners determine that the way to move people to the train station is to create larger, high-speed roadways as the most efficient way to meet mobility needs. The canal that you see in the middle could be covered with a multi-lane road. The intricate design elements of the blue/green/safe street would be erased. Over time, the disamenity of the larger road would depress property values and, with the proximity to the train station as lure for parking, tearing down the now deteriorating row houses for parking lots could seem like a reasonable idea. As these local decisions are scaled up to regions, imagine that residents who can afford it begin to move away from the center. The roads and land uses spread outward, the train becomes less important as the community sprawls, GHG emissions rise, and climate problems seem simultaneously abstract and intractable. If you are reading this book in the United States or another car-dependent place, you are probably experiencing this future as your present reality.

Now as we begin to reverse the process and plan for adaptation urbanism, the small decisions on individual streets like the one here in Rotterdam can begin to be scaled up into neighborhoods and city-scale districts with the results visible in the crash statistics, water storage, and GHG emissions of cities. A street segment or two is a good start for the local community, but not enough to make much of a dent in the larger resilience picture. A network of complete green streets like this, however, would be transformative and act as the foundation for a regional adaptation urbanism system.

Reference

NACTO (National Association of City Transportation Officials). (2017). *Urban Street Stormwater Guide*. Washington, DC: Island Press.

INDEX

www.ingramcontent.com/pod-product-compliance
Lightning Source LLC
LaVergne TN
LVHW021122300926
849160LV00010B/824
9780367134952